Kathy Kristof's COMPLETE BOOK OF DOLLARS AND SENSE

Best wishes —

Kathy Kristof's COMPLETE BOOK OF DOLLARS AND SENSE

From Budget Basics to Lifetime Plans—the Only Guide You'll Need to Manage Your Money

KATHY M. KRISTOF

MACMILLAN · USA

MACMILLAN
A Simon & Schuster Macmillan Company
1633 Broadway
New York, NY 10019-6785

Copyright © 1997 by Kathy M. Kristof

All rights reserved. No part of this book may be reproduced or transmitted in any form by any means, electronic or mechanical, including photocopying, recording, or by any information storage and retrieval system, without permission in writing from the Publisher.

MACMILLAN is a registered trademark of Macmillan, Inc.

Library of Congress Cataloging-in-Publication Data

Kristof, Kathy.
Kathy Kristof's Complete Book of Dollars and Sense/Kathy Kristof.
p. cm.

ISBN 0-02-860852-6
1. Finance, personal. I. Title.
HG179.K73 1997
332.024—dc20 96-23912
CIP

Design by Kevin Hanek

10 9 8 7 6 5 4 3 2 1

Printed in the United States of America

Dedication

To my family—ten wonderful people who make all good things possible.

Contents

Acknowledgments

There are a great number of people to whom I owe a debt of gratitude for their support, advice, and assistance with this book (and a host of other things, for that matter). However, a few people stand out.

First and foremost, thank you Moira. Once again, I've been able to grasp something beyond my reach only because my big sister let me stand on her shoulders.

Frances Pollock and Philip J. Holthouse, two busy professional people, were kind enough to read, critique, and correct every chapter. I'm also deeply grateful for the support and encouragement provided by my husband, Rich, and for the patience of my wonderful children.

Finally, I thank my mom and dad, who taught me the importance of values—the kind that have nothing to do with money.

What went right with this book is largely thanks to their help. Any remaining problems are solely mine.

Introduction

This is a book for busy people.

If you know you should get a lower-rate credit card but don't want to spend months trying to find one; if you want to buy shares in a mutual fund but don't know how to get started; if you think you need life insurance but can't decide how much to buy; if you want to get your financial life in order but would rather have a root canal than spend months pouring through a stack of financial books and articles to figure out how to do it—then this book is for you.

It will show you how to save some money; how to make some money; and how to get organized. It will give you guidance to handle life's major financial hurdles—buying a house or car, financing college and retirement—as well as financially protecting yourself and your family.

It provides phone numbers, form letters, and other organizational help to get you financially fit in short order. In other words, it's designed to save you time as well as money.

How to Use This Book

There are four ways to use this book.

1. As a guidebook: Perhaps you're trying to get started on a healthy financial future but don't know where to start. Read one chapter a day—or one a week—and fill in the worksheets. When you're done, you'll be well on your way.

2. As a do-it-yourself manual: This book teaches you how to do a simple mathematical calculation that will enable you to figure out nearly anything you need to know in the world of finance—how much you need to save for retirement; how much you ought to pay for an auto lease; whether an insurance salesman is lying to you or not; how to save a fortune on your home mortgage; and more.

   The calculation, called a present-value calculation, looks intimidating at first, but it is easy, really. But unless you're the type to do all of your long division by hand, you'll want to use something called a present-value calculator (see page 3). Better yet, visit the Macmillan Web site on the Internet at http://www.mcp.com/mgr/macmillan/dollars for simple, fill-in-the-blank worksheets. Best of all, once you understand it—and you will long before the book is done—you'll know as much, or more, about finance as almost anyone you meet. The next time a salesman says: "It's a good deal. Trust me," you won't have to. You'll know exactly how to determine whether what's being said is true.

3. For reference: Say most of your financial life is in order, but you need help with one or two things. Flip to the appropriate section, use the index to direct you to the specific item you want, spend five minutes reading, then close the book. If, later, you have another question, you can refer to the book again. But there's no reason to read a whole book when all you need is a paragraph.

4. As a bequest: *You* may know what's going on in your financial life, but does your spouse? In many families, one spouse handles the finances, while the other remains blissfully ignorant. The bliss ends, however, the moment something happens to the financially oriented spouse. All too often, the survivor or divorcee is left struggling because he doesn't know how much he's got; where it's invested; why it's invested the way it is; and who can be trusted when asking for financial advice. If you fill out the worksheets provided in this book, your spouse will know where to look for answers.

In each part—and for each individual chapter—you'll find an additional short table of contents so you can find the specific page you're looking for.

If you use this book as it is intended, it will help you cut your financial maintenance time to a bare minimum and put your financial life on automatic pilot.

Kathy Kristof's COMPLETE BOOK OF DOLLARS AND SENSE

Part One

GETTING STARTED

Do you know how much you have, spend, save—or how much you ought to be saving to get things you want in the future? If not, get started.

Chapter 1: Figuring the Cost

Most people never know how much they could save by paying a little extra on their mortgage. They wonder how much they need to save for retirement. They're stumped by how inflation affects the value of their savings. Want to be different? Want to be the person who knows how to find the answers? Start on page 2.

Chapter 2: Sweet Dreaming (Setting Goals)

Ever daydreamed about having a house at the beach? Pined after a costly sports car? Wished you were more financially secure? The first step toward getting what you want is determining what that is. For help, turn to page 11.

Chapter 3: You Are Here

You need to know your starting point to get where you want to go. This chapter is the financial equivalent of a big "X" on a map: "You Are Here" starts on page 18.

Chapter 4: I Spend, Therefore I Am

It's the dreaded B word: *budget*. But if you want things that you can't buy with your monthly income, you've got to break down and deal with it. Sharpen your pencils and turn to page 30.

Chapter 5: Money Trouble

If you don't know where your money is going, this chapter's for you. It's designed solely to help people who seem to have holes in their pockets. Go directly to page 39.

Chapter 1

Figuring the Cost

You don't have to be psychic to predict the future—at least when it comes to finance. All you need is a $20 calculator or a computer with an Internet connection.

What the chapter tells you

- You can dazzle your friends—and save yourself money—by playing a mathematical game.
- As with most games, you need some equipment to play.
- Believe it or not, it's fun.

What the chapter shows you

- How to be your own financial planner
- How to evaluate your present financial arrangements
- How to determine what your savings will be worth in the future
- How to save a fortune on your home mortgage

Where do I start?

Financial planners can dazzle their clients by telling them precisely how much they need to save today to finance some future cost. Thanks in large part to this mathematical wizardry, they're able to charge their clients hundreds of dollars to create a fairly simple savings plan for college, retirement, or any other long-term goal.

In truth, it's easy to do this calculation yourself. All you need is a present-value calculator and a little instruction on how to use it.

Better yet, knowing this calculation will help you solve dozens of financial riddles—important questions that people worry about all the time—such as:

- "How much is my retirement account going to be worth thirty years from now?"
- "Will that be enough money to live on?"
- "How much do I have to save to pay for my children's college expenses?"
- "Am I getting ripped off on my auto lease?"
- "How much money would I save if I paid my mortgage off early?"

"Euueew. Math. Not interested," you say? I guarantee that, once you learn how to do this, the benefits will dazzle you so much that you'll *like* playing with this calculator. Especially because it will save you literally *thousands* of dollars—and countless hours of worry—over time. Not to mention that it will impress your friends.

Why do I say all of this? Because by plugging four numbers into this calculator, a person with a $100,000 mortgage at 8 percent could find that by rounding their $733.76 monthly payment up to $775, they could pay off their mortgage five years faster and save a sum total of $34,678 in interest.

Feeling insecure about your retirement account? You've got $10,000 saved and want to know what that will be worth thirty-five years from now? You can find out in a few seconds—with a present-value calculator. (Assuming a reasonable 8 percent average annual return, your $10,000 nest egg would grow to $162,925. Honest.)

How much do you need to save each month to build up $100,000 in savings in twenty years? Tap. Tap. Tap. Tap. $170.

Where can you buy one of these little gems? Virtually anywhere—drugstores, office supply stores, as well as virtually any electronics store you can name. They cost anywhere from $15 to $75, depending on where you buy them and what model you choose.* Any present-value calculator will do, however, and you may even have one already.

**The least expensive model I've found is the Texas Instruments BA-35. It's available at most discount retail stores, selling between $15 and $25, depending on the retailer. If you can't find one at a local store, Texas Instruments will also sell them directly. You can call them at 800-TI-CARES (800-842-2737) to order. But it's more expensive this way. After taxes and shipping and handling charges are factored in, a BA-35 will cost almost $30 when ordered from the manufacturer.*

How do you differentiate a present-value calculator from a run-of-the-mill calculator? By looking for a line of keys that look roughly like this:

N	Number of payments
%I	Percent Interest
PMT	Payment
PV	Present Value
FV	Future Value

although not always in that order. On any given problem, you'll have to plug in four numbers—sometimes one or two are estimated—and hit four of those keys to find an answer to the question you're trying to solve.

With practice, this is easy to do. It may take some getting used to because you must plug in many numbers before you actually ask the calculator to do anything. Just remember: What you're essentially doing is talking to the calculator—telling it what's going on in your financial life. The bad news here is that to talk *to* a calculator, you have to talk *like* a calculator. The good news is the calculator won't laugh.

Let's say you wanted to find out how much money you would have in ten years if you put away $50 a month and earned an average of 8 percent interest annually. Simply tell the calculator the facts. Then ask for the solution.

In this case, you would say:

1. "I have nothing saved." To translate that to calculatorese, you hit "0" and then "PV" (present value).
2. "But I'm willing to save $50 a month." You hit "$50," then "PMT" (payment).
3. "I think I can earn 8 percent annually, but the interest is likely to compound monthly." Hit 8 and then divide it by 12 (months) = to get a result of 0.666667. While that result is still on the screen, just hit "%I" (percent interest)—because 0.666667 is the percent interest you'd earn each month.
4. "I will do this for 10 years, which, at 12 months to a year, equals 120 months." So hit "120," then "N" (number of payments).
5. "How much will that get me at the end of ten years?" Hit "CPT," then "FV" (compute future value.) Voilà. $9,147.31.

You can plug in the information in any order—and solve for any variable. Naturally, however, the "compute the answer" question must be last.

Want to know how to answer that retirement fund question—that is, how much will my $10,000 be worth in thirty-five years? First, tell the calculator how much you have now ($10,000). Hit "10,000," then "PV" (present value).

Next, tell it how much you think you'll earn on the money while it's invested. In this case, we've figured 8 percent annually, but, because interest usually compounds monthly, everything needs to be calculated on a monthly basis. So just divide the 8 by 12 (months) to get a monthly rate of interest, then hit the "equals" key. That will give you 0.666667. Punch "0.666667," then "%I" (percent interest).

Then tell it the length of time you plan to invest the money. Thirty-five years equals 420 months. Hit "420," then "N" (number of periods).

Finally, plug in how much additional money you will add to the pot each month from personal savings. (Here we figured "0," "PMT" because we only wanted to know what that $10,000 would accrue without adding anything to it.)

Then simply hit "CPT," "FV" (compute future value). Voilà. In thirty-five years, the $10,000 in your retirement fund will be worth $162,925.49.

Easy.

Okay. Painful. But it will become easier with practice. And that's just what you're going to do. ("Ah, shucks. Homework? I actually *paid* for this book to torture me?" Buck up. I promise it will be worth your while.)

So take the first step and buy the calculator—if you haven't already—then sit down with a pencil and the worksheets on the following pages.

You're going to find out:

- just how rich you are going to be at retirement
- how much you need to save to be as rich as you want
- whether it makes sense to pay a few bucks extra each month on your mortgage

You'll use all this information as you progress through the book—as well as through life.

In return, you will never again have to rely on someone else to tell you how much you're worth or how much you need to save. You'll walk into every future financial discussion with more knowledge and, consequently, the ability to make better decisions.

But how long will it take you to reach that enviable empowered state? Approximately one hour—to learn how your calculator works and to figure out how to do this formula forward, backward, and upside down will take you a maximum of one hour.

One hour for a lifetime of better decisions.

How to Do It

Any present-value calculation is made up of five elements:

1. How much you have: Present Value (PV).
2. How much you want to have: Future Value (FV).

3. The amount of time it will take to reach your goal: Number of periods *in months* (N).
4. The rate you'll earn on savings or pay on a loan: Percent Interest *divided by 12 to get the monthly rate* (%I). (In reality, you don't have to do present-value calculations based on monthly periods and monthly interest rates, but because that's how interest is usually paid [and charged], that's how we've done the calculations in this book.)
5. How much you will have to pay to reach your goal: Monthly Payments (PMT).

Whenever you pick up the calculator, simply ask yourself: "Which of the five elements do I want to know?" That tells you that you must plug in figures for the other four elements to find your answer.

In other words, if you are trying to find what something will be worth in the future, you have to "solve" the future value. That means you need to plug in figures for the remaining four elements—present value, number of months, interest rate, and monthly payments. Your final step is to ask the calculator to "compute future value."

If you want to find out what your monthly payment is going to be on a loan, you'll plug in figures for (1) "number" of months that you'll be making payments; (2) "percent interest" you're paying; (3) the "present value" of the loan (how much you intend to borrow); (4) the "future value" of the loan—which will probably be zero, because most loans must be paid off at some point. The fifth step is to solve the problem by punching "CPT PMT" (compute payment).

How do you know what figures to plug in? In some cases, you guess. No one really knows how much money they're going to earn on a mutual fund, for example. But you can guess by looking at historic returns and assuming that those returns will hold steady over long periods of time.

What happens if things don't work out the way you expected? You guess again. This is precisely why you ought to *buy* the calculator rather than borrow it. It's important to remain flexible, and to adjust your calculation to fit your updated projections.

For example, you may have figured your retirement savings based on a plan to retire thirty years from now. But you've had a bad day at the office and want to know what would happen if you retired earlier. You just plug in new numbers for the duration or "number" of periods that you'll have your money saved or invested. And plug in new numbers for how long you'll need to collect monthly payments from your savings. (See Chapter 22 for guidance.)

What happens if you didn't earn as much as you thought you would on your investments? Adjust the interest rate to the current reality, and do the calculation again.

There's no limit to the number of times you can do this. After all, it's your calculator. Play with it.

In other instances, you'll know the facts. On a fixed-rate mortgage, for example, you know how much you borrowed; you know the interest rate; you know the duration—or number of months before the loan is paid off; you know what your payments are. Once you've agreed to a mortgage deal, the five elements of the present value calculation are "solved."

If you borrowed $100,000 on a thirty-year, fixed-rate mortgage at 8 percent, for example, the elements would work out this way.

1. Present Value = $100,000 (Hit 100,000, PV)
2. Future Value = 0, since you'll pay off the loan completely over the period of the mortgage. (Hit 0, FV)
3. Number of periods, or months = 360—that's 30 years times 12 months. (Hit 360, N)
4. Percent Interest = 0.66667—the annual 8 percent rate divided by 12 months. (Hit 0.66667, %I)
5. Payment = $733.76—your bank would be sure to mention this. But, to calculate it yourself, your final step would be to hit "CPT PMT" or compute payment.

So how do you figure out what would happen if you wanted to pay off the loan early? You substitute hypothetical figures for those you've actually got.

For instance, you decide you want to pay off that mortgage in twenty years rather than thirty. How much extra do you have to pay each month to do that?

To determine the answer, you simply need to plug in a new value for "N" (Number of Payments). Instead of 360 (30 years), you'd hit 240 (20 years), N. Then you hit figures that correspond with the facts:

- $100,000, PV;
- 0, FV;
- 0.66667, %I;
- And you ask the calculator to compute the necessary payment by hitting "CPT PMT." What do you get? $836.44.

In other words, if you pay $836.44 per month instead of $733.76, you'll pay off the loan ten years faster.

How much does that save you in interest? The answer requires only simple multiplication and subtraction. If you pay $733.76 each month for 30 years, or 360 months, you pay a sum total of $264,153 ($733.76 times 360 payments).

If you pay $836.44 for 20 years, you pay a total of $200,746 ($836.44 times 240 payments).

Paying the extra $103 per month saves you $63,407 ($264,153 minus $200,746)!

Let's Pretend

Fiddling with present-value calculations is a game—an adult version of "let's pretend." Let's pretend I have an extra $100 a month. What would happen if I applied it to my mortgage?

The important difference between this version and the version your kids play is that you might just have that $100 someday. So, instead of winning play money, you save real money.

You can also play around to see what a different interest rate will do.

For instance, let's pretend you could earn 15 percent on your money every year for thirty-five years. Then what would that initial investment of $10,000 be worth? Steady . . . $1.84 million.

Let's say you needed the money in thirty years, rather than thirty-five. You'd have less than *half* what you would if you had left the money in savings for those five years. To be precise: $875,409.89.

How do you figure out how much you'd have to save each month to accumulate $100,000 in twenty years?

1. Future Value = $100,000. Punch 100,000, FV.

2. Present Value = 0 (assuming you're starting from scratch). Punch 0, PV.

3. Number of Periods = 240 (20 years times 12 months). Punch 240, N.

4. Percent Interest = (This will be a guess. If you're going to invest the money in stocks, it would be reasonable to assume that the money will earn 10 percent annually over that period. If you're going to invest in savings accounts, you'd plug in a smaller amount—perhaps 6 percent. Because you may invest in both, split the difference—compute at 8 percent, which, broken into a monthly rate [divided by 12] = 0.6667.) Punch 0.6667, %I.

5. Compute your payment by punching CPT PMT. Result: $169.77. That's how much you'd have to save every month to create a $100,000 nest egg twenty years from now.

If you've followed along, plugged these numbers into your calculator, and come up with the same answers as you saw here, you've already learned how to do this.

You can now substitute the sample numbers for the numbers that correspond with your mortgage, your savings account, or the estimated amount you want to save.

In later chapters you'll see how you can use variations of this same calculation to save yourself money or to help determine your investment strategies.

Alternate Methods

You might be wondering if there's an easier way to do this—or a way to do this without a present-value calculator. The answers on both counts are yes and no.

First: "Is there an easier way?" Sometimes.

If you just want to know how much you're going to have to pay each month on a mortgage or how much your $10,000 savings account is going to be worth in the future, you can find a simple compound–interest rate table and multiply your mortgage amount (or savings amount) by the stated "multiplier." Of course, finding a compound-interest table isn't as easy as finding a newsstand, but you can often get them from your banker or mutual fund company. Macmillan also offers present-value calculations on its Web site at http://www.mcp.com/mgr/macmillan/dollars.

To calculate how much your retirement fund will be worth in the future, however, is more complicated. You will need to use several types of interest-rate tables to get a final answer. (To see for yourself, call Dreyfus Corporation at 800-782-6620 and ask for their free retirement planner. They have one of the simplest worksheets around and it uses five charts and twelve steps.) The bottom line: It's simply easier to use the present-value calculator.

You say you don't want to buy a calculator? It's possible to do the math without it, but you have to be a whiz at calculus. If you want to try it yourself—and thus save the $20—check out *Quick Business Math*, by Steve Slavin, or any other basic calculus text in the library or bookstore.

Personally, I'd rather spend the $20.

Can you read this book without a calculator? Absolutely. Most of the chapters don't require any math at all. But if you do buy the calculator, you'll get a much more thorough understanding of your finances in the handful of chapters that explain how to calculate the costs (or rewards) of borrowing or saving over long periods.

Calculator Trouble

You bought the calculator, but you're having trouble figuring out how to use it? Chances are, it comes with a little instruction card that can signal the tricks and quirks of the particular model you bought.

On the BA-35, for example, you can't do present-value calculations unless the calculator is in the proper "mode." That's because the machine does financial, statistical, and plain vanilla math. To get it to do a present-value calculation, you have to tell it that you want the financial option by hitting the key that has a little red "fin" below it.

When you're in the financial mode a tiny fin also appears on the screen. If you try to do a present-value calculation when you're not in the financial mode, the calculator will print "ERROR" across the screen. Clear it; hit the "fin" key; and start again.

One other small but important point to make about present-value calculators: Because these calculators are designed to figure out loan payments, when you plug in both a present value and a payment, many of them will assume you are trying to pay off a debt, and will make your present value negative.

If you are trying to determine how long it will take you to pay off a loan, that works to your advantage and it saves you a step. However, if you are trying to determine, say, how much your retirement fund will be worth in the future, you already have some savings and are continuing to save every month, it will throw off your calculation.

The good news is, it's a problem that's easy to fix. Because you know the calculator is automatically going to make your present value (PV) negative, just input your payment as a negative number as well, by punching the "+/–" key after you enter the amount of your payment, but before you punch the PMT button. Your result will appear as a negative number on the screen, but you'll know it's a savings, not a debt—more important, it will be the right number. More on that in Chapter 22, "Saving for Retirement," which starts on page 239.

Chapter 2

Sweet Dreaming (Setting Goals)

Knowing what you want is the first step toward getting it.

What the chapter tells you

- Setting goals is as simple as having a conversation.
- Some goals seem nebulous. But you can make them tangible, which is the first step toward attaining them.

What the chapter shows you

- How to define your goals
- How to figure the cost

Where do I start?

What do you want in life and when do you want it?

Is your goal to have enough money to retire comfortably at age fifty-five? A college fund for the kids? A new home within five years? A fast car? More time for pleasure? Or do you aim simply for comfort, security, or freedom?

Think about it.

Every one of your financial goals is attainable. Honest.

But I won't lie to you. Attaining financial goals—particularly if you're starting fairly late in life—may require some difficult trade-offs and sacrifices.

If you want to save more money, you will either have to spend less or earn more. Before you launch into a plan to do this, you should consider what it will entail and whether it's worth it.

All too often, people make the mistake of adapting their life-style to someone else's longer-term goals. Financial planners, for example, are nearly unanimous in pushing the idea that you'll need a huge nest egg for retirement. Certainly, you'll need something socked away for your old age, but are you willing to work extra hours or give up all of today's pleasures for a fat retirement account? Maybe not.

You may prefer a modest life-style at retirement in exchange for having more time to spend with your children today. Your neighbor may decide that a seven-day workweek is a small price to pay for a Porsche. Your brother-in-law may be willing to eat a sack lunch every day to save for a house on the beach.

The point is, financial goals are personal. You have to consider what you want from your money. Setting your own goals—and considering the sacrifices that those goals require—is the first step in making money work for you rather than the other way around.

If you're married, remember that financial goals are shared. Sit down with your spouse—kids too, if they're old enough—and talk about the things you're striving to attain.

On the worksheet at the end of this chapter, in the section marked "short-term goals," family members should write down what they like to do with their money and the approximate monthly cost. The goals near the top should be those that are most precious. For instance, if dining out is something you look forward to all week—more than buying new clothes or taking vacations—list it at the top.

Under "long-term goals," write in the things that you can't afford today but hope to have eventually. Again, try to rank these goals by priority. And write down when you could reasonably expect to have them. Don't worry if you don't know exactly what they'll cost. Figuring the cost of uncertain goals, such as retirement or a child's college tuition, is an inexact science. But you'll learn how to estimate it as you progress through this book.

One suggestion: Use pencil. In later chapters, you'll be presented with ideas about how to save money and some unpleasant realities about what certain goals will cost. Both the opportunities and the grim truth are likely to affect how you view your goals.

Why Bother?

Somewhere in the back of your mind you're probably thinking that you know what you want. Why bother writing it down? Two reasons: First, your goals may be different from the goals of your spouse and you may not even realize it. Too often couples trip along thinking that husband and wife are after the same things when in fact their goals are mutually exclusive. This is one way that money can split up a marriage. If you write down your financial goals now, there won't be any surprises later.

Another reason to write down goals is to avoid some of the "shudda-wudda-kuddas." Late in life, many people lament what they didn't do. "I should have bought that investment property." "I should have saved more for retirement." "If only I'd done ———, I would have been able to spend more time with my kids."

Maybe you should be doing things differently. Maybe not. But if you never sit down and actually consider what you can do—what you want to do—you'll never know. Ideally, when you're old, you should be able to sit down and say: "We could have done that, but we decided not to. We had more important goals." No regrets.

If you are married, you and your spouse should each take a few minutes independently and fill out one of the worksheets below. When you compare them afterward, you may find you have some things to discuss. If you're single, fill out the worksheets simply to make your goals tangible and to prioritize them. This is the first step in the process of finding out how to get what you want.

Coping with Elusive Goals

Okay, you don't mind writing down your goals, but they aren't all that tangible. Perhaps you simply want to feel comfortable, secure, happy.

No problem. Close your eyes and imagine the comfort you're striving for. What do you see? Are you in your own home or is it an apartment? Is the chair you're sitting in wicker or Chippendale? Are you driving a motorcycle or a Ferrari?

Now imagine the things that make you uncomfortable. Is it bills? Is it not having enough to pay a check in a restaurant? Or to go on a nice vacation? Or is it stress from a job that you really don't like?

Once you've compiled a mental list of what you consider comfortable and uncomfortable, you'll find your goals will start to become more tangible—and you may even be able to start putting them in order.

You may, for example, decide that you're happy in an apartment with inexpensive furniture and you don't mind the motorcycle—but you really don't like your job. Your goal, then, is to make yourself financially independent: economically capable of liberating yourself from that job and surviving comfortably—in your apartment with your motorcycle and your furniture—until you find a job you like.

Your next step is to figure out what that will cost. Would it take, for example, three months to get the job you want? Or would it take six? Maybe what you want is your own company. How much money would it cost to start it? How much money would you need to live on until it was running successfully enough to support you?

You need to go through this process for each and every goal that is hard to quantify.

Today's Cost or the Future Cost?

How on earth can you estimate the cost for long-term goals? After all, retirement may be twenty years away. How are you supposed to know how much money you'll need then to be comfortable?

You aren't. To estimate a long-term goal, list how much it would cost today. For instance, if you retired tomorrow, how much would you need in the bank to generate a livable income? How do you figure that?

One simple option is to look at how much banks are paying on savings deposits, and then to multiply that amount by round numbers, such as $100,000 or $200,000. If going interest rates are 6 percent, for example, you multiply that by $100,000; then ask yourself, can I live on $6,000 annually? No. What about $12,000? You need $24,000? Okay. Divide the $24,000 by the $6,000 you could earn on your bank account. You will find that you need four times as much—$400,000 in your bank account—to generate that kind of income in interest. Later in the book, you'll learn how to adjust that figure to account for inflation so you can determine precisely how much you will need at any given point in the future.

Now, get started. And have fun. Remember, setting goals is like daydreaming—only better because you can make these dreams come true.

Goals

Who: ______________________________

Short-term goals (You want it in five years or less):

1. What: ______________________________

   When: ______________ How much: ______________

2. What: ______________________________

   When: ______________ How much: ______________

3. What: ______________________________

   When: ______________ How much: __________

4. What: ______________________________

   When: ______________ How much: __________

5. What: ______________________________

   When: ______________ How much: __________

Long-term goals (5+ years from now):

1. What: ______________________________

   When: ______________ How much: __________

2. What: ______________________________

   When: ______________ How much: __________

3. What: ______________________________

   When: ______________ How much: __________

4. What: ______________________________

   When: ______________ How much: __________

5. What: ______________________________

   When: ______________ How much: __________

6. What: ______________________________

   When: ______________ How much: __________

Goals

Who:____

Short-term goals (You want it in five years or less):

1. What: ____

   When: ____________________ How much: ________________

2. What: ____

   When: ____________________ How much: ________________

3. What: ____

   When: ____________________ How much: ________________

4. What: ____

   When: ____________________ How much: ________________

5. What: ____

   When: ____________________ How much: ________________

Long-term goals (5+ years from now):

1. What: ____

   When: ____________________ How much: ________________

2. What: ____

   When: ____________________ How much: ________________

3. What: ______________________________

   When: ______________ How much: ______________

4. What: ______________________________

   When: ______________ How much: ______________

5. What: ______________________________

   When: ______________ How much: ______________

6. What: ______________________________

   When: ______________ How much: ______________

Chapter 3

You Are Here

A picture is worth a thousand words, and you can prove it by creating a snapshot of your financial life.

What the chapter tells you

Knowing what you own and what you owe:

- will save you countless hours—and thousands of dollars—when it comes time to fill out a loan application or financial aid form, or to buy life insurance.
- is the first step in creating a viable investment plan.
- is a graphic illustration of whether you have too much or too little debt.
- is a valuable reference for your heirs, who will be able to piece together the details of your estate more quickly and easily if you happen to die unexpectedly.

What the chapter shows you

- How to determine your net worth
- How to categorize what you own in order to spread your money around, boost your returns, and make your money safer
- Where to write it all down

Where do I start?

Ever try to get somewhere without knowing where you're starting from? You simply can't. It's necessary to know where you are and where you want to end up. Otherwise, you don't know whether to turn left or right; you may move too fast; or you may not be able to move at all for fear of choosing the wrong direction.

When you start to get your financial life together, you face the same problem. Without knowing where you are, it's nearly impossible to set out for where you want to go.

The good news is that pinpointing your place on a *financial* road map is easy. It's a matter of simple addition and subtraction.

It's also worth mentioning that the few minutes you spend calculating how much you have—your "net worth"—will pay numerous dividends in the future.

It will make it easier to fill out loan applications. It will save you time when determining how much life insurance you need. It will help you invest, by showing how you have already invested. It will help you estimate how much you need to save for retirement. It will help you determine the best college savings strategies for your children. And, in general, it will serve as a mark on the wall to show where you started and how much you've grown.

What You Need

Before you get started, take a moment to pull together some of the financial records that will make this job fairly quick and easy. Specifically, you want statements that indicate how much you owe on each of these types of loans:

- Mortgage loans
- Home equity loans
- Personal loans, including student loans, a line of credit, credit card, or debt owed a family member
- Brokerage loans, which would be incurred when you buy stocks on margin
- Auto loans
- Loans against a retirement account, such as a 401(k)

Also collect bank, brokerage, and retirement account statements that indicate how much cash or equity you have in various types of investments, including:

- Savings account balances
- Value of stocks, bonds, or mutual funds you own
- Savings bonds

- Mutual funds
- Checking account balances (list only the amount you have left over after paying regular bills each month)
- Balances in IRA, 401(k) or self-directed pension plans
- Vested value of company-paid pension (list only the lump-sum amount you could receive if you left your company tomorrow)
- The market value of interests in limited partnerships and other investments

Finally, pull out a copy of your most recent tax return, to jog your memory about any investments or assets that you may have forgotten.

Categorize

In the spaces provided on the worksheets at the end of this chapter, you'll want to jot down the value of your assets and the size of your debts.

You'll notice that this listing is categorized, separating real estate, cash, stocks, bonds, insurance, and other assets such as art or collectibles. In each section you'll have space to write down the approximate value of an asset, as well as any loans made against that type of property.

You then take your total debt and subtract it from your total assets to come up with your equity for each category.

At the bottom of the worksheet, you'll add together all of the totals to determine your total net worth. Then, if you like, you can go back and calculate what percentage of your assets are currently locked up in each type of investment.

What ultimately is the purpose of categorizing? Diversification. Knowing what percentage of your assets are in different types of investments helps you wisely diversify—or spread your money around. That brings you safety and, possibly, higher investment returns.

Chapter 18 will address diversification in more detail, but for now, suffice it to say that it's the financial world's equivalent of "don't put all your eggs in one basket."

For instance, if your entire net worth is locked up in your home, you could be wiped out by a plunge in real estate values. Likewise, if all your money is in the stock market, you would get crushed if the market fell. But it's unlikely that the stock market, the bond market, and the real estate markets would fall all at the same time. So by spreading your wealth around, you've made your nest egg safer.

Determining Value

If you have a home (or investment "units" in a limited partnership that is not publicly traded) you may have a hard time putting a real value on some of what you own. Certainly you know what you paid for these things. But are they worth what you paid? Are they worth less or more?

Make an educated guess, trying to be as realistic as possible. If you need to, call a broker or other professional to help. But don't spend a tremendous amount of time at it.

Just as you don't need to know what grain of sand you're standing on at the beach to know how close you are to the pier, you don't need to count every penny in your pocket to determine whether you will meet your financial goals.

Besides, market values are fluid. There's no point in belaboring a calculation that's going to change the moment you've solved it. Try to get within a few thousand dollars of accurate. If you do, this estimate will serve your purposes as well as one that gets down to the final penny.

Personal Property

The following worksheet doesn't leave space for you to record the value of personal property, such as your furniture, paintings, crystal, and jewelry. Additionally, though you'll list the amount you owe on your car, you haven't been asked to list what it's worth. Clearly these items are valuable, so why don't you count them?

Generally speaking, you buy these things because you are using them—they're what you spend your wealth on; not items that will generate wealth for you. The only time you should worry about what your personal property is worth is when you give it to charity or attempt to sell it secondhand.

Until then, the couch is a nice place to sit. The car is a means of transportation.

There are, of course, a few exceptions. If you collect cars or art or baseball cards or jewelry—buying and selling them actively and for the purpose of making a profit—you should list them as assets. Record these items under "Collectibles, Art, and Other."

Account Numbers

This asset listing also has spaces to provide the names of your banks, brokerage firms, and account numbers. Clearly, you don't need to fill these in, but you may want to for two reasons:

One is in case of a disaster. If anything happened to you, your family could have real trouble piecing together your financial life. This listing allows spouses and children, who may be unfamiliar with the family finances, to figure out where the money is to pay the bills.

Or, if you survive a fire that consumes your savings bonds, you can get them replaced fairly easily if you know the serial numbers.

On a more day-to-day level, having bank names and account numbers handy will save you time if you ever need to fill out a loan application. Whether you're applying for a credit card, personal loan, or mortgage, chances are you'll have to list much of this same information time and again.

You've got all this stuff out now. If you spend a couple extra minutes writing it down, you won't have to sift through the bill drawer again trying to find a gazillion little pieces of paper.

Don't be casual about where you leave this book, though. If you've got larcenous relatives or friends, they could do some damage with all your financial information at their fingertips. Put this where you put other documents that you don't want tampered with or pilfered—just make sure that somebody you trust knows where that is.

So Many Spaces, So Little to Record

Your first reaction to the following worksheets is likely to be: "You've got to be kidding." The list of assets *is* huge.

That doesn't mean this is going to take forever. It just means you'll probably leave plenty of spaces blank.

Why have so many lines, when most people aren't going to need them all? It's like buying a house that has far more closet space than you need. When you've got plenty of room, things stay neat and orderly. It gets ugly when space is tight.

If you, however, are one of the lucky few who need more spaces than are provided, attach a separate sheet with your account numbers or simply copy some of these and just use the worksheet for totals.

Keep This

As a final note, make sure you save this net worth worksheet—for the long haul. If you eventually throw away this book, try to remember to take this listing out, date it, and stick it with your permanent personal papers.

Why? Someday you'll be miles from here, financially speaking, that is. This listing will give you a clear illustration of how far you traveled.

That's important because there are times when you'll feel that financial prudence is all work and no reward. You may scrimp and save for years, and feel as if you've made sorry progress. Sure, you've paid off a few credit cards. Maybe you've put some money in a retirement plan. But your bank account is empty. Stock brokers don't seem interested when you tell them how many shares you want to buy.

That's the time to do this net worth listing again, to see how far you've come. If you realize that, in reality, you're $10,000 or $20,000 richer than you were before, you may feel inspired enough to keep up the good work. On the other hand, if you find that you are standing still—or falling backward—you may want to scrutinize your finances more closely to see where you are going wrong and why you can't seem to get there from here.

Assets

Cash

Checking acct. balance $____________________

Bank:____________________ Acct. #: ____________________

Checking acct. balance $____________________

Bank:____________________ Acct. #: ____________________

Savings acct. balance $____________________

Bank:____________________ Acct. #: ____________________

Savings acct. balance $____________________

Bank:____________________ Acct. #: ____________________

Certificates of deposit $____________________

Bank:____________________ Acct. #: ____________________

Certificates of deposit $____________________

Bank:____________________ Acct. #: ____________________

Certificates of deposit $____________________

Bank:____________________ Acct. #: ____________________

Money market account/fund $____________________

Bank:____________________ Acct. #: ____________________

Money market account balance $____________________

Bank:____________________ Acct. #: ____________________

Treasury bills* $______________________

Located:______________ Serial #: ______________

Savings bonds* $______________________

Located:______________ Serial #: ______________

Other cash $______________________

Description: ______________________________

A. Total cash investments: $______________________
(Add all preceding amounts)

Personal loans

Credit-card balance $______________________

Issuer:______________ Card #: ______________

Number to call if lost or stolen:______________________

Credit-card balance $______________________

Issuer:______________ Card #: ______________

Number to call if lost or stolen:______________________

Credit-card balance $______________________

Issuer:______________ Card #: ______________

Number to call if lost or stolen:______________________

Credit-card balance $______________________

Issuer:______________ Card #: ______________

Number to call if lost or stolen:______________________

Personal line of credit (balance) $______________________

Bank:______________ Acct. #:______________

**If you have more than one, attach a list of serial numbers and dollar values.*

Other unsecured personal loan $ ______________________

Issuer:______________________ Acct. #:______________________

B. Total unsecured debt: $ ______________________
(Add all balance due amounts)

C. Net cash (A minus B): $ ______________________

% of total assets in cash:** ______________________

Real Estate

Market value of your home: $ ______________________

Rental or vacation home: $ ______________________

Shares in real estate investment trusts: $ ______________________

Broker:______________________ Acct. #:______________________

Mortgage-backed securities $ ______________________

Broker:______________________ Acct. #:______________________

CMOs and other real estate $ ______________________

Broker:______________________ Acct. #:______________________

D. Total real estate assets: $ ______________________

Loans Secured by Real Estate

Mortgage loan balance $ ______________________

Bank:______________________ Acct. #:______________________

Mortgage loan balance $ ______________________

Bank:______________________ Acct. #:______________________

***Calculate this after you finish the entire worksheet by dividing your net cash result by your total assets (line S). (In other words, if line C—net cash—is $1,500 and line S—total assets—is $10,000, you divide $1,500 by $10,000 to find 15% of your assets are in cash.)*

Home equity loan balance $________________

Bank:________________ Acct. #: ________________

Other real estate loans $________________

What:________________ Where:________________

E. Total real estate loans: $ ________________

F. Net assets in real estate: (D minus E) $ ________________

% of assets in real estate*: ________________

Stock

Brokerage account value $________________

Broker:________________ Acct. #: ________________

Brokerage account value $________________

Broker:________________ Acct. #: ________________

Equity mutual fund value $________________

Fund:________________ Acct. #: ________________

Equity mutual fund value $________________

Fund:________________ Acct. #: ________________

401(k)-amt. in equity option $________________

401(k)-amt. in equity option $________________

Other stock investments $________________

What:________________ Where:________________

G. Total stock assets: $________________

**Calculate this after you finish the entire worksheet by dividing your net assets in real estate by your total assets (line S). (In other words, if line F—net assets in real estate—is $30,000 and line S—total assets—is $100,000, you divide $30,000 by $100,000 to find 30% of your assets are in real estate.)*

Securities Debts

Margin loan balance $____________________

Lender:____________________ Acct. #: ____________________

Other securities loans $____________________

What:____________________ Where:____________________

H. Total securities debts: $____________________

I. Net stock investments: (G minus H) $____________________

% of assets in stock*: ____________________

Bonds

Treasury notes/bonds** $____________________

Maturity:____________________ Serial #: ____________________

Corporate notes/bonds** $____________________

Maturity:____________________ Serial #: ____________________

Municipal notes/bonds** $____________________

Maturity:____________________ Serial #: ____________________

Bond funds** $____________________

Company:____________________ Acct. #: ____________________

401(k), assets invested in bonds $____________________

401(k), assets invested in bonds $____________________

**Calculate this after you finish the entire worksheet by dividing your net stock investments by your total assets (line S). (In other words, if line I—net stock investments—is $1,500 and line S—total net worth—is $20,000, you divide $1,500 by $20,000 to find 7.5% of your assets are in stocks.)*

***If you have more than one, attach a list of serial numbers and dollar values.*

Other bonds/fixed income $________________

What:________________ Where:________________

J. Total bond/fixed income: $________________

Loans Secured by Bonds

Loan balance $________________

Lender:________________ Acct. #: ________________

K. Total loans against bonds: $________________

L. Net bond assets:
(J minus K) $________________

% of assets in bonds: ________________

Insurance

Cash value life insurance Insurer:________________

Policy #:________________ Surrender value:________________

Variable annuity Insurer:________________

Policy #:________________ Surrender value:________________

M. Insurance surrender value: $________________

Policy Loans

Loan amount $________________

Policy #:________________ Insurer:________________

Loan amount $________________

Policy #:________________ Insurer:________________

N. Total policy loans: $________________

O. Net insurance assets:
(M minus N) $________________

% of assets in insurance: ________________

Collectibles, Art, and Other

What:________________ Value $________________

Where:____

What:________________ Value $________________

Where:____

P. Total value of "other": $ ________________

Loans Against Collectibles, Art, and Other Assets

Lender:________________ Amount:________________

Acct. #:________________

Lender:________________ Amount:________________

Acct. #:________________

Q. Total "other" loans: $ ________________

R. Net other assets: $ ________________
(P minus Q)

% of assets in "other": ________________

S. NET (TOTAL) ASSETS: $ ________________
(Add: C, F, I, L, O and R)

Chapter 4

I Spend, Therefore I Am

It's a miserable job. But you've got to budget—at least if you want to do more than get by each month and especially if you want to be comfortable when you retire.

What the chapter tells you

- You may need a budget to help limit your spending. But you definitely need a budget to help plan for your future.
- Budgets don't need to imply deprivation. They're better if they encourage moderation.

What the chapter shows you

- What you need
- Where to record it

Where do I start?

You might as well know now: This is the toughest chapter in the book. This is where you're supposed to put together your budget—or, as financial planners euphemistically call it, your "spending plan."

Not only do budgets take time to compile, they make you face all your financial demons. Those demons are niggling expenses that you've ignored for years. One at a time, they probably seem insignificant. But once you write them down, and note the frequency, you can't ignore them anymore. They're not little expenses. They're big, gaping money pits. You've either got to board them up or accept the fact that you'll be feeding them—and little else—for the rest of your life.

Maybe your demon is a hobby, like fixing up old cars that constantly need one more $40 part. Or maybe it's going out to dinner two or three nights a week. Or lunches with your pals at work. Perhaps you're hooked on short vacations—one more $500 weekend isn't going to hurt anybody, right? Or clothes. Or music. Or maybe it's as innocent as never getting your rented videos back on time. Whatever it is, you'll find it here. And you'll have to deal with it.

The good news is, you don't have to give up all your expensive habits. Most people just need to scale them back a bit. In fact, it's a bad idea to try to completely cast aside the costly things you love. Money, after all, is a means to an end. And that end is to make you happy, secure, and comfortable—now *and* later.

You do need to feed your long-term goals by saving. But your long-term goals don't have to consume your short-term happiness. A good budget is Aristotle in action: "Moderation in all things."

What You Need

So get started by pulling out twelve months' worth of check registers and credit-card receipts, as well as a copy of last year's tax return. You'll need these things to remind you of your monthly, annual, and semiannual expenses.

You thought you were going to make up a "projected" budget based on what you think you're spending?

Nah. People who try to make up budgets without looking at their actual expenses are kidding themselves. The amount you think you're spending—or think you ought to be spending—is almost always less than what you are actually spending. Chances are you're paying more for entertainment or dry cleaning or cable or utilities or gasoline or nail polish than you've ever considered.

After you've finished reading this book, you can do a second "projected" budget that incorporates savings that you've discovered—or costs that you've only now become aware of—but you need the real budget first.

Why Do I Need It?

In addition to the obvious reasons to create a budget—like figuring out where you're spending your money—completing a current budget is the first step in determining how much money you'll need for retirement. It will also help you estimate how much life insurance you'll need.

How so? Both your retirement needs and your insurance needs are based on your actual expenses. You figure out how much you spend, look at the assets you could tap to finance that spending, and then save (or insure) enough to finance the gap. Without a clear idea of how you spend your money, you really don't know whether your retirement gap is an abyss or a pothole. If you're saving for an abyss when the gap is modest, you're forgoing today's pleasures to make your heirs rich. If, on the other hand, your gap is wider than you think, your golden years could turn decidedly leaden.

How to Do It

You'll notice that each entry on the worksheet at the end of this chapter has a space for each month and a separate space for the annual total. In some cases, you won't need to fill in all those spaces.

For instance, unless you have an impound account, you pay your property taxes and insurance bills just once or twice a year. And utility companies often bill for two or three months of service at a time.

If you're troubled by the fact that you're flush with cash in some months and broke in others, you should carefully jot down every expense in the month it's paid. That should help you ferret out the problem expenditures and better plan for them.

Otherwise, you can be more casual about how you fill in the worksheet. If you've got a fixed monthly expense—such as a fixed-rate mortgage—you can annualize the cost and simply record it at the end, rather than writing down the same number twelve times. You can also round figures to the nearest dollar. There's no reason to be counting pennies.

Make sure to use pencil when you're filling in the spaces. Chances are you'll find expenditures that you forgot about after you've filled in a few spaces. You may also want to have a scratch pad handy because there's not enough space here to record every movie and every trip to the grocery store. Use this listing just for the monthly totals.

In the end, you'll compare your total expenses to your total income. There's a good chance that there's a gap between the two.

If you earned less than you spent, the difference is what you financed on credit cards or personal loans during the year.

If what you spent appears to be less than your income, but you have no savings or loose cash, you've found the depth of your personal money pit. You may want to complete the worksheet in the following chapter, titled "Money Troubles," as well. It will help you find out where your money is actually going.

Sharpen your pencils and get to it.

Annual Budget

	Jan	Feb	Mar	Apr	May	June	July	Aug	Sept	Oct	Nov	Dec
Income												
Wages	___	___	___	___	___	___	___	___	___	___	___	___
Tips	___	___	___	___	___	___	___	___	___	___	___	___
Interest	___	___	___	___	___	___	___	___	___	___	___	___
Dividends	___	___	___	___	___	___	___	___	___	___	___	___
Annuities	___	___	___	___	___	___	___	___	___	___	___	___
Social Security	___	___	___	___	___	___	___	___	___	___	___	___
Capital gains	___	___	___	___	___	___	___	___	___	___	___	___
Rentals	___	___	___	___	___	___	___	___	___	___	___	___
Other	___	___	___	___	___	___	___	___	___	___	___	___
Total income	___	___	___	___	___	___	___	___	___	___	___	___
Expenses: Housing Related												
Mortgage/ rent	___	___	___	___	___	___	___	___	___	___	___	___
Property taxes	___	___	___	___	___	___	___	___	___	___	___	___
Water	___	___	___	___	___	___	___	___	___	___	___	___

	Jan	Feb	Mar	Apr	May	June	July	Aug	Sept	Oct	Nov	Dec
Electric	____	____	____	____	____	____	____	____	____	____	____	____
Gas	____	____	____	____	____	____	____	____	____	____	____	____
Garbage	____	____	____	____	____	____	____	____	____	____	____	____
Phone	____	____	____	____	____	____	____	____	____	____	____	____
Newspaper	____	____	____	____	____	____	____	____	____	____	____	____
Cable	____	____	____	____	____	____	____	____	____	____	____	____
Home insurance	____	____	____	____	____	____	____	____	____	____	____	____
Repair	____	____	____	____	____	____	____	____	____	____	____	____
Other	____	____	____	____	____	____	____	____	____	____	____	____

Expenses: Food/Clothing/Transportation

Groceries	____	____	____	____	____	____	____	____	____	____	____	____
Clothes	____	____	____	____	____	____	____	____	____	____	____	____
Shoes	____	____	____	____	____	____	____	____	____	____	____	____
Car payments	____	____	____	____	____	____	____	____	____	____	____	____
Auto insurance	____	____	____	____	____	____	____	____	____	____	____	____
Car repairs	____	____	____	____	____	____	____	____	____	____	____	____
Other transport	____	____	____	____	____	____	____	____	____	____	____	____

	Jan	Feb	Mar	Apr	May	June	July	Aug	Sept	Oct	Nov	Dec
Taxi	____	____	____	____	____	____	____	____	____	____	____	____
Train	____	____	____	____	____	____	____	____	____	____	____	____
Plane	____	____	____	____	____	____	____	____	____	____	____	____
Other	____	____	____	____	____	____	____	____	____	____	____	____

Expenses: Personal Insurance

Life	____	____	____	____	____	____	____	____	____	____	____	____
Health	____	____	____	____	____	____	____	____	____	____	____	____
Disability	____	____	____	____	____	____	____	____	____	____	____	____
Other	____	____	____	____	____	____	____	____	____	____	____	____

Expenses: Personal Debt Payments

Credit card	____	____	____	____	____	____	____	____	____	____	____	____
Personal loan	____	____	____	____	____	____	____	____	____	____	____	____
Other	____	____	____	____	____	____	____	____	____	____	____	____

Expenses: Children

School/ daycare	____	____	____	____	____	____	____	____	____	____	____	____
Baby-sitting	____	____	____	____	____	____	____	____	____	____	____	____

	Jan	*Feb*	*Mar*	*Apr*	*May*	*June*	*July*	*Aug*	*Sept*	*Oct*	*Nov*	*Dec*
Activities (ballet/ tennis/karate/ art/etc.)	___	___	___	___	___	___	___	___	___	___	___	___
School supplies	___	___	___	___	___	___	___	___	___	___	___	___
Other	___	___	___	___	___	___	___	___	___	___	___	___

Expenses: Entertainment/Miscellaneous

Dinner out	___	___	___	___	___	___	___	___	___	___	___	___
Lunches out	___	___	___	___	___	___	___	___	___	___	___	___
Breakfasts	___	___	___	___	___	___	___	___	___	___	___	___
Movies	___	___	___	___	___	___	___	___	___	___	___	___
Concerts	___	___	___	___	___	___	___	___	___	___	___	___
Plays	___	___	___	___	___	___	___	___	___	___	___	___
Health club	___	___	___	___	___	___	___	___	___	___	___	___
Vacations	___	___	___	___	___	___	___	___	___	___	___	___
Housekeeper	___	___	___	___	___	___	___	___	___	___	___	___
Gardener	___	___	___	___	___	___	___	___	___	___	___	___
Pool service	___	___	___	___	___	___	___	___	___	___	___	___
Other	___	___	___	___	___	___	___	___	___	___	___	___

	Jan	*Feb*	*Mar*	*Apr*	*May*	*June*	*July*	*Aug*	*Sept*	*Oct*	*Nov*	*Dec*
Expenses: Vacation/Rental Property												
Mortgage												
Insurance												
Utilities												
Maintenance												
Taxes												
Other												
Expenses: Taxes												
Federal income												
State income												
Social Security												
Disability												
Other												
Regular Contributions to Savings												
401k												
IRA/SEP IRA												
Keogh												
Thrift plan												

	Jan	*Feb*	*Mar*	*Apr*	*May*	*June*	*July*	*Aug*	*Sept*	*Oct*	*Nov*	*Dec*
Bank	____	____	____	____	____	____	____	____	____	____	____	____
Broker	____	____	____	____	____	____	____	____	____	____	____	____
Mutual fund	____	____	____	____	____	____	____	____	____	____	____	____
Total expenses	____	____	____	____	____	____	____	____	____	____	____	____
Discretionary income*	____	____	____	____	____	____	____	____	____	____	____	____

**Subtract total expenses from total income (page 33). This is the money you can play with.*

Chapter 5

Money Trouble

If you fight about money—or are dissatisfied with what you've got, even though you're earning a reasonable income—this chapter is for you.

What the chapter tells you

- Most minor money woes are caused by wasting small amounts of money consistently.
- You can solve these woes by finding your personal money pit and boarding it up—or at least making the hole a bit smaller.

What the chapter shows you

- How to find the hole

Where do I start?

Do you fight about money? Are you overextended and still unhappy about your life-style, about how much (or how little) money you have? Are you not sure where your money goes? Do you have trouble making minimum payments on all your monthly bills?

If you answered yes to any or all of those questions, this chapter is for you. It will start you thinking, and lead you on a month-long odyssey that should help you spend your money in ways that will make you happier.

Sound like a dream? Well, it's not quite a nightmare. But it will require some work.

Specifically, you will need to fill out a daily expense log, writing down every dollar—every dime, even—that you spend during a day. Why? Because every one of us wastes some money. We spend money on snacks or overdue videos or trinkets that are cast aside in a matter of days. In most cases, you're not even aware of how much you're spending or precisely what you're spending that money on.

Consider a common scenario: You go to work in the morning with $20 and come home with $3. You remember spending $5 on lunch, but other than that, the money seems to have disappeared.

Were you robbed by a particularly sadistic burglar who left that $3 just to confuse you? Or did you actually spend the other $12 and just not remember how? No need to ponder. The expense log will help you to figure it out.

How to Do It

When you start out in the morning, you need to actually take stock of how much you've got in your wallet, your pocket, or your billfold. Then detail every dime you spend. There's no worming your way out by using checks or credit cards, either. Whether you bought gas, lunch, or stamps—regardless of whether you used cash, credit cards, or change—every dime you pay out needs to be recorded.

This may seem like overkill, but breaking bad habits in finance is just like breaking any other bad habits. It's like bad eating habits: You think you're starving yourself just because you haven't had a satisfying meal in days. But you're gaining weight. How could it happen?

What you probably failed to realize is that you ate every piece of candy in your coworker's Valentine basket. And you scarfed down a bowl of mixed nuts while you were waiting for a nondieter to finish a fish sandwich. You end up chunky, dissatisfied, and ready to ditch it all. But if you'd just been keeping track of all those little snacks, you would have spotted the problem, eliminated it, and gone for the less caloric five-course meal instead.

It's the same with money. You don't realize it, but at times, you're spending money on mixed nuts. And you don't even like them.

You need to figure out where that $12 is going. And then decide whether those purchases are making you happier—or just poorer. In many cases, you'll decide you still want to buy the same things—you just wouldn't buy as much if you were paying attention to the cost.

To help you figure out just what happened to the $12 and the rest of the money you spend each day, make copies of the worksheet at the end of this chapter. Then start using them—one per day, every day. Write in the date and each and every expenditure you made during the day. Follow the program for a month, which should be enough time to recognize wasteful spending patterns. However, if you're a binge spender—you go along frugally for months, but suddenly blow everything on diamond tiaras, beaded gowns, or lavish vacations—you may need to keep track of your expenses for longer periods.

Remember, the expenses you write down here are not your monthly bills, such as your mortgage and utility payments. Those items are part of your monthly budget. This listing should show where you spend your pocket change, which, often, isn't change at all—it's big bucks.

Bigger Trouble

If you are in a position where you cannot pay all of your bills each month—perhaps because you've built up more debt than you can handle—you need more than a daily expense log. You need a credit counselor. If things are really dire, you may even need a bankruptcy attorney.

To find a credit counselor, check the phone book for a local chapter of the Consumer Credit Counseling Service. This nonprofit organization can sometimes negotiate lower interest rates on your debt, help you work out payment plans with your creditors, and set up a budget. They can also help explain what your options are when things have gotten too bad to handle with these simple measures.

In most instances, CCCS provides basic counseling services for free. However, some offices charge nominal fees—usually from $10 to $25—if your problems require a lot of time and attention.

Dogged by Past Troubles

If your money problems are largely behind you, but you can't seem to shake the long-lasting ill effects of a scarred credit record, see the "Establishing Credit" section in Chapter 7 (page 59). It will explain how you can reestablish credit, what it costs, and roughly how long it takes.

Daily Expenses

Date:________________

Meals Out		***Transportation***	
Breakfast	$__________	Bus fare	$__________
Lunch	$__________	Plane tickets	$__________
Dinner	$__________	Gas	$__________
Coffee	$__________	Boat	$__________
Snacks	$__________	Concorde	$__________

Entertainment		***Clothing/Trinkets***	
Movies out	$__________	__________	$__________
Videos	$__________	__________	$__________
Sports	$__________	__________	$__________
Other	$__________	__________	$__________

All other (What/How much)

__________	$__________	__________	$__________
__________	$__________	__________	$__________
__________	$__________	__________	$__________

Part Two

BANKING AND CREDIT

Everybody needs some banking services and access to a certain amount of credit. Here's how you get what you need at a reasonable cost.

Chapter 6: Bargain Banking

You may think deposit rates, fees, and loan costs are immovable. Think again. Your banker is willing to bargain. You just have to learn the ropes. See page 45.

Chapter 7: Give Yourself Credit

Credit cards are nearly impossible to live without in today's society. You need one to order flowers over the phone, reserve a hotel room, or rent a car. The trick is getting the right card at the right cost. Here's how, page 54.

Chapter 6

Bargain Banking

Learning to deal effectively with your banker can pay valuable dividends.

What the chapter tells you

- You're probably spending too much on bank charges, credit-card rates, and other financial fees.
- What, besides loans, your banker is peddling

What the chapter shows you

- The approximate amount you're spending on a checking account and why that may not be necessary
- How to monitor your credit needs and find the best loan to suit them
- How to determine how safe your bank investments are
- What to do with your statements
- How to boost the return on a certificate of deposit
- How to reduce the agony of applying for a loan

Where do I start?

Remember: When it comes to banking, everything is negotiable.

People tend to walk into the marbled halls of their local financial institution thinking that it's the last bastion of conservatism. They wouldn't expect their gray-suited banker to be bartering like a pumpkin salesman on the day after Halloween. In fact, bankers do wheel and deal. You don't even have to be a high roller to participate—although your bargaining power does tend to rise with your balance. For instance, anyone can do the following:

- Bargain up the advertised interest rate on a certificate of deposit
- Get the banker to eliminate fees on a checking or savings account
- Get a "free" credit card
- Have fees "waived" on everything from bounced checks to over-limit penalties on your personal loans

It's important to note that rates on certificates of deposit have been negotiable for years, but your banker's propensity to bargain on other types of accounts is a fairly recent trend that's growing every day. Why? The regulatory walls dividing banking from industry are coming down. Banks are suddenly competing with mutual funds, insurers, and investment banking firms. This gives the banks new opportunities to sell these same services to the thousands of checking and savings account customers that they've taken for granted for decades.

The result is that your banker would like to forge a "relationship" with you—the kind of bond that bankers assume can be leveraged into a series of profitable transactions. If you're smart, the relationship you develop can be *mutually* beneficial.

Choosing a Bank

The first step to developing a profitable relationship is choosing the right kind of bank. That comes down to knowing what you need and want from a financial institution. If the answer is: "A checking account and lots of automated tellers so I can get cash whenever I need it, no matter where I am," you'd be wise to look to big banks.

If, on the other hand, you're looking for a bank that would be willing to finance your small business, you're probably better off with a small "niche" bank that's willing to get to know you and to accommodate your schedule and needs with a minimum of fuss and red tape.

If you are willing to put up with some inconvenience in order to get better rates on your deposits and lower fees on checking and savings accounts, you'd be wise to check out credit unions.

Credit unions are member-only organizations that are similar to Bailey's Building and Loan in the Frank Capra movie *It's a Wonderful Life*. They're usually less convenient than using a big bank because they typically have just one office and limited office hours, and they are less automated than the big boys. However, they're far more likely than a bank to offer a "free" account; when they charge for services, they usually charge less; and their loan rates are often better than the rates you'd pay at a commercial bank or savings and loan.

Credit unions are usually available to government employees, teachers, union members, members of some trade groups, members of many professional organizations, and employees of many large companies. In the last few years, credit unions have also expanded their membership by letting in relatives and, sometimes, friends of members. Today more than half of all adult Americans have access to a credit union. Check with your employer, professional group, and relatives to see if you're among them.

What about savings and loans? For the most part, savings and loans have become very similar to consumer-oriented banks. They don't usually offer business loans, but most do offer checking accounts, savings accounts, and mortgage, auto, and credit-card loans. You can assume that big savings and loans are similar to big banks; small ones are similar to small banks.

What You Have to Offer

Once you consider what you want, you'd be wise to realistically assess what you have to offer a banker. The benefits that you can bring to the table are a key issue when sitting down to negotiate the best possible deal.

What could you possibly offer a banker?

- Deposits—bankers particularly like the multiple-digit ones
- Good credit—your willingness to borrow and pay back loans
- Your demographic profile, which may make you a ready market for a spectrum of bank-offered products and services

And, of course, the more business you do with the bank, the more attractive you become as a customer, and the more bargaining power you have.

There are a number of ways you can do business with a bank. You can:

- Open a checking account.
- Open a savings account.
- Buy a certificate of deposit.
- Open a retirement account, such as an IRA or roll-over IRA.

- Get a credit-card loan.
- Secure a mortgage loan or home equity line of credit.
- Take out a personal loan.
- Buy investment and insurance products through the bank's nonbank affiliate.

Chances are, you have several different types of accounts already. If they're at different institutions, you should consider consolidating them with your favorite bank to boost your bargaining power.

Bargaining with a Banker

Before you go shopping for a bank, jot down the average balance you'd normally maintain in your checking account and about how many checks you write each month. If you have a savings account, too, jot down the balance. Do you have a credit card? If so, jot down the type, the interest rate, the annual fee, and a rough approximation of your revolving balance.

Checking balance: $________________________
Number of checks written in a month: __________(approx.)
Do you use the ATM or usually go in to see a teller?
ATM:______ Teller:_______
Do you want your canceled checks returned to you or are you willing to have the bank keep them and simply send you a statement?
Want them back:______ Bank can keep them:_______
Savings balance: $________________________
Credit-card interest rate:______% Annual fee: $_________
Credit-card balance: $________________________

Now, start to shop over the phone. Because it's faster than going to a branch in person, you can check with more institutions. Call several local banks; ask for a new accounts officer; explain that you're shopping around and need to know the best deal you can get given the way you use the bank. Then rattle off your basic banking information—without mentioning the interest rate and annual fee amount that you pay on your credit card—that's listed above.

What You Should Expect

If you are willing to maintain a minimum balance in your standard checking account of $500 to $1,000, you should expect the bank to waive monthly service charges on your checking account.

If you are willing to keep a minimum balance of $300 or more in your savings account, you should expect monthly service charges on that account to be waived too.

If you are a good credit risk and use your credit card at least once or twice a year, you should also expect the bank to waive the annual fee on your credit card. That's simply because there are plenty of fee-free cards. If your bank refuses to waive the charge, you can easily take that business elsewhere. In addition, if your interest rate is above 18 percent, there's a good chance you can get the bank to lower your interest rate as well. (For more details, refer to Chapter 7, "Give Yourself Credit," which starts on page 54.)

What do these "waivers" mean to you in dollars and cents? About $145 annually. To be specific: The average annual fee on checking accounts is more than $7 per month. Banks frequently charge smaller fees—about $3 per month—for your savings account. And the average annual credit-card fee is $25. If your banker waives these fees, you save about $145 a year.

What if the minimum balance required to have the fees waived is higher—say $1,000 or more? Keep shopping.

When you can afford it, it makes sense to maintain a balance of a few hundred dollars in your checking and savings accounts. The balance provides a cushion that helps ensure that you don't bounce checks and that you have a few bucks that can be tapped in an emergency. But keeping a large balance in a checking account simply doesn't make sense because most banks pay little or no interest on these accounts.

Fee-for-All

But monthly and annual fees on basic checking, savings and credit-card accounts are only the beginning of the ways banks nickel-and-dime-and-dollar you to death today.

Banks now commonly charge fees—usually $1 to $2—for each use of "foreign" automated tellers (that's any ATM machine that isn't directly owned by your bank). They charge fees for "point-of-sale" transactions, when you buy gasoline or groceries using your automated teller card. POS fees are often $1 or $2 as well.

You'll get charged anywhere from $2 to $15 if you want a money order or cashier's check, or if you want to transfer money electronically to another person or another bank.

Depending on the type of account you have, you could also get zapped with additional charges if you visit a human teller, write more than a set number of checks in a month, or have your canceled checks returned to you.

And those fees are pikers when you compare them to the penalty fees you pay if you break bank rules. Overdraw your checking account and you could get hit with a fee ranging between $10 and $25 per bounce. Pay your mortgage late and the fee could astound you. It's not unheard of to get hit with $50 to $100 late payment penalties on a mortgage, for example. Go over your credit-card limit and you could face a $10 to $15 fee. Make your credit-card payment late, and not only could you be hit with a fee, the bank could hike the interest rate on your card by several percentage points. And the higher interest rate would apply to your entire revolving balance, which could force you to pay hundreds of dollars more over time.

The good news is that most of these fees are simple to avoid. All you have to do is be aware of them and be careful about how you handle your finances. That means you have to occasionally balance your checkbook. If your bank isn't right around the corner, you may have to plan ahead when you think you'll need cash. You may even have to defer a purchase or two to avoid bounced checks or point-of-sale fees.

It's true that none of these fees are so big that they'll bankrupt you. But paying them is the equivalent of dropping dollar bills out the window as you speed down the freeway. It's money permanently lost. You get absolutely nothing of value in return.

Dialing for Dollars

If you have money to deposit in the bank, you'd be wise to also shop around for the best type of account—and best bank—to deposit it in.

Shouldn't you keep that deposit in your primary bank to build your banking relationship? Not necessarily.

If you have established a friendly relationship with your banker, you should always give your primary bank the opportunity to get or keep your business—if the terms of the deal are comparable to what you could get elsewhere.

Let's say, for example, that you have a $10,000 certificate of deposit at Security First Federal. Security First is paying 5 percent per annum on your deposit. But, when the account matures, you notice an advertisement from Financial First Federal, which is offering 6 percent on their one-year CDs. That would pay $100 more per year.

Before you switch, you should call Security First and ask whether they're willing to match the 6 percent rate. There's a very good chance that they will—or that they'll at least come close.

If not, switch. After all, unless you've got such a tight relationship with your banker that he's taking you out to dinner, $100 is worth walking across the street for.

It is worth mentioning, however, that bankers don't have negotiating room with every type of account. Money market accounts, for example, are offered at a set rate, and everyone who has one gets the same rate. The same holds true for most passbook savings accounts and rates paid on interest-bearing checking accounts. So, while your banker can waive any annual or monthly fees on the account to forward your relationship, he or she usually can't strike a special deal on the interest rate just for you.

Time deposits—usually called certificates of deposit—are the most noteworthy exception. With a CD, you strike an individual deal with the bank. The bank is under no obligation to give another customer the same deal that it gave to you. So if you're a special customer—a person of impeccable banking relationships—you can usually get your banker to boost a CD rate by a few tenths of a percentage point at least.

Early Withdrawal Penalties

The one drawback to certificates of deposit is that they lock your money up for a set period of time. If you attempt to pull your money out before the established "maturity" date, you'll get hit with a penalty.

How much? That depends on the bank, the term of the deposit, and how early you wish to withdraw. It is not uncommon, however, to give up between one and three months' worth of interest earnings if you withdraw money early from a one-year CD; nor is it unheard of to lose six months of interest if you take money out of a five-year CD too soon.

Before you buy a CD, ask the banker about the early withdrawal penalties and whether there are specific circumstances where the bank would agree to waive the fee. Then assess your chance of having to withdraw the money early. If there is a good chance that you'll have to take your money out before the account matures, consider depositing your funds in a shorter-term account, even if that means a somewhat lower interest rate.

If the banker promises not to charge a fee if you withdraw your money early, be sure to get that promise in writing. Years from now when you find you need to rely on that promise, you don't want your money riding on your banker's memory.

Safety and the FDIC

One of the primary reasons people like to deposit money in banks is because they know the federal government stands behind every dollar deposited—up to $100,000—through the aegis of the Federal Deposit Insurance Corporation.

That means you can't lose principal or accrued interest of up to that amount, in the unlikely event that your bank fails.

In fact, you can deposit far more than $100,000 in a single bank—and have every dollar federally insured—if you set the accounts up properly. However, unless there is a compelling reason to do so, you'd be wise never to let your accounts at a single bank amount to more than the $100,000 limit.

Why? Mainly, delays. Normally, if a bank or savings and loan fails, federal regulators will open the bank and pay off depositors on the spot. However, if you have several accounts that combined add to more than $100,000, your payoff may be delayed while regulators sort out whether all of these accounts are fully covered by FDIC insurance. More often than you'd realize, there are mistakes that can cause a portion of your deposits to lose their FDIC insurance coverage.

In addition, if your accounts are held in a living trust, there is a chance that some or all of your deposits are not FDIC insured. The reason has to do with the complicated language and wishes of the trustees. If your bequests are contingent on anything other than age, for example, it's likely that the successor trustee named in that contingent bequest would be denied FDIC coverage. In addition, if the trust names itself as the beneficiary of the account, it is also likely to lose FDIC coverage. That's simply because the FDIC protects people from loss—it doesn't protect legal entities from loss.

After literally hundreds of unsuspecting people lost billions of dollars during the mid-1980s because of this type of legal glitch, the FDIC came out with an eleven-page rule book for how the agency handles the insurance of living trusts. However, the rules are complicated, and you should not count on your banker to fully understand them. If you have a living trust, make sure you deposit no more than $100,000 per financial institution. If your trust is set up just right, you may feel as if you're being unduly and overly cautious. But, particularly when you're dealing with thousands of dollars, it's better to be safe than sorry.

Loans

If you are a good credit risk—someone who pays bills on time and isn't financially overextended—there is a wide array of loans that you can get from your local bank.

In general, these loans fall into two categories: secured and unsecured. Home mortgages, home equity lines of credit, and auto loans are all secured loans. Credit-card loans and personal lines of credit are unsecured.

Generally, secured loans are cheaper than unsecured loans. The downside, of course, is if you fail to pay on your loan, the bank can seize the collateral that secured the loan. Default (stop paying) on a home loan, and the bank will foreclose on your house. Fail to pay on an auto loan and the bank will repossess your car.

Most people will require just four types of loans: mortgage loans, home equity loans, auto loans, and credit-card loans. Information on how to find these loans at reasonable rates and terms are included in Chapters 7 ("Give Yourself Credit"), 8 ("Buying a Car"), and 11 ("Home Sweet Home").

The New Frontier of Bank Products

Banks are increasingly selling an array of new products—ranging from mutual funds and securities to insurance—in their lobbies. In most cases, these are nearly identical to the products you could buy at a brokerage or insurance agency.

However, bank customers are often confused about what they are buying simply because of long-standing perceptions of how banks operate.

Some people think that every product sold in a bank lobby is federally insured, for instance. Some people assume they can't lose principal when they buy a product from a bank representative. Some assume that bankers are highly trained financial professionals who can give you trustworthy, unbiased advice about different products that are available.

For the most part, all of these assumptions are dangerously inaccurate.

Here are the facts: The federal government insures deposits of up to $100,000, which makes it virtually impossible to lose principal on a savings account or CD placed in a federally insured bank or savings and loan.

However, if you buy a mutual fund or a bond or an insurance policy, the federal government is *in no way* standing behind the principal in your account. Some of these investments are insured by nongovernment entities. Insurance policies, for instance, are backed by state guarantee funds. Securities purchased through a registered broker/dealer are backed by the Securities Industry Protection Corporation.

However, neither bears even a remote resemblance to the FDIC.

When a bank fails, the FDIC can tap the massive resources of the U.S. Treasury to pay off depositors on the spot.

When an insurance company fails, state guarantee funds ask healthy insurers to kick money into a pot to pay off policyholders of the failed company. That doesn't happen overnight. In fact, policyholders have often had to wait years before they are paid.

When a brokerage company fails, SIPC ensures that the company's customers get physical possession of their securities (worth up to $500,000) and are returned any cash they had on deposit up to $100,000. However, SIPC does nothing to protect you from a loss of principal caused by market fluctuations.

What about Treasury bills, notes, and bonds that you can purchase at a bank? Aren't they backed by the federal government?

The federal government promises to pay back every dollar of principal and promised interest on these bonds, if you hold them to maturity. If you sell them before they mature, they may be worth more or less than what you originally paid.

Do not be lulled into a false sense of security because you happened to buy an investment product through a bank. Investment products purchased in a bank are no more and no less risky than investment products purchased anywhere else.

To be sure you know what you are buying and the risks you're taking, ask for disclosure statements when you consider purchasing an investment product. Read them. If you don't protect yourself, your banker—no matter how polite or well-meaning—won't either.

Chapter 7

Give Yourself Credit

Want a credit card but don't want to pay ridiculous rates? There are smart ways to get and manage your credit that can drastically lower the interest charges you pay.

What the chapter tells you

- Too much credit can hamper your ability to get a low-rate card.
- Bad credit shouldn't preclude you from getting a card.
- When conventional means don't work, there are some unconventional ways to establish credit.
- You can "repair" your credit yourself. It's fast, easy, and free.

What the chapter shows you

- How to find low-rate cards
- How to establish a credit record
- How to evaluate your credit needs
- Ways to monitor and correct your credit report
- What to look for in a credit agreement

Where do I start?

The credit-card industry used to be a pretty dull place.

A handful of big companies dominated the market. They all charged interest rates ranging from 19.8 to 21.9 percent. (Where they got those figures, no one knows.) They all exacted more than $25 in annual fees. Consumers simply paid up and shut up.

That's history.

There are several reasons why: The 1986 Tax Act took away tax deductions for credit-card interest payments. The recession of the early 1990s pushed interest rates on everything—except credit cards—down; congressional leaders started investigating credit-card rates and considered legislation to cut them; cardholders began to get downright snippy about the high cost.

A couple of intrepid card issuers responded by offering variable-rate cards, which declined in cost as interest rates continued to fall; a few others started to "tier" their rates, giving better deals to better customers; then annual fees started to disappear here and there. Consumers flocked to the less expensive issuers in droves.

Credit card–rate wars ensued, with issuers rapidly slashing rates and fees. Now consumers are clearly in the position to be victors—if they understand the vast differences among the various card terms and fees.

What do you need to know?

The Basics

There are essentially three different types of general-purpose plastic cards: credit cards, charge cards, and debit cards.

Credit cards—your Visa, Mastercard, and retail credit cards—provide you with a flexible personal loan, allowing you to make a purchase and pay the cost off over time.

Charge cards, like the traditional green American Express card, are for convenience only. You can use the card to make a purchase, but you're billed for (and required to pay) the entire amount at the end of the month.

Debit cards, such as your automated teller card, are the equivalent of writing a check—but faster. To make a purchase, you (or a sales clerk) run your plastic card through a computerized machine. The amount of the purchase is automatically, and nearly immediately, deducted from the balance in your bank account.

Why You Need a Credit Card

Although some people may want charge or debit cards, *everybody* needs a credit card. There are three reasons why: (1) emergencies, (2) convenience, and (3) credit history.

If your car breaks down in the middle of nowhere; if you want to cash a check; or if you need to buy something over the phone or rent a car, a credit card is likely to be your best option. (Sure, you can use a charge card for many of the same things. But the credit card offers additional flexibility—just in case your emergency is too expensive to pay off in one fell swoop.)

Having a credit card also allows you to establish a credit history—a written record showing how much you've borrowed in the past and how good you were about paying it back. That will eventually help you qualify for bigger and better things, like an auto loan, a mortgage, and possibly a personal line of credit.

Important, too, is that although people criticize high credit-card rates, having a credit card doesn't have to cost you a single penny. You can get free credit if you choose and use your cards wisely. How? Start by considering just how you plan to use the card.

Self-Evaluation

The card-holding public falls into two basic camps: people who carry balances and people who don't.

About 30 percent of the nation's cardholders use their credit cards like charge cards. They use them for purchases, but they pay off the full balance each and every month. This is, without a doubt, the most cost-effective way to use a credit card—assuming you choose the right card. The "right" card, in this case, is one with no annual fee that offers a so-called "grace period." Grace periods give you a set period of time to pay off the balance before interest charges accrue. Roughly 90 percent of the nation's card issuers offer grace periods that average twenty-five days. Literally dozens of companies offer no-fee cards.

For a convenience user, a no-fee card with a grace period provides easily accessible short-term loans *absolutely free*. Because this consumer pays off the balance before interest charges accrue, the interest rate on the card doesn't matter.

The other 70 percent of Americans leave balances on their cards. For them, interest rates are at least as important—and probably more important—than annual fees.

But they get no mileage out of grace periods. That's because grace periods generally don't apply to cardholders who carry a balance. (Check the fine print on your credit-card agreements, if you don't believe me.) Almost every major card, with the exception of American Express's True Grace, starts charging interest on new purchases immediately if you maintain a revolving balance.

The Interest Rate

Interest rates on credit cards can be either variable or fixed. However, a fixed-rate card is not like a fixed-rate mortgage. The rate on a fixed mortgage cannot change during the life of the loan. But the only procedure necessary to change the rate on your fixed-rate credit card is fifteen days' written notice by the issuer.

It's worth mentioning that issuers rarely raise rates on fixed-rate cards. The ability to do so is only there to help issuers cope if interest rates ever skyrocket. Nonetheless, you should know, when you're considering whether to get a fixed- or a variable-rate card, that this possibility exists.

The interest rate on a variable card "floats" above an index. Most commonly, that index is the prime rate—that's the interest rate that big banks charge their best customers. Banks then add a "margin"—a set number of percentage points—above the index to determine the rate you pay. A common deal, for example, would be a variable card with a published rate of prime plus 9. In this case, when prime is at 6 percent, the credit-card rate is 15 percent—the "index" of 6, plus the "margin" of 9.

A few banks tie their card rates to the so-called London Interbank Offered Rate, or LIBOR, index. That's the rate that banks in Europe charge when they lend each other money. LIBOR may be lower or higher than prime.

The interest rates on variable-rate cards generally adjust at set intervals, such as every three to six months. The current rate will be reflected on your credit-card statement each month.

One other rate-related tidbit you should know: Increasingly, credit-card issuers are trying to get customers in the door by offering "teaser" rates—super-low interest deals of anywhere from 5.9 percent to 9.9 percent that last only a few months.

The teaser rate often has little to do with the ordinary interest rate on the card. So be cautious. These cards can provide true savings to someone who needs very short-term credit—and who meets all the conditions. But be sure to read the fine print. If you end up with a balance after the teaser period is over—or you break one of the rules—you could end up paying more in interest or penalties than you saved.

Annual Fees

Annual fees on credit cards range from a low of zero to highs exceeding $100. In today's market, it's easy to find an issuer that doesn't charge an annual fee. However, you may be willing to pay a fee if the credit-card company is offering some valuable *extra*—a remarkably high credit limit or premiums such as frequent-flier miles, free gasoline, or added insurance coverage.

Realize, however, that premiums aren't always worth the cost of the fee. Frequent-flyer miles, for example, have an average value of just 2 cents per mile, according to *CardTrak*, an industry newsletter. In most cases, you get one frequent-flyer mile for every dollar you charge. Consequently, you'd have to charge more than $1,750 on your credit card in one year to get miles worth $35—a typical annual fee. If you leave that $1,750 balance on your credit card—in other words, you don't pay off the balance right away—you'll pay far more in interest charges than the frequent-flyer miles are worth.

The Caveats

The things you need to be wary of are all neatly encapsulated in something called the disclosure box. On credit-card solicitations, this box is normally located on the top of the second page.

Here's where you will find out how long your teaser rate lasts and how much the interest rate will rise when it's over. It will also tell you whether or not there's an annual fee.

Other things to look for:

- Is the low advertised rate only given to those who maintain a balance?
- Is there a higher rate charged for cash advances?
- How long is the grace period? Does it apply when you carry a balance? Does it apply to cash advances?
- Will your rate jump if you make a payment late? Is there a late-payment fee?
- Is there a fee if you go over your credit limit?
- If the interest rate adjusts: When does it adjust, what index is it tied to, and what's the margin over the index?

More than anything, the disclosure box should give you a good idea of what you can't do with this card. If the interest rate on cash advances is 22 percent versus 15 percent for purchases, chances are you'd want to avoid that type of borrowing except perhaps in the most dire emergency.

Be sure to consider how you use credit when scanning the disclosure box and evaluate how you would fare under the terms of the agreement. There are plenty of credit-card offers. Make sure the cards you choose actually suit the way you like to do business.

Finding a Low-Rate Card

Okay. Some of that basic stuff was worth knowing. But what you really want to know is how to find a low-rate card, right?

The quick and easy way is to buy an issue of a monthly credit-card newsletter called *CardTrak*. It's timely, accurate, well-organized, and fairly comprehensive. Why can't I just list low-rate credit cards here? Because issuers change their rates and fees all the time based on how badly they want new business. Last year's rates mean nothing in today's market.

CardTrak sells single issues for $5 a copy. Each issue includes separate rankings for lowest-rate standard cards, lowest-rate gold cards, no-fee cards, and secured cards. The issuers are listed by rates or fees (depending on the chart) and are flanked by information about where cards are issued and their toll-free phone numbers. To order an issue, send $5 to *CardTrak*, Box 1700, Frederick, MD 21702. You can also call the company's consumer information line at 800-344-7714. (If your hearing is impaired, call the company's TTY at 301-695-5804.) There's a form letter at the back of this chapter that can be used to order a copy, if you're so inclined. (And no, I'm not making a commission on referrals. Nor do I have a stake in the company.)

If you have Internet access, you can get low-rate card information for free at Ram's Web site at http://www.cardtrak.com. The site also has hot links to a handful of low-rate issuers, who will allow you to apply on-line.

Establishing Credit

If you've never had credit before—or if you had it and abused it—you may need to establish or reestablish credit by getting a secured credit card.

A secured card works in the following manner: You agree to put a set amount of money in a bank account—say $500. In turn, the bank agrees to give you a card with a $500 (or less) credit limit. The bank usually pays you a small amount of interest on your deposit. Meanwhile, they charge you a fairly stiff—anywhere from $20 to $95—annual fee. And, if you maintain a balance on the card, they charge interest ranging from 9.9 percent to 22.8 percent on the balance. It's a rotten deal.

The good news is, if you handle a secured card well—you make all payments on time and never exceed your limit—you can usually graduate to a regular card fairly quickly. If you're establishing credit for the first time, expect to move into a standard card within a year. If you once had credit, but abused it, it may take longer.

Coping with Credit

In a perfect world, no one would keep a balance on their credit cards. They would realize it was high-cost debt and that it was not tax deductible; and they wouldn't be so stretched that they needed to tap into it. In the real world, people do maintain credit-card balances that average somewhere between $1,700 and $3,300, depending on the time of year and the state of the economy.

If you are among the balance-carrying masses, one simple piece of advice will save you thousands of dollars: Pay more each month than the minimum due—even if it's only a few dollars more. Why? Interest charges and minimum payments are calculated in such a way that the minimum payment barely covers the interest that's accruing each month. As a result, you stay indebted for years—even with a relatively small balance. Pay just a touch more and you could knock years—and hundreds of dollars—off your bill.

For example, according to Bankcard Holders of America, if you had a $1,700 balance on an 18 percent card, it would take nearly fourteen years—and cost you $1,973 in interest—if you paid only the 2.5 percent minimum payment each month. On the other hand, if you paid just $10 more per month than the minimum, you'd have paid off the bill in less than four years and you'd save $1,319 in interest.

Overextended

If you find yourself over your head, unable to pay your bills each month, and worried that you're headed toward bankruptcy court, call an organization called Consumer Credit Counseling Service. CCCS is a nonprofit organization that has offices all over the country. They're listed in both the white and the yellow pages of your phone book.

Their credit counselors are trained to help you budget and to negotiate with your creditors when you simply can't pay all that's due. In many cases, they've been successful at working out lower monthly payments and even getting interest charges waived. In some cities, CCCS provides its services for free. In others, it charges a nominal fee—usually $5 to $25 depending on whether you need simple debt counseling or more time-consuming budget help.

Stolen Card

If your credit card is stolen, the most you can be held responsible for is $50 in bogus charges. However, many issuers won't even charge you that if you report the loss promptly. *Prompt* is a subjective term, however. If you're robbed at gunpoint or have your purse snatched—in other words, you know immediately—you're expected to call the credit-card company fairly quickly. Sure, call the police first. Call your family second. But do call the credit-card company third. If you're unaware of the theft (e.g., a seldom-used card is taken out of your desk drawer), "prompt notification" would boil down to calling the credit-card company as soon as you notice suspect charges on your credit-card bill.

Who to Call

Card issuers provide you with a phone number to report problems and thefts when they send your card. Since these little slips of paper can be easy to lose, you'd be wise to write the information down when you receive the card.

At the end of this chapter you'll find a form where you can list your credit-card issuers and the toll-free numbers they provide to report lost and stolen cards.

Credit Denied

If you are turned down for credit, chances are there's a problem with your credit report. Three big credit bureaus keep files on the payment histories of everyone who borrows from a bank or retailer. Each time a new credit issuer considers giving you a loan, they'll pull a copy of this report.

Reasons for denying credit usually boil down to one of three:

1. You have no credit history.
2. There is derogatory information on your credit report.
3. You have too much credit already, or too many "inquiries" on your file.

Any of these problems is fixable—in most circumstances. But it takes some work.

Creating a History

If you are denied credit because you have no credit history, you have three choices: You can get a secured card; you can get a co-signer—a parent, relative, or close friend who is willing to pledge their money to pay your bills if you default; or you can try to establish a credit history from less conventional sources.

There's no formula for establishing a history when you haven't had official credit. It's a matter of thinking back and determining whether you have ever paid a debt over a period of time—a doctor's or dentist's bill, perhaps. If you have—and you were responsible about it—ask that credit grantor to report your payment history to a credit bureau.

Never even borrowed a sweater? Then, if you haven't already, open a checking or savings account to establish a relationship with a bank or credit union. In some cases, the bank will offer you a credit card immediately. In others, you'll have to apply and they'll have to consider your application based on what kind of customer you are.

In any case, even if the rate on the card is higher than you were hoping for, take it. Use sparingly. Pay promptly. It will help you establish a record, which will allow you to get a better deal the next time around.

What about advertisements that promise a credit card no matter how bad (or lacking) your credit history? Be wary.

Many of these offers are deceptive. Some provide cards that can only be used to buy overpriced merchandise from the same company that issues the card.

Others are pure scams. The issuer claims: "We'll give you credit if you send us a $25 application fee." So you send the fee and never see the card.

Derogatory Information

If you are turned down for credit because of negative information in your credit file, you are entitled to a free copy of your credit report. Order this report from the credit bureau immediately and check the information to make sure it's accurate. (Credit bureau addresses and a sample form letter are located on page 66–67.)

Do not make the mistake of hiring some company to "clean your credit record." Most of these companies charge substantial fees and do nothing for you that you can't easily do yourself—if they're complying with the law.

A few more dubious companies actually fabricate new Social Security numbers for their clients, which does, in fact, "clear" their client's credit records. Unfortunately, it's also fraud. You could be required to pay a hefty fine or even be sent to jail if you participate.

Errors

What should you do if you discover inaccurate information on your credit report?

Start by identifying the incorrect item, and write *on the report* that it is inaccurate. If you know why, say so. (You could write a letter explaining what items on the report are inaccurate, and attach a copy of the credit report. But there's really no need to bother with stationery.)

If you have a common name or are a "junior" or "senior," some of the reported information may simply belong to someone else. This should be fairly easy to fix. Write on the report: "This item is not mine. It may belong to my dad, John Smith Sr., or some other John Smith. In any case, I have never had credit dealings with this company [or bank]."

If you are divorced, you may be tarnished by your ex-spouse's credit woes. This should be a fairly cursory correction as long as you officially severed all ties—that is, canceled joint accounts and paid off joint bills. If you divorced but didn't cut your financial ties, see a lawyer. You could be on the hook for any credit that was issued to the two of you if it was not officially canceled.

Other mistakes may be due to a disagreement or misunderstanding with an issuer of credit. In such instances, it is wise to write to the credit issuer—usually a retailer or bank—as well as the credit bureau.

For example, let's say the bank that held your student loan reported a late payment. You, however, recall that the reason the payment was late was because the bank sent the bill to the college dorm rather than your home address. It was the bank's error because you had sent them a change-of-address card months before. The bill and a pile of late notices shuffled through sixteen college mailboxes before your former roommate stumbled on it and sent it to you. You paid the bill right away but, thanks to their address error, it was late.

This is clearly not your fault, but it is up to you to remind the bank what happened. Call or preferably write the bank to let them know you've been denied credit because of *their* mistake. Politely ask that they refrain in the future from besmirching your pristine reputation.

Correcting this type of error with the creditor (rather than just the credit bureau) is necessary because credit bureaus simply reiterate information that they've received from someone else. If you dispute information on your credit report, the credit bureau is required to "investigate." What this investigation boils down to is going to the source of the bad information and asking whether it is accurate. If that company insists the information is correct, it's nearly impossible to remove it. In some cases the information will be removed temporarily because the creditor was slow in responding to the bureau, but will reappear once the creditor finally answers. Correcting errors at the source can resolve them permanently.

Once you have identified and noted any and all inaccurate items on the report, send it back. Ask the bureau to correct the erroneous items and to send you an updated copy when they're through. If you haven't received a corrected copy within sixty days, call or write the bureau again. If necessary, mention that the company is required by federal law—the Fair Credit Reporting Act—to give you a copy of the corrected report.

What if there's a late payment on your record and you think it shouldn't be there, but the credit grantor won't agree to stop reporting it? You can send a short letter, not more than a hundred words, to each credit-reporting company detailing the dispute and circumstances. The credit bureau is required, by federal law, to attach it to your credit record. Anyone who requests your credit report will receive it.

The sort of disputes that may fall into this category include these examples:

- You paid late because you ordered merchandise by mail and it was broken when it arrived. You refused to pay the bill until the problem was corrected.
- The bank that held your student loan and sent the bill to the wrong address says it doesn't care whose fault it was that you paid late. You were late. You should have paid. The bank refuses to clear your record, despite the fact that it was arguably the main cause of the problem.

It's worth mentioning that you ought to be careful about what you say in these statements. Three types of people can get copies of your credit report: Credit grantors, such as banks, thrifts, credit unions, and retailers; insurance companies, who are considering issuing you a policy; and prospective employers.

If you don't want an employer, insurer, or credit grantor to know that you had a serious illness or a flaky husband or a stint in the state penitentiary, don't include that information in your statement. Remember, it goes out to whoever requests your credit file and it stays attached to your credit record for a long time. In fact, when you determine whatever derogatory information you were responding to is no longer important, you may have to be aggressive about deleting it from your file.

Delinquencies and late payments stay on your credit record for seven years. Bankruptcy filings and foreclosures are listed for ten years.

Too Much Credit

Some people can't get new credit because they already have too much "available" credit. It doesn't matter whether or not they're actually indebted. As far as bankers are concerned, they're overextended.

For instance, if you have a never-used credit card with a $10,000 credit limit, other issuers may deny you an application for a loan because you would be overextended if you hit the limit on that card and their card too. In another case, you may be deemed to be overextended because the "available" credit on your credit report could include a card that's long been canceled.

If you're planning to apply for a big loan, get a copy of your credit report and check to see that your outstanding credit is truly outstanding. As a general rule, you should always cancel cards that you don't use—even if you aren't charged an annual fee. You do need at least one credit card; having twenty could hurt you later on.

Too Many Inquiries

When you apply for a loan, the creditor will pull your credit report. This will be marked as an "inquiry" on future credit reports. If there are numerous recent inquiries, it gives a bank, credit union, or retailer reason enough to turn down your application for credit. In their mind, you could be applying for a dozen loans to fund a wild buying spree and a one-way ticket out of the country.

Therefore, you'd be wise to apply for only one loan at a time. It is tempting to fill out numerous applications at once, figuring that by having a choice you would be able to select the loan with the best rate. But you can see how this strategy could shoot you in the foot. Shop for rates before you apply. Then apply selectively.

Preapproved Cards

You need not worry about all of those "preapproved" credit-card solicitations you receive in the mail each month. Those "inquiries" will not affect your chances of qualifying for a home loan. They don't show up as inquiries unless you accept one of the preapproved cards.

In fact, these issuers have never even pulled your personal credit report. They got your name and address from a prescreened list, which could have been screened in any number of ways: people with a lot of credit, no delinquencies, who once ordered merchandise from a catalog; people who have less than two credit cards, estimated income above $50,000, and who live in certain ZIP codes; college graduates with no student debts—you get the idea.

If you accept a preapproved card, the issuer will at that time pull your credit record and set your credit limit based on what it says. In some cases, a "preapproved card with up to $6,000 in available credit," will land you a real card with a credit limit under $600. Don't be a chump. If you know you could never qualify for a $6,000 unsecured loan, don't expect to find a miracle in the form of a preapproved card.

Free Credit Report

If you haven't been denied credit, but still want a copy of your credit report, you can get one by sending a request and a check to most credit bureaus. The three national bureaus usually charge an average of $8 per report, but the cost can vary by credit bureau and state law. Additionally, married couples need two reports—one for each spouse—so their fee is double.

The good news is the Credit Reform Act that passed last year somewhat expands the group of people who are entitled to a free report. In addition to those who have been turned down for credit in the past sixty days, people who are on welfare are assured free copies of their credit reports starting in October, 1997.

To request this free copy, simply write the credit bureau. Your letter needs to include the following:

- Your full name, including middle initial and generation (Junior, Senior, II, III, etc.)
- Your current address, including ZIP code; if you've moved in the past five years, you also need to include your previous address(es)
- Your Social Security number
- Date of birth
- Spouse's name, if married
- Verification of your current address, which can come in the form of a copy of a driver's license, state identification card, or utility bill

Companies require this information to ensure that the person requesting the report is truly requesting it for themselves, not simply to check up on a neighbor or relative. (See sample request letter at the end of this chapter.)

Where do you send the request?

Experian National Consumer Assistance Center
P.O. Box 949
Allen, TX 75013
Phone: 800-392-1122

Equifax-Consumer Affairs Dept.
P. O. Box 740256
Atlanta, GA 30374-0256
Phone: 800-685-1111

Transunion-Consumer Relations Dept.
P.O. Box 7000
North Olmstead, OH 44070
Phone: 800-851-2574

What should you say in the letter? The next page is a form letter, where all you have to do is fill in your personal information and mail.

Form Letter (Been denied, need the report)

Date: ______________________

Credit bureau:____________________

____

____

Dear Sirs:

Please provide me with a free copy of my credit report.

I was denied credit on ______________(date) by __________________

(company) as a result of negative information included in my credit report.

My name is:____________________________

Address:_______________________________

____

Phone:________________________________

Date of birth:___________________________

Social Security number:______-______-________

Previous address (if it has changed within five years):

____

____

Thank you for your prompt attention to my request.

Sincerely,

Credit-Card Contacts

Who do you call if your card is lost or stolen—or you simply want to cancel or change your credit limit? This information is found on a letter or notecard you receive when you are first sent a new credit card. Record it here, so you won't have to search for it later.

Card/issuer	***Phone Number***
1.____________________	____________________
2.____________________	____________________
3.____________________	____________________
4.____________________	____________________
5.____________________	____________________
6.____________________	____________________
7.____________________	____________________
8.____________________	____________________
9.____________________	____________________
10.____________________	____________________

Part Three

HOUSES AND CARS

Houses and cars are big things that most of us want. Here are strategies to obtain and protect these costly possessions.

Chapter 8: Buying a Car

Americans are sentimental about their cars—but they hate to buy them. How do you buy a car without getting ticked off or ripped off? Turn to page 70.

Chapter 9: Leasing a Car

Auto leasing is becoming increasingly popular. But to lease without knowing the risks is to get slaughtered. The risks and rewards of leasing start on page 81.

Chapter 10: Auto Insurance

There's nothing glamorous about auto insurance, but it protects you, your passengers, and your car. You need it. You want it. You just have to figure out how to get it at a reasonable cost. Details on page 90.

Chapter 11: Home Sweet Home

Many renters say they would rather buy than rent. But how do you buy if you don't have the money for a big down payment? Where do you get a loan and what will it cost? See page 100.

Chapter 12: Insuring Your House

What you don't know about your home-owner's insurance can cost you if you're ever unfortunate enough to have to make a claim. Here's what your policy covers and how to determine how much insurance you ought to have, on page 124.

Chapter 13: Home Inventory

If you're lucky, you'll never suffer a fire, theft, flood, earthquake, or other catastrophic disaster that requires filling out a home-owner's insurance claim. But if you're not lucky, having a detailed home inventory can help you collect on your home-owner's policy in a quick, efficient manner. Turn to page 130.

Chapter 8

Buying a Car

A car is usually the first big purchase in most Americans' lives. If you do it right you could save thousands of dollars.

What the chapter tells you

- There are three ways to get a car—buy new, buy used, or lease. The right choice depends on how you drive.
- The best way to save money on a car is to visit the public library.
- Nearly everybody makes a few car-buying mistakes. Knowing what they are can help you avoid them.

What the chapter shows you

- How to find the dealer's cost

Where do I start?

Americans are so sentimental about what they drive that most people can tell you the year, make, model—and often the "name"—of the first car they ever bought. Yet the process of buying a car consistently ranks as one of the most onerous tasks of adulthood.

In most dealerships, it takes two hours and numerous delays (while the salesman goes to "check with his manager") before you can break out with a vehicle.

Horror stories abound.

- One woman says a dealer asked for her driver's license before a test drive, but then refused to give it back when she wanted to leave.
- Another consumer negotiated the purchase of a small truck, making it clear that air-conditioning was essential. "No problem. You've got it," the salesman said. But later, the buyer couldn't figure out where the switch was or how to turn it on. Embarrassed, she returned to the dealership and asked. The salesman flipped open the back window and said: "There. You've got air."

Such egregious cases are the exception rather than the rule, of course. But even sophisticated buyers complain about prices and terms changing at a dizzying pace and about salespeople who appear more intent on generating a sale than satisfying a customer. To make matters worse, no matter how long or hard you battle over the price, there's a decent chance that someone else bought the same car, better equipped, for less.

In short, it's not surprising that so many consumers leave auto dealerships feeling ripped off or ticked off.

The solution: Learn to be a good negotiator. You may still get ticked off, but it will drastically reduce the chances of getting ripped off.

Assessing the Choices

There are three ways to get a car in your driveway. You can buy one new; you can buy one used; or you can lease.

Although buying new was once the most popular option, today it accounts for a relatively small fraction of annual car sales. Precise figures are hard to come by, but industry experts estimate that only around 30 percent of cars are purchased new, more than half are bought used, and about 10 to 15 percent are leased.

The appeal of buying used is clear: It's cheaper.

You give up the prestige of driving a perfect, brand-new car; the enjoyment of breathing that new car smell; and the mixed blessing of adding the first dings to the doors or bumper. In return, you shave about $10,000—far more with a luxury car—off the sticker price.

It is the perfect option for somebody who is price-conscious, not overly concerned with impressions, and willing to deal with auto maintenance. The importance of auto maintenance to a used-car buyer cannot be overstated. Consider buying used only if you have a good mechanic, can fix the car yourself, or are comfortable about your ability to handle needed repairs in some other fashion.

Leasing is more complex.

It can save savvy negotiators a lot of money and allow them to drive late-model luxury cars that they otherwise couldn't afford.

Negotiating the deal, however, is complicated and fraught with peril. You could end up paying thousands more for a lease than you would for a comparable car purchase—and not even know it. Worse yet, getting out of a lease early is harder than getting paroled from prison. If you want to back out, it will cost you a fortune.

Additionally, leasing companies will require you to have high limits on your auto insurance and maintain the car to a "reasonable" degree. If you put multiple dings in the doors or tears in the upholstery, you'll get hit with a fine when you return the car at the end of the deal.

If you are willing to brush up on your algebra (see Chapter 9 for a quick review), and are willing and able to abide by the terms of the contract, leasing could be a suitable and economical option.

Everybody else is a buyer.

Once you've decided how you want to get your hands on the keys to a car, your next step is to research and prepare before approaching a dealer to negotiate. The next sections will show you the sources to access and the steps to take to determine the right price to pay and the pitfalls to avoid. If you do your homework before meeting with the dealer, you will greatly diminish your chances of being ripped off.

Buying New

Step One: Select a Model

If you're like most people, you have a good idea of the type of car you want—whether sedan, sportscar, utility vehicle, or truck—before you ever start looking. However, there are dozens or hundreds of cars in each class, and you must try to limit your choices to a handful.

Aside from chatting with friends and taking preliminary test drives, the best way to narrow the field is to take a look at the most recent *Consumer Reports* April Car-Buying Guide. This guide rates new cars on a variety of factors, including their safety, quality, and maintenance records.

Narrowing the field to five or six cars will allow you to do more thorough investigating, which will ultimately help you when negotiating the price.

Step Two: Call Your Insurance Agent

Waffling among a handful of different cars? Your insurance agent may just help you to make that decision.

Cars that you might consider fairly similar can have vast disparities when it comes to insurance costs. And the premium difference between a "muscle" car, such as a Camaro, and a standard family sedan, such as a Ford Taurus, can knock your socks off.

Consider a hypothetical consumer—Ann—who lives in Santa Monica, California, and insures with State Farm. If she buys the Taurus, she will pay $812 semiannually—$1,624 per year—for auto insurance. However, if Ann buys the Camaro, she'll pay $1,334 semiannually, or $2,664 per year. The Camaro costs a stunning $1,044 more in annual premiums.

To put it another way, assuming both cars cost exactly the same to purchase, your car-related payments are $87 per month higher on the Camaro because of the difference in insurance premiums.

Precise differences in insurance rates will depend on numerous factors, including the car you choose, where you live, your age, driving record, marital status, and how many members of your family use the car.

The good news is your insurance agent will give you preliminary quotes on any type of car you are considering. Make sure you ask about premium discounts for optional safety features you plan to buy—such as airbags and antilock brakes.

Step Three: Determine the Dealer's Price

One of the biggest mistakes car buyers can make is not knowing how much the dealer paid for the car. The dealer's cost has little relationship to the price on the window, but it is pivotal in determining just how much the salesman is able to dicker.

Finding the dealer's price is easy. There are two invaluable sources for this information. You can either look through a copy of the *Kelly Blue Book for New Cars*—nearly every public library has one—or you can spend a few bucks on a buyer service, which will give you a full report on a single car for a fee. Don't consider even preliminary negotiations before you have looked into one or both of these sources.

The advantage of the *Blue Book* is that it's comprehensive and—if you borrow the library copy—it's free. It lists virtually every make and model sold in the United States, and it reveals the price of the car and the prices of all the manufacturer-offered options.

However, what the *Blue Book* doesn't include is information about periodic factory rebates available to the dealership. These rebates are important because they effectively lower the dealer's price by hundreds—even thousands—of dollars below the invoice prices that you'll see in the *Blue Book*. With luxury cars, in particular, these rebates can make or break a deal.

Most car-buying services do include rebate information—as well as car-buying tips. However, you pay a per-request (or per-car) fee ranging from about $5 to more than $15.

For example, *Consumer Reports* offers a national service (800-933-5555) that costs $12 per car and provides car-buying tips as well as invoice prices and rebate information. Many credit unions and regional auto clubs offer similar packages to their members—sometimes for less. If you are a member of an auto club or credit union, check to see if they offer the service, what it costs, and what it includes.

If you're technologically oriented, there are also a number of on-line services, such as AutoQuot-R, AutoNet, and AutoVantage. Call or message your on-line service for more information.

Step Four: Choose Your Options

The base price of most cars is just the start of what the car is going to cost you. That's because most people want costly extras, such as air conditioning, power steering, antilock brakes, and a functional radio.

Before you visit the dealership, determine which of these options you want and which options don't matter. Check the prices (in the *Kelly Blue Book* or the report from your car-buying service) and add up the totals. In other words, car price + option price + option price + option price = total cost.

Realize, however, that some manufacturers "package" options, rather than selling them all separately. You will not be able to take options out of a standard package. Conversely, if you want an option that isn't included and don't want to upgrade to a package that includes it, you'll probably have to add that option at the dealership rather than the factory. Choose—and price—the package that best suits your needs.

One cautionary note: Salespeople may try to talk you into options that happen to be included on a car that's parked in their lot. That's to their advantage for many reasons. Don't allow yourself to be talked into options that you don't want, regardless of whether it's a relatively small item, such as tinted windows, or a big one, such as an extended warranty. (Take it if the dealer is offering to throw it in for free, of course. But if you're paying the tab, stick with the options you choose.)

It's true that your dealer may not have the specific car—loaded with the specific options—that you want on their lot. It can be ordered, or you can look elsewhere. There are plenty of cars; plenty of dealerships.

Just as you wouldn't buy a suit that you didn't like and wouldn't use—even if it was cheap—you shouldn't stock your car with options that will only gather dust.

Step Five: Value Your Trade-in

Your local public library should also have a copy of the *Kelly Blue Book for Used Cars*. This edition has both wholesale (dealer) and retail (consumer) prices. Consider your current car's condition, mileage, and options to determine a reasonable selling price for your used car.

Also check classified advertisements in your local newspaper to see how other people have priced cars like yours. Though the *Blue Book* is the definitive guide, car prices—like prices on nearly everything else—vary somewhat according to market conditions. The health of your local economy and the regional popularity of your vehicle could have an impact on how much you can reasonably expect to get for your trade-in.

Step Six: Consider the Financing

Unless you've got thousands of dollars in your checking account or sock drawer, you'll probably have to borrow some money to buy a car. The question is: Do you want to borrow from the dealer or a bank? The answer will differ given the circumstances.

If you are a good credit risk, it is very possible that the dealer will have a better financing rate than the bank. That's because car manufacturers' so-called "captive" financing arms sometimes offer super-low-rate deals in an effort to boost car sales.

However, you'll never know whether the dealer's rate is reasonable unless you check what others are offering. Call around to see what banks, thrifts, and credit unions are currently charging for auto loans. If you own a home and have substantial equity in it, you may also want to check rates and availability of home-equity loans (for more on home equity loans, see page 120). They're often cheaper than auto loans—and the interest on home equity loans of up to $100,000 is tax deductible.

Then, when the dealer quotes a financing rate, you are in a position to determine whether the rate is attractive or if you should get your financing elsewhere.

Step Seven: Do the Math

Okay, now you're ready to buy. You know the car you want; the options you want; what it should cost; how much your trade-in is worth; and what you should expect to pay for financing.

But if you want to make sure that a fast-talking salesperson won't take advantage of you in the showroom, take a few minutes more to write everything down. (The following worksheet should help.) Then pull out your calculator and do the math.

Car-Buying

Car price: $____________

Options

What: ____________ $____________

____________ $____________

____________ $____________

____________ $____________

Total dealer's cost $____________

Plus reasonable profit for dealer + $____________

My cost = $____________

Plus tax and license fees (vary by state) + $____________

Total cost = $____________

Minus the value of my trade-in – $____________

Minus any additional down-payment amount – $____________

Total amount to be financed = $____________

Today's financing rate ____________%

Number of months on the auto loan ____________

My monthly payment should be*: $____________

**To calculate your monthly payment, pull out your present-value calculator. Punch in the number next to "total amount financed" and hit "PV." Then hit "0, FV" because you're going to pay off the loan eventually. Punch in the number of months of the loan (i.e., 36 for a three-year loan) and hit "N" for number of payments. Then divide the annual interest rate figure by 12 to get a monthly interest rate, and punch the "%I" key. Now hit "CPT PMT."*

For example, the "total amount financed" equals $10,000, current financing rates are 10%, and you want a three-year (thirty-six-month) car loan. Punch in "10,000, PV"; "0, FV"; "36, N"; 10 divided by 12 equals 0.8333, "%I"; "CPT, PMT." In this case, the monthly payment should work out to $322.67.

Buying Used

There are several ways to buy a used car. You can buy one through a dealer; you can buy one from a private seller; or you can buy at auction.

Good deals can be found at auto auctions, but they're not recommended for most used-car buyers for a simple reason: Auctions are fast-paced and sales are final. In addition, there are no warranties on the car's condition. The auctioneer usually won't even guarantee that the mileage reading on the odometer is accurate. If you're not certain you can determine the car's physical and mechanical condition before the gavel strikes, play it safe and use one of the other two methods that are examined more thoroughly here.

Step One: Select a Model

Savvy new-car buyers check with friends, relatives, and the *Consumer Reports* April car-buying issue to determine what makes and models are top-notch in driver satisfaction, dependability, and style. This is also the first step a used-car buyer should take. It will help narrow the field to a reasonable number of cars you'll want to check out more thoroughly.

Mechanics warn that used-car buyers should be particularly wary of obscure models that are no longer being made. Many of these models were shelved because of severe design problems. With others, it's simply impossible to get replacement parts when something wears out.

Step Two: Determine a Reasonable Price

Used-car buyers can find suggested retail and wholesale prices in the *Kelly Blue Book for Used Cars*, which is available in most public libraries. This book can serve as a guide to price both the car you want to buy and your current car (if you have one for sale). Realize, however, that unlike a new-car buyer, you are not going to be able to pick and choose options. The original buyer of the car did that already. However, you will need to take them into account when determining the price you'll be willing to pay.

Step Three: Set Up Financing

If you're planning to buy from a dealer, the dealer may offer financing. However, more than half of the used cars sold are sold by private parties. If you want to consider a private sale, you should research sufficiently, and arrange your financing in advance.

That may be as simple as deciding to put the car purchase on your home equity line of credit, or get a cash advance from your credit card. Be aware, however, that your financing rate will have a dramatic impact on the total cost of the car.

How much does the financing rate matter? Consider someone who buys a used car, which costs $4,000—including taxes and license fees. If the buyer pays cash, the total cost is the purchase price: $4,000. If they finance the car through a 9 percent auto loan over three years, they'll pay a total of $4,579.16. If they finance the purchase through a credit-card cash advance at 21 percent and pay off the loan over three years, they'll pay $5,425.21.

Car cost, when paying cash: $4,000

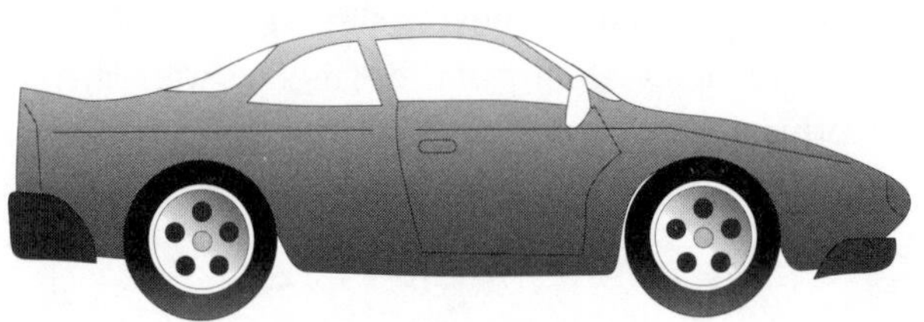

When financing at 9%: $4,579

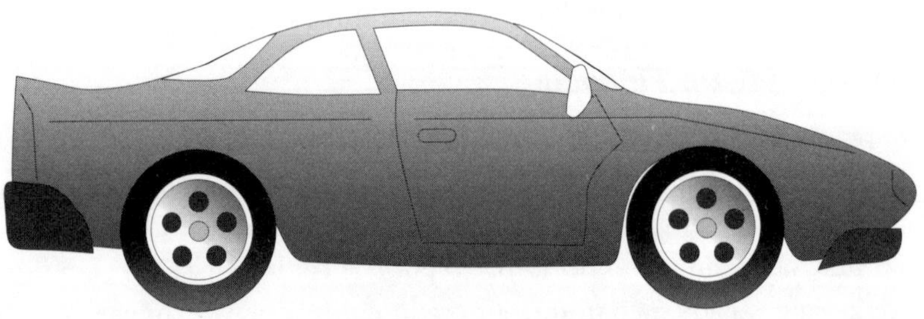

When financing at 21%: $5,425.21

Step Four: Troll for Bargains

To buy a used car for a great price, you have to plan on taking your time. And you must become an avid reader of newspaper classified advertisements.

There's no formula. You simply start reading every ad that pertains to the car you want. Over time—the amount of time depends on how long you're willing to wait—you'll recognize when a car is selling for less than the going market price.

Step Five: Do a Mechanical Check

A thorough mechanical check can spell the difference between buying a great car at a great price and buying a lemon that spends more time in the shop than your driveway. It's arguably the most important step in buying a used car and very simple to do.

How do you do it? Start the engine and keep it running while you go through the following battery of tests, suggests Scott Kilmer, an auto mechanic and author of *Everyone's Guide to Buying a Used Car.*

1. Scrutinize the car in full sunlight to see if the body and paint appear even, with no irregular spacing between joints. Uneven joints or paint can indicate that the car has been through a major repair—a warning sign of a possibly undisclosed wreck.
2. Open and close all the doors, including the trunk, and check for signs of rust.
3. Stand back from the hood and look to see that the tires are evenly spaced. One tire shouldn't be closer to the fender than the others, for example.
4. Climb in and check out the gadgets—blinkers, windshield wipers, air-conditioning, heat, radio, and all the gages—to see if they're working.
5. Shift the gears several times to see if you hear any odd sounds, such as a scraping or clunking. Those sounds can indicate that the transmission is failing—a clear sign that you should forget this car.
6. Check under the car for major leaks.
7. Check the exhaust to make sure it's not dripping water or spewing clouds of black smoke.
8. Assuming that all this looks good, and that the car hasn't overheated while you were checking it out, take it for a test drive to check the brakes, steering, power, and suspension.

Beware of any overheating problems, Kilmer adds. There's no way to know in advance whether overheating is caused by a $5 hose or a $500 engine breakdown, he says. If the car overheats, skip it unless the seller agrees to fix the overheating problem before you buy.

If you like what you see, consider taking the car to your own mechanic for a second, more thorough check before you buy.

Step Six: Consider the Warranty

Private sellers generally don't offer guarantees on the condition of the car they sell you. However, a dealer may. Dealers are required to post a "Buyer's Guide" on the window that says whether the car is covered by warranty or is being sold "as is."

Some cars, particularly late-model vehicles that have been released from a short-term lease, also may be covered by manufacturer's warranties. These warranties can be remarkably valuable.

Consider a recent California appeals case: A woman bought a BMW that had been used as a "demonstrator vehicle" from a dealer. The car had just 7,565 miles on it when it was purchased, with a three-year, 36,000-mile warranty.

Shortly after the purchase, the buyer noticed a shimmy in the braking system. She brought it back to be fixed seven times. When all these attempts proved unsuccessful, she asked BMW to replace the car or refund her money. BMW refused. She sued, citing state lemon laws. The court ruled in her favor, saying that lemon laws—which had previously only been used to protect buyers of brand-new cars—apply to used cars that are still under a manufacturer's new-car warranty. This buyer received $88,000 in damages.

With information about the car, the dealer's cost, and the financing rate, you have all the ammunition you need to get a good deal at the car lot.

Chapter 9

Leasing a Car

Leasing has become one of the fastest-growing areas of car sales. However, it's much riskier than buying, and if you're not careful—and fail to do your homework—you'll get creamed.

What the chapter tells you

- Some leasing deals *sound* good, but they're not.
- To lease wisely you have to know how much you plan to drive and how you'll use your car. If you don't, you're likely to pay too much.

What the chapter shows you

- How to evaluate the potential back-end costs of a lease
- How to translate the language of leasing
- How to recognize which negotiating tricks work against you and which can work in your favor
- How to determine what you're paying for a lease

Where do I start?

If you approach a lease without knowing how to use a present-value calculator, you should consider yourself a lamb in a feed lot, bleating: "Slaughter meeeeee. Meeeeeee next." You would be so unprepared that it would require the soul of a saint not to overcharge you. Because Mother Teresa doesn't own an auto dealership, you'd better have a calculator. (If you don't have one, flip back to Chapter 1, "Figuring the Cost," for information on where you can find an inexpensive calculator and other reasons you'd want to buy one.)

Here's why: The cost of your monthly payments on a lease is based on how much you put in as a down payment (which can include the value of your trade-in), the interest rate, the number of months you'll pay on the lease, the current price of the car, and the value the car will have when you decide to trade it in.

That's not too hard to follow, right? The tricky part is, the dealership won't necessarily disclose *any of these numbers*. (Actually, that's not *completely* true. They'll tell you how many months you have to pay—they don't want any misunderstandings about that.)

That leaves customers exceptionally vulnerable to being cheated by an unscrupulous salesperson. Indeed, a recent news investigation found that several undercover reporters were overcharged on leases by amounts ranging from $2,000 to $7,500—not exactly small change.

That happens because very little of the deal is written down, and what *is* written down is written in a language few understand. As a result, auto dealers can manipulate the numbers by changing one of the variables without actually changing the price. Leasing laws have changed recently, requiring more disclosure, but they won't take full effect until late 1997. Even then, the interest rate, a key component in how much you pay, won't necessarily be disclosed.

You may think you're wheeling and dealing just as you would when you buy, but in fact, all that's changing is your attitude.

Let's say, for instance, that you tell the dealer that the $300 monthly payment on a two-year lease is too high. You want a better deal.

"Okay," he replies. "I'm going to take $1,000 off your residual and put you into a three-year lease. I'll also cut your payments to $250 per month." How much have you saved?

If you don't buy the car at the end of the period, this deal will cost you $1,800 *more* than the first one. If you do buy the car at the end of the period, it will cost you $800 *more* than the deal you started out with.

Quipped one leasing industry executive, who (not surprisingly) asked not to be quoted by name: "Most people get their 'faces ripped off' when they try to lease a car."

On the bright side, if you learn how a lease works and learn to do a quick-draw with that present-value calculator, you can actually save a fortune by leasing rather than buying. But to understand how to do it, you have to know some of the jargon and how a lease differs from a purchase.

Step One: Beware of Potential Back-end Costs

A closed-end lease is not a purchase. It's more like a long-term rental where you have the *right*, but not the obligation, to buy the car at the end of the deal.

However, because you're essentially renting rather than buying outright, the company that *owns* your car has a say in how many miles you can drive, the amount of auto insurance you must carry, and the condition the car must be in when it's returned.

If you drive more miles than allowed, you get charged. If you buy too little insurance, the leasing company may buy insurance for you—and charge you for it. If you turn the car in looking shabby, dinged, or dented, you get charged again. Specifically:

Insurance. Leasing firms generally require that you buy a minimum of $100,000 per person; $300,000 per accident in liability insurance protection. If you'd normally have that much insurance, this isn't anything to be concerned about. If not, you should check with your insurance agent—before signing on the dotted line—to see just how much this is going to cost you.

Mileage. Just as you get a certain number of "free" miles when you rent a car, you get a mileage allowance when you lease. If you exceed your mileage allowance, you get charged for each mile you drive over the limit. Typically, you're allowed to drive about 15,000 miles per year without any additional payments. But some leases allow more mileage; others allow less.

The mileage count is done just once at the end of the lease. So you don't have to worry about going over the yearly allowance, as long as you don't drive more than the total mileage limit over the course of the deal.

What happens if you do? Leasing companies charge a fee that usually ranges between 10 cents and 25 cents per additional mile. Let's say your three-year lease allows you to drive 45,000 miles and charges 15 cents per mile for additional mileage. If you drive 53,000 miles—a mere 8,000 miles more—before you turn the car in, you'll owe $1,200 in excess mileage charges.

Wear and tear. The most subjective item on lease contracts are charges for "excess wear and tear." When you turn in a leased vehicle, somebody will inspect it. He'll note any dings, stains, or rips in the upholstery or dashboard, and then he'll decide whether the condition of your car is "reasonable" given the length of your lease. If it's not, the dealer will charge you.

How much? There's no telling. It depends on how bad the car's condition is. However, if you take fairly good care, maintaining the car as if it were your own, you probably don't have to worry.

Early termination. Let's say you leased a car for four years. You suddenly decide you can't afford it; don't like the color; wish you'd bought a different model; or otherwise simply want out of the deal. Bad news.

In many leases, you can't exit the deal without paying the leasing company an amount equal to the remainder of your monthly payments. A lease is a binding civil contract. Unless you are on the brink of bankruptcy, the leasing company is unlikely to renegotiate your deal to let you out early.

Step Two: Translate the Terms

When you buy, you have a purchase price, a down payment, and an interest rate—words you understand. When you lease, you deal with the "residual," the "capital cost reduction," and the "lease factor"—terms you've probably never used before and will never use again.

What Do They Mean in English?

- **Residual.** The residual is how much the car will be worth—and the amount you can purchase it for—at the end of the lease term on a closed-end lease. When you're calculating how much you're paying to lease a car, you should consider this the "future value."
- **Capitalized cost.** This is how much you're paying for the car, before you account for the cost of financing. This is equivalent to the sales price, and—in what's considered a major step forward in consumer protection—some leasing companies are now disclosing this amount on lease contracts.
- **Capitalized cost reduction.** This is your down payment, plain and simple. It can include the value of your trade-in. It may be just the cash that you put into the deal; or it may both of those, plus the value of a manufacturer's rebate. In any case, this amount is a credit against the purchase price.
- **Lease factor.** This is a ridiculous figure that you can multiply by another number to come up with your actual interest rate. Ignore it. Instead, before you negotiate a lease, find out what market interest rates are for auto loans. You'll use the going market rate (divided by 12 to get a monthly rate) to determine what your monthly payment should be.
- **Open-ended lease.** This type of lease is rare today, but if you see it on your contract think: "Run, Forrest . . . ruuuun!" It can be remarkably dangerous to your financial health. On an open-ended lease, you are responsible for the car's depreciation. If the

value of the car, when you trade it in, is less than the residual you negotiated up front, you pay a back-end fee to make up the difference.

- **Closed-end lease.** This simply means that you have the right to buy the car at the residual value you negotiated up front at the end of the deal. If the car is worth more than the residual, you can buy it and resell it immediately and turn a profit. If it's worth less when you turn it in, the leasing company suffers the loss.

Step Three: Negotiating Basics

To negotiate a good price on a lease, you have to start like a buyer. In other words, go through steps 1 through 6 in Chapter 8, "Buying a Car"—that is, choose the model and options you want, find out the cost of insurance, the cost of financing, the dealer's price and what your trade-in (if any) is worth.

You also have to consider how you drive when determining whether or not you'll run into any of the back-end costs of leasing, such as additional mileage, higher insurance, or "wear and tear" fees.

There's not a lot you can do to change the insurance or wear-and-tear issues. They'll simply help determine whether you are or aren't a good candidate for a lease.

You *can* negotiate the amount of miles you get to drive. If the lease contract stipulates just 10,000 miles per year, for example, and you know you drive about 15,000 miles per year, have them add in 5,000 additional "free" miles so you can drive your normal amount and not face back-end fees.

Additionally, you can avoid termination fees by never agreeing to lease a car for a longer period of time than you'll want it. If you know you only want a car for two years, do not lengthen the term under any circumstances.

Step Four: Figuring the Cost

Time to pull out your present-value calculator.

To figure out what a lease costs, you have to know the capitalized cost (price); the residual (the amount you'll owe at the end of the lease, if you decide to buy the car); market interest rates; the number of months on the lease; and the amount of the monthly payments.

However, before you step into a dealership, you should know how to do leasing math. That entails being able to juggle all of these numbers around to come up with the payments and terms you want.

It's easy as long as you keep your eye on the ball. Just like juggling, all it takes is practice.

Here's what you need:

1. Determine a reasonable price to pay for the car by checking with a car-buying service or the *Kelly Blue Book* (as described in the "Buying New" section of Chapter 8, "Buying a Car"). Enter the figure here: $________________________
2. Decide how much of a down payment you can come up with, including the cost of your trade-in, but minus any up-front fees, such as tax and license fees that are exacted at the time of sale. Enter the down payment here: $________________________
3. Subtract the result of number 2 from number 1 to determine how much of the purchase price you'll need to finance. Enter the result here: $____________________("PV")
4. Determine a reasonable residual value of the car. This can be as simple as asking the dealer. Or, you can determine a reasonable residual by checking advertised leases in the newspaper. (If there are advertisements for the car you wish to lease, they almost always disclose the residual or "purchase option price" in the fine print.) Enter it here: $____________________("FV")
5. Determine a reasonable financing rate by checking with a handful of auto lenders (banks and credit unions usually offer auto loans). Enter the financing rate here: ________________%
6. Divide the financing rate by 12 to get a monthly rate. Enter the result here: ____________________("%I")
7. Determine how many months you want to lease the car. Typical lease terms will be anywhere from two years (twenty-four months) to seven years (eighty-four months). Enter the number of months you prefer here: ____________________("N")
8. In the lines above, you'll notice there are codes—"PV," "FV," "%I," and "N" after numbers 3, 4, 6, and 7. To find the amount of your monthly payment, plug in the result on that line and hit the code following it on your present-value calculator. Once you've plugged in all the numbers, followed by the appropriate symbols, hit "CPT, PMT" for "compute payment."

   Enter your expected payment here: $____________________
9. To determine the total cost of the car, multiply your monthly payments by the number of payments (result on line 8 times the number on line 7), then add the number you've noted on line 2 (your down-payment amount). Then add the residual amount (line 4).

   This total will be higher than the cost of a straight purchase because it includes the cost of financing. However, it should be close to—or less than—the cost of a similar

purchase once you include the cost of financing. (In other words, it should be equivalent to the amount of your monthly payments times the number of payments you make when you buy, because that amount will also include the cost of financing.)
Total cost of the car: $____________________

Step Five: Beware of Negotiating Tricks That Work Against You

There are several ways a dealer can lower your monthly payment on a lease without decreasing the total amount you will ultimately pay. They will often *increase* the total amount, and you might not realize it until after it is too late.

The dealer can do this in the following ways:

- Stretch out your payments over a longer period of time.
- Require a larger down-payment amount to "buy down" your monthly payments.
- Reduce your "free" mileage to virtually nothing, making it likely that you'll pay walloping back-end fees. One recent advertisement for a luxury car lease, for example, offered a terrific monthly payment and a very reasonable down-payment amount. However, in the fine print, it noted that consumers were allowed just 10,000 miles per year and were charged 15 cents per mile for each additional mile they traveled. Most people drive about 15,000 miles per year—which is the mileage allowance in most leases. If you leased this car for three years and drove 15,000 miles per year instead of 10,000, you'd owe $2,250 in mileage charges at the end of the lease. This is equivalent to boosting the payments by $62.50 per month.

Step Six: Learn Three Negotiating Tricks That Work in Your Favor

The bright side is there are a few tricks that can work in your favor too. If you know how to play the game, you can actually get a better deal on a lease than a comparable car purchase.

How?

First determine what you think the monthly payments should be given the dealer's price, market interest rates, what you expect for your down payment, and so on. (Refer to the worksheet under "Step Four: Figuring the Cost.") Then learn how three factors can be manipulated to lower your cost. The dealer, however, is likely to agree to only one of them. The three factors:

1. Boost the value of your trade-in. This effectively hikes your down payment or "capitalized cost reduction" and lowers the amount you have to pay over time. But it's tough to get dealers to be flexible with this because they will not be able to resell the car for

more than the going market price. They'll also have expenses to pay for advertising it and for a salesman. Those overhead costs are reflected in the trade-in price a dealer will offer you.

2. Cut the interest rate. If the dealer has captive financing, and is anxious to sell cars, it might possibly cut the rate as much as 2 or 3 percent.
3. Boost the residual value. The cost of your payments is based on the difference between the price of the car (minus your down payment) and the value of the car at the end of the lease period. The more the car is worth at the end of the lease, the smaller the difference between the current price (the present value) and the future price (future value)—which means lower monthly payments for you.

Dealers are usually willing to increase the residual value somewhat because when you lease a car, a leasing company buys the car from the dealer and then leases it back to you. This transaction—the purchase by the leasing company and lease back to you—is fairly invisible and mostly incidental to you. But as far as the dealer is concerned, it's pivotal. It passes the risk of having to resell the car at a loss sometime in the future from the dealer to a third party that isn't directly involved in making the deal.

Leasing companies do set guidelines on how high they'd be willing to go on the residual. At some point, you'll hit the leasing company's topmost limit and not be able to boost the residual any higher. But, strive to hit that limit. It pays off nicely for you.

Here's why: With a closed-end lease, you are not obligated to buy the car at lease end. You simply have the *option* to buy it at the residual price. If the residual price is too high, the leasing company takes the hit, not you.

What if you do want to buy the car at the end of the lease? One of the best-kept secrets in leasing is that residual prices can be renegotiated at the end of the lease.

Consider, for example, a Woodland Hills man who leased a Porsche for five years. He loved the car. But according to his agreement he'd have to pay $29,000 for it at the end of the lease term. That was substantially more than what similar cars were selling for used. He was ready to return the car when his leasing company offered to pare the residual by $6,500, allowing him to buy his pristine white-and-tan Porsche for $22,500—the going market rate. He did.

Why would the leasing company do that? Because if you don't buy the car, they're going to have to sell it to somebody else. And nobody else is going to pay more than the car is worth either. Besides, the leasing company already knows you. They know you've made your payments on time. Better yet, they don't have to spend money advertising to find you.

Just how much does boosting the residual cut the monthly payments? It varies, of course. But here's a quick example that can help illustrate. You can plug in your own numbers, too, using the worksheet on page 86 and your present-value calculator.

Consider someone who leases a $30,000 car for thirty-six months. The financing rate is 9 percent; the residual is $10,000. He pays $711 a month.

Now if he can get the dealer to boost the residual value to $12,000, he would pay only $662 per month—a $49 monthly, or $588 annual, savings. If he can convince the dealer to boost the residual to $15,000, he would pay only $589.50 per month—a savings of $121.50 per month, or $1,458 per year.

Residual Math

How do you do the calculation to see just how much boosting your residual saves you? Follow the steps of the above example to see.

Low Residual Value

Car cost: $30,000. (Hit "30,000, PV" on your calculator.)
Financing rate: 9 percent. (Divide by 12 months to get a 0.75 percent monthly interest rate and hit the percent interest—"%I"—key on your calculator.)
Residual value: $10,000. (That's the future value of the car. Hit "10,000, FV.")
Number of months on the loan: 36. (Hit "36, N.")

Then hit "CPT PMT" for compute monthly payment. You get: $710.99, which I rounded up a penny to $711.

High Residual Value

Car cost: $30,000, PV.
Financing rate: 9% divided by 12 (months) = 0.75, %I.
Residual value: $15,000, FV.
Number of months on the lease: 36, N.
Monthly payment: $589.50.

Chapter 10

Auto Insurance

Auto insurance protects you and your car. You need it. You want it. You just have to find a way to get it at a reasonable price.

What the chapter tells you

- What your policy covers
- How insurance companies determine rates

What the chapter shows you

- Where to start when you're shopping around
- How to cut your rates by changing your image
- How to cut your rates with discounts
- A low-cost way for high-end consumers to get more protection

Where do I start?

Now that you have a car, it's time to insure it.

If you're young, live in a big city, drive a nice car, or have had a few accidents, your insurance rates will be e-x-p-e-n-s-i-v-e. There are ways you can dramatically reduce them. You just need to learn the ropes.

Coverage Basics

An average auto insurance contract covers six things: bodily injury liability; property damage liability; medical payments; losses caused by uninsured motorists; collision; and comprehensive losses. To cut your costs, you have to examine the protection offered in each component. In some cases, you'll realize that you don't need one specific coverage—or at least could live with less of it—which would provide you with easy money-saving opportunities.

Starting at the top:

Bodily injury and property damage liability coverages are packaged together on your policy under the title "BI/PD." This pays the cost of injuries and damages for anyone you hit. It protects you from losing your house, car, and other assets if someone sues you following an accident. The liability protection covers passengers in your car as well. If your passengers are hurt in an accident and they sue you, claiming you were driving negligently, your liability coverage would kick in again. However, be aware that nearly every type of insurance policy excludes coverage for willful and illegal acts. If someone cut you off in traffic and you got annoyed, figuring, "Hey, I'm driving a Volvo, the safest car in the universe. I'm just going to smash that annoying little Miata like a bug," your insurance company would have the right to deny your claim.

On the policy, the coverage will be listed with three numbers, looking something like this: BI/PD 100/300/50. This indicates that your liability protection covers up to $100,000 per person and $300,000 per accident, for which the property coverage is capped at $50,000.

If you have significant assets, income, or earning capacity—in other words, you think you'll earn a lot of money in the future—you probably need a significant amount of liability coverage. If you don't, you can live with less. In some cases, all you need is the amount that state law—if any—requires you to buy.

Medical payment coverage pays doctor and hospital bills for you and any passengers in your car in the event that you are hurt in an accident. There is usually no deductible on this coverage, which means you won't face any out-of-pocket costs for medical visits caused by a crash. However, if you have adequate health insurance, this may be an area where you could trim costs.

Comprehensive is a catch-all coverage that pays to repair or replace your car when it is damaged while parked, no matter whether the damage was caused by theft, hurricane, flood, earthquake, tornado, fire, or another "peril." The only limit on this coverage is the value of the automobile. However, you usually have a deductible—an amount that you must pay before coverage kicks in. The higher your deductible, the lower your premium.

Collision coverage is similar to comprehensive, but it pays if the car is damaged while moving.

Uninsured and underinsured motorist policies pay for your—and your passengers'—injuries and property damage if you are hit by an uninsured or underinsured motorist. In some states, insurers are required to offer this coverage, but you are generally not required to buy it. Uninsured motorist coverage also duplicates, to some extent, your medical payment coverage. However, it can also provide compensation for lost wages and pain and suffering. Medical payment coverage only pays for doctor and hospital bills and prescription medicines.

How You Rate

Your auto insurance premium is going to depend on a wide variety of factors including your age, sex, marital status, the car you drive, where you live, how far you drive, the coverage you choose, and the amount of your deductible.

Once you've filled out an application, an insurance underwriter is going to draw up a mental image of you from the information you've provided on the form to determine how likely you are to get into an accident or file a claim. Your rates will reflect, to a certain degree, a sort of organized, statistical stereotyping. You can lower your premiums by molding yourself into a duller person, at least as far as insurance goes.

Consider, for example, an eighteen-year-old boy who we'll call Tom—an average student who buys a new Mustang and wants to get his own insurance policy.

An underwriter is going to look at his application and say: "Hummm . . . kid. Very little driving experience. Wants a flashy car, so he can peel out, drive fast, impress the girls. That's the kind of car you'd take to clubs at night—concerts, parties, bars. His friends, who probably drive Hondas and Tempos, are going to be piling in the back anytime they want to go somewhere. So, if Tom has an accident, there will also be five kids with him. Five kids, each with forty years of future earnings potential. [Million-dollar liability judgments are often based on the lost earnings potential of the victims.] . . . Big risk."

The underwriter scans a little further: "Hummm. . . He wants his own policy, huh? Not trying to insure with Mom and Dad. Maybe that means he's moving out. Maybe that means they're not that involved with him. Maybe they've lost control. Thrown up their hands. Said, 'Do whatever you want. We give up on you.' Maybe Tom's a problem child."

The bottom line: If Tom lived in Los Angeles, he would pay roughly $5,000 annually for auto insurance.

Changing Tom's Image

If he boosted his grade-point average, bought the "passive restraints"—air bags or automatic seat belts—got antilock brakes, and bought insurance with Mom and Dad, he would suddenly qualify for rates that are between 20 and 30 percent lower.

Raise the deductible, and his rate drops further. (The underwriter says: "Sure, he wants a Mustang. But he's a good kid. Straight-A student. You can see from his high deductible that he's willing to take responsibility for his actions.")

Now if Tom were willing to trade in the Mustang keys and buy a more sedate vehicle—a Chevy Corsica, perhaps—his premium would drop drastically. If he and his family moved to the suburbs, it could drop even more.

One insurer who provided rates for this hypothetical driver said Tom's premium could drop as low as $1,258—from a stunning $5,390 starting rate.

Discounts and Special Deals

How can you shave your auto insurance premiums? Here's a list of items that can have a dramatic impact on how much you pay for auto insurance—but you may not be willing to change them all.

Marry. Married couples pay less for insurance, on average, than similarly situated singles. Why? If you're single, you probably have a social life. Maybe you go out at night. Dancing. Clubs. Bars. Drinks. Maybe somebody at one of those clubs notices the cool stereo you've got in your car. Maybe they covet it. Maybe they steal it. Maybe you don't drive as carefully after clubbing late at night as you would if you just went home to your family right after work.

In any case, you're more likely to file a claim than that married couple that lives down the street from you whose car rarely leaves the garage.

Move. Live in the country, or the less-populated suburbs, and you'll probably pay lower rates. The more densely populated your town, the more accidents and robberies there are likely to be—the higher your rates, insurers say. Setting premium rates by ZIP code remains one of the most controversial and contentious issues facing auto insurers. Nonetheless, for policyholders, it's a fact of life.

Avoid "points." If you are a good driver—no tickets, no accidents—you'll qualify for the lowest rates. That's because you have no "points" against your driving record, which allows you to get good driver discounts that can range from 10 to 40 percent of the premium. So if you get a ticket, consider traffic school. Usually, this costs you time because you have to spend a Saturday, or several evenings, attending the equivalent of a driver's education class, but it saves you money because completing the class keeps the points off your record.

Choose cars carefully. Two cars that cost the same amount to buy can vary dramatically when it comes to the cost of insurance. Certain cars are expensive to repair, are hot targets for thieves, and are more likely to suffer serious damage in an accident, according to insurers. The good news: You can get an inkling of which cars are likely to cost a lot to insure by writing to the Insurance Institute for Highway Safety, 1005 North Glebe Road, Arlington, VA 22201. This trade group does an annual survey of highway loss data, which is used to determine rates for different types of cars.

Or you could just ask your insurance agent. If you are planning to purchase a car, call and have your agent do a quick premium price comparison on the different models you like.

Raise your deductible. The deductible is the portion of the loss that is uninsured—the amount that you, rather than your insurer, must pay. If you have a $100 deductible and make a claim because somebody broke into your car and caused $500 in damage, the insurer would pay $400. You would be expected to pay the $100 deductible amount.

In many cases, drivers set these thresholds low—at $100 or $250 on a car that's worth $20,000 or more. But that can be costly.

When you have higher deductibles, your insurance company assumes—probably accurately—that you'll take a little extra care with how you drive and where you park. That makes you less likely to file a claim, which lowers your insurance rate.

How much does it cut the rate? It varies widely by the type of car you drive and where you live. However, in many cases, it can lower your costs by hundreds of dollars annually. In many cases you could save more in premiums by raising your deductible than you'd risk from a loss.

If you don't file a lot of claims—and a one-time loss of $500 or so wouldn't derail your financial plan—consider hiking your deductible. Ask your insurer how much it would save you.

Look for discounts. Insurers offer discounts for a wide array of reasons. The discounts can range from relatively modest breaks—5 to 10 percent off a portion of the premium—to substantial—20 percent or more off the entire cost of insurance. However, discounts aren't offered by every insurer in every state. And they're not always automatic. In many cases, you have to ask whether discounts are available or are reflected in your premium. Some of the more common discounts:

- **Loyalty/persistency discounts.** If you've insured with the same company for several years—usually more than three—and have a good driving record, you could get a loyalty discount that will shave 20 percent off your overall rate. If you insure your house with the same company, or insure other cars on the same policy, you may also qualify for good-customer or multicar discounts.
- **Defensive driving discounts.** If you are over the age of fifty-five, most insurers will pare your rate 5 to 10 percent if you complete a defensive driving course. In many states, insurers are required to offer these discounts.
- **Good-student discounts.** If you, or someone on your insurance policy, is a student, realize that good grades can save you a small fortune. Keeping a grade-point average of a B or better can qualify you for good-student discounts ranging from 10 to 20 percent. A hypothetical Chicago driver with a sixteen-year-old son would pay $2,939 to insure his Ford Taurus, for example. But if Junior got good grades, the premium would drop to about $2,258.
- **Safety feature discounts.** Get antilock brakes, passive restraints, or antitheft devices installed on your car, and you could qualify for savings ranging from 10 to 40 percent off the medical payment, liability, or comprehensive coverages.
- **Nonsmoker discounts.** A handful of insurers will give you substantial premium discounts if you're a nonsmoker.
- **Low-mileage discounts.** If you drive less than five miles to work each day, you may qualify for a modest break—ranging from 1 to 5 percent of the premium amount.

Shop Around

Naturally, you know there are many insurers out there, and that comparison shopping can save you hundreds of dollars on your annual premium.

However, what you may not know is that your state insurance department may be willing to help. Insurance regulators frequently track auto insurance rates—particularly in high-rate states—and have a fair amount of survey data that they're normally willing to share with consumers. Frequently, the survey data will examine the cost of a fairly standard auto insurance policy—for a fairly standard driver—and compare prices in a variety of zip codes with a variety of insurers. Of course, your insurance costs will be different. But the surveys can give you an idea of who is offering the lowest rates in your neighborhood.

Additionally, insurance regulators in most states also track complaint data. If you want to know how many of your insurance company's policyholders griped about the insurer's willingness to pay claims, you may be able to get it with one phone call.

The phone number of your state insurance department should be listed in the government section of the phone book.

Before You Shop

Before you start shopping around, take a moment to determine just how much insurance you need in each of the major categories mentioned. Also consider how large a deductible you can handle.

Recognize that some coverage limits will be dictated by state law—in California, for example, you must carry at least $15,000 per person/$30,000 per accident in liability insurance and at least $5,000 in coverage for property damage.

Other coverage amounts may not be mandated, but your insurer is likely to sell standard "packages," particularly when it comes to liability coverage. Coverage amounts are almost always rounded to the nearest $5,000 or $10,000. If you are buying a big policy, they'll be rounded to the closest $50,000 or $100,000.

Stick with standard amounts. It will be easier to get competitive quotes and, consequently, cheaper insurance rates.

Otherwise, your decision about how much coverage you need should be based on what you own, and how worried you are that your assets could be put at risk if someone sued you following an accident.

If you have a junker car, you could easily save hundreds of dollars in premiums by dropping collision and comprehensive insurance coverages. Then what do you do if you have an accident? If you were to put the amount that you would have paid in insurance premiums in the bank or a mutual fund, there's a good chance (unless you have an accident or natural disaster right away) that what you save on premiums will more than pay to replace your rust-riddled 1962 Ford Fairlane. Indeed, though an insurer will pay only enough to replace the precise car you have—and only if it's destroyed—if you are able to save the premium costs for several years, you may be able to buy a better car regardless of whether or not the car is destroyed.

Likewise, if you have good health insurance with a low deductible, consider lowering or canceling the medical payment coverage on your auto insurance. Sure, that means that your auto insurer will not pay your medical bills if you are hurt in an accident. But, if your health insurer will, all you're out is the deductible.

The following worksheet should help organize your notes.

Auto Insurance Rate Comparison

Coverage	***Insurer***	***Insurer***	***Insurer***
	________	________	________
Bodily Injury			
$________per person			
$________per accident	________ (rate)	________ (rate)	________ (rate)
Property Damage			
$________	________	________	________
Comprehensive			
$________ (deductible amount)	________	________	________
Collision			
$________ (deductible amount)	________	________	________
Medical Payment			
$________	________	________	________
Uninsured Motorist			
$________per person			
$________per accident	________	________	________
Total Premium	________	________	________

Help for the High End (Read This Only If You're Rich)

If you are a high roller—somebody with hundreds of thousands of dollars in assets—you may need exceptionally high liability limits on both your auto and home-owner's insurance policies.

Instead of buying them separately—which costs a fortune—consider buying an "umbrella" policy.

Umbrella policies are separate liability policies that overlay most other insurance you may have—with the possible exception of professional liability coverage. Typically, they'll add $1 million in liability insurance on top of other liability insurance you've purchased on your home, car, or boat.

In other words, if your auto policy offers $100,000 in liability protection and your home-owner's liability limit is $300,000, one umbrella policy would boost the liability coverage on your car to $1.1 million and your home-owner's protection to $1.3 million.

It's important to stress that an umbrella policy does not help you if the house or car is destroyed in a fire, flood, or theft. It only kicks in when you are sued. For that reason, it's fairly cheap—often far cheaper than buying high liability limits on separate home-owner's and auto policies.

To be specific, a forty-year old man who drives a Ford Taurus in South Philadelphia would pay $3,550 annually if he bought a no-deductible policy providing $500,000 in liability coverage. But an astounding $1,880 of the cost is for liability protection. He could cut his auto insurance premium by $500 annually—and get better liability protection—if he slashed the auto insurance liability limits to $100,000 per person/$300,000 per accident and bought an umbrella policy.

The umbrella policy would supplement the coverage in his standard auto policy—and his home-owner's insurance too. In this example, it would boost his auto insurance liability coverage to $1.1 million per person/$1.3 million per accident. Yet, in this case, the umbrella policy costs about $200 per year. Because he's saving $500 on the auto insurance and spending just $200 on the umbrella policy, he gets more insurance for $300 less a year.

Why wouldn't he just slash his auto liability limits to nothing, buy the $1 million umbrella, and save even more? Because he couldn't.

Insurers that sell umbrella policies require you to have a minimum amount of liability insurance on both your home and car before they'll sell you an umbrella. And if the umbrella is covering a boat, vacation home, or some other property, they'll require minimum liability thresholds there too. In fact, the reason these policies are cheap is because they're rarely used. The people who buy them are usually very well insured, but they have so much money or assets to protect that they need the additional security.

It is also important to mention that not everyone can buy an umbrella, partly because these policies will also include their coverage on a wide variety of other "perils," such as defamation lawsuits and false imprisonment.

Let's say, for example, that our Philadelphia driver is shopping at Dillard's department store. He thinks he sees another shopper steal something and flee the store. He yells, "Stop, thief!" He grabs the woman and holds her until store security guards arrive. When security comes, they find that this woman not only didn't steal anything, she's a minister at a local church. She sues Philadelphia driver for all he's worth. His umbrella policy opens.

Insurers hate that.

So if they think you're unusually likely to shout "Stop, thief!"—maybe because you are a radio talk show host, a commentator, or a journalist—they probably won't sell you an umbrella policy. If you have all-terrain vehicles, jet skis, speedboats, or other amusing but fairly dangerous adult toys, again, your chance of being able to buy an umbrella policy is slim. If you are able to find one, chances are you'll pay substantially more for it.

Nonetheless, if you are a fairly average person who is just lucky enough to be really rich, you may benefit from such a policy. Check with your insurance agent for price quotes and more information. But be sure to read the policy language carefully to make sure there are no important exclusions. A few of these policies define coverage so narrowly that they're virtually worthless.

Chapter 11

Home Sweet Home

Buying a home is the first big financial goal of the average American family. When you're smart and a bit lucky, it makes for a nice investment, too.

What the chapter tells you

- The benefits and detriments of home ownership
- Whether or not you can consider your home as an investment

What the chapter shows you

- How to determine how much house you can afford
- How to determine the cost of closing
- How much you can save by paying a little extra each month
- How to get a house with little or no down payment
- How to choose the right loan
- How to get the equity out of your home when you need it

Where do I start?

Most renters say they'd rather buy than rent. And even Congress presumes that the American Dream includes home ownership. But how do you get a house if you don't have a lot of cash? How do you determine whether you're better off by buying or renting? How do you choose a loan if you do decide to buy? And once you have a home, how do you determine when—or if—you ought to refinance?

Start with the facts.

Ownership = Commitment

In their enthusiasm to encourage home ownership, many people conveniently forget the fact that a home isn't a simple purchase or investment. It's a way of life.

Once in, home owners rarely leave the house except to work or buy groceries. There's a practical reason for that. They can't afford to. Between the mortgage payments, the roof repairs, the home improvements, and the water and utility payments, many home owners find themselves with very little cash to spare. The good news is that they're often so busy puttering in the garden that they don't have time to think about what they might be missing.

You're a home owner. Your renter friends are hopping off to Bermuda. Water skiing. Dining out. You're spackling. Hanging pictures. Starting a vegetable garden. But, oddly enough, you're probably happy. Numerous surveys indicate that home owners are just plain contented. When the renters drop by with their vacation photos, the home owner—blissful and oblivious—may just counter with something like: "Hey, have you seen our new stove?"

In other words, your life changes when you buy a home. It ties you down. It commits you. It's similar to getting married. You can back out, of course. But if you do, it's likely to cost you.

Why is that? Realtor's commissions. The average real estate broker will charge between 5 and 7 percent of the home's sales price to represent you in the sale of your home. Not to belabor the point, but that's not a percentage of your profit. That's a percentage of the entire selling price of the home.

So you plunk down your $10,000 life savings and buy a house for $110,000. After living there for a year, you decide you hate it. You hire a real estate agent who is able to sell the house for $112,000. The realtor pockets 6 percent of that $112,000 ($6,720), and about 1 percent more—$1,120—will probably go toward so-called closing costs, which leaves you with $104,160. Then once you pay the bank back the $100,000 you borrowed, the escrow company will return to you the balance of the $10,000 you invested, amounting to $4,160.

Even though your house actually rose in value, you lost $5,840.

What about all those payments you made? Didn't they reduce your loan enough to build up your equity in the house? ("Equity" is the difference between the value of the house—what you could sell it for today—and the amount you owe on it in mortgage and home equity loans.) Probably not.

To illustrate, let's say this mortgage was at a thirty-year, fixed-rate loan at 8 percent interest. That means your payments amounted to $734 a month, or $8,805 per year. How much of that paid down your principal? $835. The rest—$7,970—paid interest on the loan.

In other words, it wasn't tremendously different from paying rent.

But you heard you'd make a fabulous profit by buying a home? On occasion, that happens, but usually not in short periods. In most cases, as in the example above, if you buy and sell within a few years, you'll pay more in trading costs than you'll get back in price appreciation and built-up equity.

Is Your Home a Long-Term Investment?

In the late 1980s, home owners saw the value of their real estate soar by double digits—sometimes nearly overnight. In the early 1990s, that trend reversed. Home values plunged. Millions of home owners not only lost their equity—the down payment—but also found their mortgage amounts were higher than the value of their real estate.

So is a home a good investment or a bad one? Neither. It's a forced savings plan.

Over short periods of time, residential real estate prices can roller-coaster up or down. There's no reliable way to predict it.

Over long periods, values tend to rise somewhat faster than the rate of inflation. There are also some tax breaks and leverage involved in owning a home that can offset the trading costs. Home owners therefore tend to do a bit better in the long run than people who put their money in savings accounts.

Residential housing *appears* to be a great investment because home owners are compelled to save. They build up substantial equity because they have no choice but to pay the mortgage. (Okay, they have other choices—default, foreclosure, or bankruptcy. But they're not good ones.) No one is going to force a renter to put their money in a savings account or a mutual fund, which makes saving difficult, because it's a lot more fun to spend money.

For that reason alone, home owners tend to be better off in the long run than non–home owners. It's not necessarily that they've made some sage investment by buying a home. It's that they've saved money by socking it against a mortgage month after month. Your non-home-owning friends are likely to have spent their investable cash on things like vacations.

Renting vs. Buying

Eventually, everybody hears the argument that if you rent, you're throwing your money down a hole. If you buy, you're building equity. Naturally, it's better to buy than rent, right? Sometimes.

The fact is, when you buy you often end up spending more than when you rent. In addition to a mortgage—which may or may not be more than your rent—you spend money on property taxes, improvements, repairs, insurance, and utilities. Many of these expenses are significantly lower—or nonexistent—for renters.

Moreover, as mentioned above, if you sell quickly or sell in a bad market, you may not be building equity at all. You only build equity if the value of the home rises enough to cover the real estate commission and leave you with a profit.

When you consider this issue of renting versus buying, you should be thinking about life-style, not finance.

Do you want to have the option of living in a home indefinitely? If you have a landlord you risk being kicked out if they decide they want to sell the property—or want to live in it themselves.

Do you want to be able to paint the walls without having to consult a landlord about the color? Do you want to rip out your carpets? Or invest in flower bulbs for the garden—and generally feel that the improvements you make are going to be long-lasting and yours alone?

Do you want to be responsible for choosing your own plumber? Maintaining your own yard? Or do you want somebody else to handle both the cost and the hassle of home maintenance and repair?

If you're the type of person who gets hooked on your own surroundings, and if you like stability and the idea of growing old in one place, home ownership is probably for you.

If, on the other hand, you value the freedom of being able to pick up and move to another city, state, or country at any given moment, you'd be nuts to buy.

In other words, the rent versus buy analysis is best done without a calculator.

The Tax Breaks

Another common argument for home ownership is the tax breaks. Uncle Sam allows you to deduct mortgage interest and property-tax payments from your income. That reduces your taxable earnings and the amount of income tax you pay.

These tax breaks can be substantial if you buy a big home, are in a lofty tax bracket, or pay a fortune in interest. However, for first-time home buyers who buy inexpensive homes at reasonable interest rates, the tax breaks are nothing to brag about.

To clarify the point, let's take a closer look at the buyers of the $110,000 home with a $100,000 mortgage. We'll call the buyers Sam and Suzie Home Owner and assume they received mortgage interest deductions for the entire year of 1994. (In other words, they were making mortgage payments for twelve months, paying the full $7,970 in interest.)

To qualify for this loan—$100,000 at 8 percent interest—they'd have to earn about $32,000 annually. As a married couple they file jointly, which lands them in the 15 percent tax bracket.

Because they bought the home, they'll itemize deductions. Between mortgage interest payments of $7,970, their property-tax payment of $1,100, and their charitable contributions of $250, their total itemized deductions add up to $9,320. They also subtract the value of two personal exemptions (worth $2,450 each in 1994) from their $32,000 annual income. Their taxable income is $17,780. They pay $2,681 in tax.

What would they have paid if they never bought the house? $3,116. Buying the house saved them $435 in federal income taxes, which works out to a savings of $36.25 per month. They may also get a break on state income taxes, but it wouldn't be enough to talk about.

The bottom line: If the cost of the home owners' mortgage, property taxes, insurance payments, and repairs exceeds about $40 per month more than their monthly rent payments would have been, they're net losers.

Tax breaks don't start getting lucrative until you're in a higher tax bracket, you have a bigger mortgage, or you have many other itemized deductions that you wouldn't claim without the boost of the mortgage interest expense.

Want It Anyway

All right, so buying your first home isn't going to make you a millionaire. It still may be a great way to spend your money. If you'd like your own home, not because you have some unrealistic belief that it's going to soar in value or save you a fortune in rent, but because you like the idea of living in it—then it's time to sharpen your pencils and figure out just what you can buy.

What Can You Afford?

Determining how much house you can afford pivots on three things: Your income, how much you have saved for a down payment, and current mortgage interest rates.

If you have a "traditional" down payment (20 percent of the home's purchase price), most banks figure you can afford a mortgage payment of between 28 percent and 35 percent of your gross monthly income. The higher your income, the more banks will be willing to increase the percentage.

How much house will that buy? For that you need a calculator, a banker, or a "multiplier." If you have already read the chapter on present-value calculations and have bought the calculator, the worksheet below will be simple.

How Big a Loan Can I Get?

Complete the worksheet and rev up your calculator. You can refer to the example as a guide. It is based on a person with a $30,000 annual income looking at a thirty-year loan at a mortgage rate of 8 percent.

		Example
1. Gross monthly income (before deductions):	$__________	$2,500
2. Multiply line 1 by 28 percent or 0.28:	$__________	(PMT) $700
3. Estimated mortgage rate _____ divided by 12 months	________	(%I) 8 = 0.6667
4. Years of the mortgage _____ multiplied by 12 months =	______	(N) 30 = 360
5. Future balance on the mortgage (always "0")		(FV) 0
6. Compute loan amount*: (CPT, PV)=	____________________	$95,395

Multipliers

If you don't have a calculator, look for mortgage interest–rate charts in your local daily newspaper. Often, mortgage-rate charts are actually detailed advertisements that list a number of mortgage lenders, the interest rates they charge, and the lenders' phone numbers. Not all papers publish these listings, of course, but many include them in weekly real estate or Sunday business sections.

These charts also often include "multipliers" after the interest rate. You can multiply the figure in that column by your mortgage amount (rounded to thousands) and get the

To compute loan amount: Pull out your present-value calculator. Enter the figures you've recorded on lines 2, 3, 4, and 5, followed by the key listed next to each. For example, the Example Person would hit: "700, PMT"; "0.6667, %I"; "360, N"; "0, FV." Then hit "CPT, PV" for compute present value.

The result: Barring bad credit or other unusual circumstances, a bank would approve this person's application to borrow up to $95,395 to buy a home.

approximate monthly payment for that loan. For instance, if the multiplier is $7.65 and you are considering a $167,000 loan, you would multiply 7.65 by 167 to find the monthly payment on this loan would be $1,277.55. If that's less than 28 percent of your gross monthly income, you would probably qualify for the mortgage.

The Banker Approach

If you can't find a mortgage multiplier and you don't have a calculator, you can get your banker to do the math for you. (Because they like to get new business, they are generally very accommodating.) Call and tell the lending officer the amount of your gross monthly income—that's income before deductions for taxes, insurance, and retirement plans. Then ask her how much house you can afford.

Your lender's answer will probably sound something like, "Well, assuming you have a 20 percent down payment, you could qualify for . . . " It shouldn't take more than a few seconds to get the answer.

The Down

The biggest trick to getting a house, however, is finding the money for a down payment.

According to traditional lending standards, a person who wants a $100,000 home would have to have $20,000 in cash—20 percent down payment—up front. The lender would then finance the $80,000 difference.

It's possible to buy a house with a smaller down payment. You can even buy a house with no down payment at all, although it will substantially limit your options (as we'll see in the next section).

Why? Because lenders want to protect themselves. The bigger the down payment, the more they're protected. Simply put, if you can't make your payments and they have to foreclose, they will already have a large portion of your money.

If you have 20 percent to put down on a house, you can go to virtually any lender. They'll most likely compete for your business, which means you'll get a better interest rate, better terms, and whatever house you want—that is, if it's in your price range.

No-Down Deals

What do you do if you don't have any down payment? You could save. You could borrow or beg money from a rich friend or relative. You could ask a seller to "carry back paper." Or you could look for a hard-to-sell foreclosed property.

Because you wouldn't be asking the question if you wanted to save—or had a rich and generous relative—we'll skip right to carrying back paper and foreclosures.

Carry-Back

What does it mean to "carry back paper"? It means that the sellers loan you the money to buy their home. Realize that this isn't going to happen unless the sellers know and love you—or unless their house is a touch difficult to unload. It would be a rare seller who would even consider carrying back paper on a hot-selling property. She simply wouldn't have to.

And practically speaking, many people can't do it because they already have a loan on the property. They need you to pay cash to them so that they can pay back their lender. They might allow you to "assume"—or take over—their loan. But that also requires lender approval. If you don't have any cash in the deal, the lender is likely to balk—unless he's convinced his other options are worse. In other words, the lender might go along with this kind of deal if you're highly creditworthy and the seller is on the verge of default.

The only home owners who are in a position to carry back paper for you are those who are rich or who have lots and lots of equity (most of their mortgage is already paid off).

However, if you find such a seller, you may have something attractive to offer. You can pay her a steady stream of income at a better interest rate than she could find elsewhere. Assuming you are a good credit risk, and the seller has reason to trust you, that's a good deal.

Moreover, by selling her property on an "installment" basis rather than flat out, the seller doesn't face a walloping tax bill. She's only required to pay tax on the payments she receives—not on the entire built-up profit in the home.

Let's say, for example, that you are renting a home that you like. You pay your rent on time each and every month. The owners are an elderly couple who support themselves on the income from their investments. You want to buy the home. The owners are not adverse to selling. You get a real estate agent (or two) to estimate the market value of the home. (Real estate agents do this all the time—for free—as a way of marketing their services.)

Once you've established the market value of the home, you should investigate interest rates by calling several lenders or finding an interest rate chart in your local newspaper. Now plug these figures into your present-value calculator.

Let's say, for example's sake, that the house is worth $130,000. Interest rates for thirty-year mortgages are at 9 percent.

You hit: "130,000, PV"; 9 divided by 12 (months) equals "0.75, %I"; "360, N"—for number of payments you'll make over thirty years; "0, FV," because you'll pay off the loan on the 360th payment. Now punch "CPT, PMT." Your monthly mortgage payment would be $1,046.

Now consider how that amount compares to your current rent payments. If it is less than you are paying in rent, the owners are probably not going to agree to the sale. They'd have no reason to. If it's more, you have to determine whether it's affordable on your budget. Assuming both answers are yes, you present your idea to the owners and see what happens.

What if the owners say they'll sell, but they think the interest rate should be 10 percent? What if they're willing to sell, but think your assessment of the home's value is too low?

Plug in the numbers they suggest and determine whether you are willing to go along with their counteroffer.

You should know, however, that unless you are in a high tax bracket and need big mortgage interest deductions, you may be better off paying a little more for the house than hiking your interest rate. If you hiked the sales price to $140,000, for example, but left the interest rate alone, your monthly payment would be $1,126.47.

If you left the sales price alone, paying $130,000, but raised the interest rate to 10 percent, your monthly payments would be $1,141—about $15 per month more.

If you hiked both the sales price and the interest rate, you'd pay $1,229 per month.

Carry-back caveats. The risk of these deals is that both buyer and seller usually represent themselves. There's no realtor involved and, in most cases, there's no real estate attorney looking at the deal. Naturally, the lack of experts saves you money. But it also presents risks to the unwary. The biggest problems you could face is not getting the deal in writing and not planning for contingencies.

What happens if somebody—buyer or seller—wants out of the deal? What happens if, five years down the road, the buyers want to move and pay off the loan? What happens if two years into it, the seller has a financial hardship and needs all the cash from the home sale?

Because buying a home is a huge purchase, involving hundreds of thousands of dollars, these are not questions to be taken lightly. The fact is, almost anything could happen in a thirty-year period. And, even though you think the seller and the buyer agree on everything, financial disagreements occasionally pop up—even among relatives and friends.

You need to hire a skilled adviser—most likely a real estate attorney—to write up your contract. Before you faint over the potential cost, realize that although anticipating all the potential pitfalls of this type of deal is difficult for you, it's what a real estate attorney does for a living. A good attorney is going to have handled transactions like this one a dozen times before. She's probably got a workable "form" contract in the office word processor. All she has to do is check to see if there's something unusual about your arrangement. Unless there is something unusual about your deal, this should take a maximum of a few hours and cost you less than $1,000.

Foreclosures

Let's say there's a house in your neighborhood that's empty. It was taken back through foreclosure. It's been on the market for a while. Nobody is buying, perhaps because it's in bad shape. It needs a lot of fixing up.

If you're not adverse to the house or the work, do your present-value calculation and see if you can make the bank an offer. You should be cautioned, however, that banks are usually bureaucratic and slow—particularly when it comes to dealing with their foreclosed real estate. Making a deal, if it can be done, will probably take longer than you expect.

Bankers also hesitate to accept no-down offers, even when they have virtually nothing to lose. (After all, a worst-case scenario leaves them with the same property they've got now, later. And in the meantime, they've at least collected some monthly payments.) Also, even in the best case, buying a foreclosure will involve some up-front closing costs. If you are exceptionally lucky—or you're buying a serious dog of a property—the bank may finance these, tagging them on to the cost of the loan. But, in most cases, you should be prepared to come up with at least 1 or 2 percent of the purchase price in advance to pay these fees, which are for sundry items such as title insurance, appraisals, and attorneys' fees.

Because you may have to come up with 1 to 2 percent of the purchase price in cash even when buying a foreclosed property, you might want to try to save just a little bit more. That will allow you to qualify for low–down payment mortgages.

Low-Down Programs

The difference between buying a property with a low down payment versus no down payment is choice. When you don't have any money saved, you have to look for a seller that's desperate or oddly accommodating. They're not easy to find.

But, if you can come up with just 5 percent of the purchase price either through your own savings or "gifts" from family members, your options soar. Suddenly, you go from being able to buy just one house out of the hundreds in your price range to being able to consider any house that's for sale and affordable.

The 203k Plan

There are now two nationally available programs that allow buyers to purchase a home with a 3 to 5 percent down payment. One is a government-sponsored program called the 203k plan, which is geared toward low-income borrowers who want to buy low- to moderate-priced homes. The program is specifically designed to help inner-city borrowers who buy fixer-uppers.

If you are considering a property that needs considerable improvements, and that is listed for sale at a price lower than most homes in the area, you may want to investigate this program.

The reason you can only consider these loans under these limited circumstances is because 203k loan limits are low. They vary by where you live, but they are lower than median-priced homes in the same areas.

But if you and the property you are considering qualify, such a loan can allow you to put just 3 percent down on a house and finance both the purchase and remodeling costs in one loan.

The downside to 203k loans is that they're somewhat more expensive than loans that require a large down payment. Typically, you'll pay between one and three "points"—one point equates to 1 percent of the loan amount—in processing and insurance fees over what you'd pay on a loan with a larger down payment.

The other catch is that not all lenders offer these loans. Although the program has recently been revamped to make it easier for borrowers and lenders alike, many lenders simply think that government-sponsored loans require more paperwork than they're worth. As a result, they can be fairly hard to find.

However, Countrywide, one of the nation's biggest mortgage banking companies, now offers the loans nationwide. You can call them at 800-669-6659 to check rates, fees, and terms.

The Department of Housing and Urban Development (HUD) can also tell you what other lenders in your area offer these loans. HUD, which administers the 203k program, has offices in many major cities. The agency is listed in the government section of your phone book.

Community Homebuyers Program

A more widely available and flexible low–down payment mortgage plan is the Community Homebuyers Program, sponsored by the Federal National Mortgage Association, which is better known as Fannie Mae.

Technically, this program requires buyers to come up with 5 percent of the purchase price in cash. However, they're fairly flexible about where part of that cash came from. A portion of the money could have been a "gift" from a friend or relative, for example.

Loan amounts on this program can go up to Fannie Mae's "conforming loan" limits, which are currently a bit over $200,000. Fannie Mae does not make loans directly. Instead, you hook into this program by going through virtually any bank or savings and loan in your area.

Make sure to shop around. Although a variety of lenders may all offer the same basic program, they're all likely to charge different rates. It's like seeing the same suit at two different retailers—the markup can vary widely from store to store.

FHA/VA Loans

It would be remiss to talk about low–down payment programs without giving at least passing mention to the government's benchmark FHA and VA mortgage loans.

VA loans offer qualified veterans the ability to borrow up to $184,000 with no down payment. The program is offered only to veterans, through the Veterans' Administration. If you're a veteran and don't know about this program, call the VA and ask for a brochure.

The Federal Housing Administration also sponsors a low-down program with maximum loan limits that go up to $151,750. In theory, at least, there is no limitation on who can qualify for these loans. However, in practice, hefty FHA insurance premiums can discourage many borrowers from using the program.

To be specific, FHA charges a 2.25 percent mortgage insurance premium at closing. That can be financed in the loan, but it boosts your overall loan amount. In other words, instead of borrowing $100,000, you'd be borrowing $102,250 to account for the $2,250 insurance premium. In addition, the government agency assesses monthly insurance costs. On this loan, the monthly insurance premium would amount to about $43.

The FHA monthly insurance premium lasts the life of the loan. Borrowers cannot cancel the mortgage insurance when their equity rises above 20 percent—as they can with a nongovernment low-down mortgage.

In addition, the FHA, in all its bureaucratic splendor, also must approve the deal, which can sometimes stall the escrow.

Some FHA officials have been lobbying to streamline the process and cut costs. So there may be hope in the future. But, for the moment, the low-down payment plans offered by banks look better than the ones offered by the government.

Private Mortgage Insurance

If you get a low–down payment loan, your lender is likely to require you to buy something called "PMI" or private mortgage insurance.

PMI is not for you. It's for your lender. It simply insures that if you default on the loan, the insurance company will step in and make your payments. This doesn't, incidentally, get you off the hook. If you have assets, the PMI company may come looking for you to reimburse them for their losses.

However, the real trouble with PMI is that it's expensive. The actual cost depends on the PMI company, the amount of your down payment, and the type of loan. But it's not unusual for annual premiums to amount to between .5 and 1 percent of your loan balance. In other words, on a $100,000 loan, you could be paying anywhere from $500 to $1,000 in annual insurance premiums. Since you pay the premiums monthly, that boosts your monthly mortgage cost by roughly $42 to $83 per month.

Because these premiums are high, but vary lender to lender, PMI can be a pivotal issue when searching for the lowest-cost loan. Make sure you find out the total cost of monthly payments, factoring in PMI, interest, principal, and any other monthly amounts that are required when you are comparing loan costs.

Also inquire about the lender's policies regarding canceling PMI.

Most lenders allow you to cancel the insurance after you have built up a certain amount of equity, or after you have been paying on the house for a set period of time. However, if you have been promised that the PMI will be canceled at a set point—when your equity reaches 80 percent, for example—make sure you get the promise in writing.

Many borrowers complain that bankers are reluctant to cancel PMI—even when such a cancellation is clearly within their lending guidelines. And since there is no law that says a lender must cancel PMI at any given point, you're in the unenviable position of trying to force a bank to follow its own rules. That's a lot like trying to get a three-year-old to stay in bed. But if it's in writing—part of your contract—you have the law on your side.

Impound Accounts

Many lenders will also require low-down borrowers to set up impound accounts to pay their property taxes and home-owner's insurance premiums. Without an impound account, you would normally pay both home-owner's insurance and property taxes in lump sums once or twice annually. With an impound account, you remit these costs monthly along with your mortgage payments.

Lenders require impounds for a simple reason. If you don't pay your property taxes, state tax authorities can place a lien on your residence. That lien must be satisfied, or paid off, if the residence is sold. If the lender takes your house back in foreclosure, their ability to resell the house could be hampered by the lien. Meanwhile, if there's a fire and you haven't been paying your home-owner's insurance premiums, both you and your lender could lose everything.

From the buyer's perspective, impound accounts can be a convenience. They force you to budget for necessary expenditures. However, if you don't need the prodding, they're costly and bureaucratic—something you may want to do without.

How are they costly? Impound rules in most states allow lenders to maintain a "reserve" in the account in the event that you don't make a necessary payment—or you don't make your payment on time. In many cases, lenders are not required to pay interest on that reserve at all. In some cases, they must pay interest, but at a very low rate. What that means is you could have several hundred dollars locked up in this account—inaccessible and unproductive. If you could be investing that money at a better rate of interest, you're losing money by keeping it locked in impound.

Traditional Mortgage Loans

If you have enough cash to put 20 percent of the home's purchase price in a down payment, you can qualify for a traditional mortgage.

A traditional mortgage is typically less expensive and requires fewer hassles than a low- or no-down payment program. You usually don't have to bother with impound accounts or private mortgage insurance. And, because your lender feels relatively secure that you're not going to walk away from such a big down payment, they'll probably offer you a better interest rate, too.

Traditional loans come in myriad varieties. There is the benchmark thirty-year, fixed-rate mortgage; fifteen-year, fixed-rate mortgages; twenty-year; forty-year; loans that require balloon payments. And there are literally dozens of different types of adjustable-rate mortgages, from the so-called "two-step" mortgages that offer a fixed rate for a while and then convert into an adjustable loan to the traditional adjustables that offer "floating" rates from start to finish.

The choices may seem dizzying. But before you close escrow, you've got to choose a lender and a loan, and get the loan approved and funded. There's no time to waste.

Choosing the Right Loan

How do you choose a loan?

Consider why you are buying the house. Is this where you plan to grow old? Or is this a temporary starting place before you move on to bigger and better things? How long do you expect to live in the home? And how certain are you that you're right?

The reason these questions are important is because some loans—adjustable-rate mortgages, for example—can be vastly cheaper in the first few years, but then they can rise in price until they significantly exceed the cost of a comparable fixed-rate mortgage.

If you are certain to move or refinance in a short period, an adjustable-rate loan would probably save you money. But if you expect to stay in the home for a long time, you may be better off with a fixed rate.

Fixed-Rate Loans

Fixed-rate loans are fairly simple. They're easy to shop for because there are just two numbers to watch: The interest rate and "points"—or up-front fees that are calculated as a percentage of your mortgage amount.

Your interest rate is set for the life of the loan. You know the number of months you need to pay. You know the payment amount. You get a payment booklet, or a monthly bill, and you pay it. Simple.

The standard fixed-rate loan must be paid off in thirty years.

How to Save by Paying More

The only other thing that you really ought to know about fixed-rate mortgages is what happens if you pay a little extra toward the principal with every monthly bill: You save a fortune and you shave years off your debt.

Consider Suzie, a home owner with a $200,000 thirty-year, fixed-rate loan at 9 percent. Her monthly payments amount to $1,609.25. If she pays as scheduled—in other words, 360 payments of exactly that amount—she'll pay back $579,330 over the life of the loan. (The $1,609.25 monthly amount times 360 payments.)

What happens if she rounds her payment up to $1,700 monthly? She shaves more than six years off the length of her mortgage and saves an astounding $92,450 in interest expenses.

How much can *you* save by paying a little extra against the mortgage each month? If you've got a present-value calculator, do the worksheet and see. (Or go to the Macmillan Web site at http://www.mcp.com/mgr/macmillan/dollars.)

Prepayment Savings

How much will you save by paying more than required against your fixed-rate mortgage? Finding the answer is a two-step process.

Step One: Determine how quickly you'd pay off the mortgage with a higher monthly payment			***Example***
1. Enter the original amount of your mortgage	$__________	(PV)	$200,000
2. Your annual interest rate______ percent divided by 12	__________	(%I)	9 = 0.75
3. Proposed payment (Current payment + ________)	$__________	(PMT)	$1,700
4. Loan balance at payoff (always 0)	$0__________	(FV)	0
5. Compute number of payments: (CPT, N)	__________	(N)	286.4

Step Two: Figure your savings	***Example***
1. Multiply your required monthly payment by the number of months you agreed to pay on the loan	360 × $1609.25 = 579,330
________________ × ________________ = ________________	
2. Multiply your revised monthly payment by the number of months you'd have to pay to pay off the loan.	286.4 × 1,700 = 486,880
________________ × ________________ = ________________	
3. Subtract the result of line 2 from the result of line 1. This is your savings: $________________	$92,450

Fifteen-Year, Fixed-Rate Loans

Naturally, if paying enough to cut six years off your mortgage saves you a bundle, then paying off the loan in fifteen years will save you even more. Amortize this same loan over 180 monthly payments instead of 360 and you save $214,195 in interest.

The catch, of course, is that the payments are stiffer. You'd pay $2,028.53 each month instead of $1,609. If you can afford that, it's worth doing. But, if you're not certain you'll be in a position to pay that much each and every month, stick with the thirty-year loan and just pay extra whenever you can.

Balloons

The idea behind balloon payments is this: The average person doesn't stay in the same house for thirty years to pay off their mortgage. They sell in five to ten years, paying off the mortgage balance with the proceeds of the sale.

Why finance the purchase over thirty years if you're only going to stay for five? Because lenders charge more for locking themselves in for long periods, as they do on thirty-year loans, you could get a lower interest rate if your payments were based on a thirty-year term, but you agreed to pay off the balance completely in just five (or seven or ten) years—like you would if you sold.

The reason balloon-payment mortgages have never really caught on is because life is not that predictable. You may think you're moving in five years, but a thousand little things may not happen precisely as you expect, so you don't.

But if you have a balloon-payment mortgage, you have to pay the loan off at the end of the period anyway. That means you'll have to sell or refinance. And refinancing at the wrong time can be costly.

Adjustable-Rate Mortgages

As a result, people who think they may move or refinance within a few years, but aren't sure, may be better off with any one of a number of adjustable-rate mortgages, called "ARMs" for short.

Adjustable mortgages come in all shapes and sizes. No matter what kind you choose, you need to know about a few key issues. Specifically:

- How often does the rate adjust?
- How is the adjusted rate calculated?
- Are there any limitations on how high the rate can go at each adjustment period or over the life of the loan?
- Are there limitations on how much the payment can rise at each adjustment?
- What "index" is your loan rate tied to and how has that index performed over time?

Adjustment Periods

When you're considering an adjustable-rate loan, the first thing you should consider is how frequently the interest rate adjusts. In bankerspeak, these are the "adjustment periods." On most ARM loans there are two adjustment periods to look at: the initial adjustment period and subsequent adjustment periods.

For instance, on a "5/25" loan, the first adjustment period is five years from the date the loan is made. After that, the interest rate may change monthly, every six months, once a year—or at some other specific interval.

On the other hand, if you choose a one-year Treasury loan, the initial adjustment period and the subsequent adjustment periods may be the same. A standard Treasury-bill loan, for example, may adjust just once (or twice) a year—every year—from the date the loan is made until it's paid off.

Other ARMs, such as the so-called COFI loans, usually have an initial adjustment period that's three to six months from the date the loan is originated. Subsequent interest-rate adjustments often are done monthly.

If you prefer stability, look for a loan with infrequent adjustment periods.

Interest Rate Caps

A key consumer protection on adjustable-rate mortgages are annual and lifetime interest-rate caps. What rate caps do is limit the amount your interest rate can rise—or fall—over specific periods of time. That protects you from seeing your loan rate—and payments—skyrocket over short periods of time.

Commonly, adjustable loans will have two interest-rate caps: an annual cap and a "lifetime" cap. For instance, the T-bill loan—an industry benchmark—offers a 2-percentage-point annual interest-rate cap and a 6-percentage-point "lifetime" cap.

What that means to you: In a worst-case scenario, your 6 percent loan can jump no higher than 8 percent within a year's time. And, no matter how high rates go over the life of the mortgage, you'll never pay more than 12 percent on this loan.

On the other hand, when rates are dropping sharply, the rate on your loan can't drop by more than 2 percentage points in a year either.

Payment Caps

Some lenders give less in the way of interest-rate caps and instead offer payment caps. Payment caps limit how high your required monthly payment can rise.

For example, so-called COFI (Cost of Funds Index) loans often stipulate that your monthly payments will never rise more than 7 percent per year. In other words, if your monthly payment is $1,000 in year one, it can't jump to more than $1,070 in year two.

However, payment caps are an artificial barrier that do not actually insulate you from the rising cost of a mortgage. What happens when a payment cap kicks in is your lender bills you for less than what you actually owe, given the rise in interest rates. The difference—what the payment should have been minus what they charged you because of the payment cap—is tacked on to the balance of your mortgage.

For example, let's say interest rates have risen by 2 percentage points since you got your $100,000 ARM at 7 percent. But you have a 5 percent annual payment cap. Your monthly payment, which starts out at $665.30, cannot rise by more than $33.27 in the first year. So your payment tops out at about $732.

However, because you have no interest-rate cap, the interest charges on your loan are actually accruing at a 9 percent rate. The amount you owe adds up to about $805 per month—$73 more than you are actually paying. If you pay at the "capped" rate of $732, the $73 difference is tacked on to your loan balance. At the end of the year, instead of paying down your principal, you find your loan balance has risen.

This unpleasant phenomenon is called "negative amortization."

The Index

When you start looking for adjustable-rate mortgages, you'll hear bankers talk about the rate "floating above an index."

What that means is the rate on your loan is linked to another rate—such as the bank's cost of funds, or prime rate, or the rate the U.S. Treasury pays on Treasury bills. The particular interest rate that your loan is linked to is called the "index."

There are several indexes that adjustable loans could be linked to: the one-year T-bill index; the so-called Cost of Funds (or COFI) index; the London Interbank Offered Rate (or LIBOR) index; the six-month certificate of deposit (or CD) index. Or, simply, "prime rate."

These indexes have varying characteristics. The T-bill and CD indexes, for example, are often lower than the COFI index. However, they also move faster. It's not unusual for the T-bill index to jump—or drop—by 3 percentage points in a single year, for example. The COFI index, on the other hand, tends to lag, changing by fairly small increments each month at a pace that's far more leisurely than the T-bill index.

There is no one index that's better than the others. But you may certainly be more comfortable with how one index moves than you are with the others. If you are uncertain which index is best for you, ask your lender for a history of how the various indexes they offer have performed over time.

The Margin

However, the rate on your loan will not be the same as the index rate. Instead, your loan will "float above" that index. The difference between the rate on your loan and the index rate is called the "margin."

For instance, your loan may float 2.75 percentage points above the T-bill index. Then, when the T-bill index is at 4 percent, your loan rate would be 6.75 percent. The 2.75 percentage points between the index and your loan rate is the "margin."

Putting It All Together

The tricky part of getting an adjustable loan is linking all the separate elements together into one package you can live with.

That means finding a loan with a reasonable margin, an index you can track, and interest rate or payment caps that make you feel comfortable.

The good news is that these loans are prepackaged in fairly standard ways.

Loans that are tied to the one-year Treasury-bill index traditionally come with 2-percentage-point annual interest-rate caps and 6-percentage-point lifetime interest-rate caps. Usually, payment caps are not offered on these loans.

Loans that are tied to the COFI index, on the other hand, usually have payment caps and lifetime interest-rate caps, but no annual interest-rate caps. These loans often allow negative amortization—the unpleasant phenomenon where you pay faithfully, but end up owing more than you originally borrowed.

The "margin" on nearly every standard adjustable loan ranges between 2 percentage points and 3 percentage points. If you're a bad credit risk, you may have to pay more. If you are a stellar risk and are getting a special deal, you may pay less.

Things to Do Before You Apply

If you want to make the application process quicker and easier, there are two things you should do in advance: Put together a financial statement by listing your assets and liabilities. (If you completed Chapter 3, you've already done this.) And check your credit report. (If you didn't do that in Chapter 5, now's the time.)

Why? When you apply for a mortgage, your bank will require you to detail your financial life on the mortgage loan application. Having your financial statement handy makes this as simple as transposing numbers from one form to another.

Your bank also will pull your credit report. If there are negative items on that report, you will be asked to explain them. In some cases, these will be simple mistakes. (Some consumer groups maintain that the majority of credit reports contain errors that range from minor to pivotal.) The credit bureau may have picked up negative information from somebody whose name or Social Security number was similar to yours, for example. You'll respond by saying that it wasn't you. Your bank will then try to verify that your explanations are valid. In the meantime, your escrow is languishing. The seller considers backing out.

If it's unclear whether you or the reporting company are telling the truth, the bank is likely to err on the side of caution. That means they don't approve your loan.

If you check the report and correct errors before you start the mortgage process, you preclude the possibility of being turned down because of a simple mistake.

Incidentally, your bank will also require a copy of your latest tax return to verify that the information you provided about your assets and liabilities is correct.

Cautions

Do not lie, exaggerate, or "pad" your loan application. This advice is more than a lesson in morality.

Somewhere in the fine print of that loan form is a release that gives your bank permission to view your personal financial records to determine that all the information you provided on the loan application was true, accurate, and correct. If the bank discovers that you lied to get a loan, you can be prosecuted for loan fraud, which carries heavy civil and criminal penalties. Or the bank can "call" your loan, requiring it to be paid off immediately. What if you can't pay? The bank will most likely foreclose.

Even if you're larcenous to the core, you have to accept that the chance of getting caught is very high. It's not worth it. *Don't lie.*

Things to Consider After You Buy

Borrowing Against Your Home Equity

One of the few tax breaks that survived the 1986 tax "simplification" bill was mortgage interest deductions for so-called home equity loans. In addition to writing off the interest payments on your mortgage, you can borrow up to $100,000—banker willing—to use for any purpose. The interest you pay on that loan is tax deductible.

This is worth mentioning because interest expenses on other types of consumer debts—auto loans, boat loans, and credit-card loans, to name a few—are no longer tax deductible.

However, you can buy a car with the money received from a home equity loan and deduct the interest—assuming the loan isn't for more than $100,000. And since home equity loans are secured by your house, the bank will probably offer you a better interest rate than it would on an unsecured loan.

That makes home equity borrowing comparatively inexpensive.

There's only one catch. If you can't make the payments, you can lose your home. So despite the tax breaks, you should be careful about racking up too much debt.

Refinancing

At some time or another, nearly every home owner considers refinancing their mortgage. There are lots of reasons you might want to:

- You have a balloon-payment mortgage and are contractually obligated to refinance.
- You have an adjustable rate and you'd prefer a fixed-rate loan because you think it could save you money over the long haul.
- Interest rates have dropped and you think refinancing could save you money.

If your purpose in refinancing falls into the first category, you're not deciding *whether* to refinance. You must. Your job boils down to finding a loan.

However, most refinancers are opportunists. They consider refinancing because interest rates have fallen since they obtained their original loan, which allows them to trade in an adjustable loan for a fixed-rate loan—or to simply secure a lower rate and lower monthly payments.

In either case, refinancers need to recognize there are some substantial costs associated with trading your loan in for a new one. If you are contemplating a refinance simply to save money, you have to consider whether the savings you'll get will more than compensate for these costs. If they do, you're wise to refinance. If they don't you're wasting both time and money.

How do you do the analysis? You compare the cost of refinancing—if you ask, the bank will spell out their fees in advance—to your monthly savings. If you plan to stay in your house long enough for the monthly savings to exceed the costs, you do the deal. If not, don't.

What are the costs? They vary. However, here's a checklist that you can run through with your banker. Fill in the appropriate items and add them up. Then calculate your monthly savings by comparing monthly payments on your new loan to your old one.

Beware: Many people inadvertently lengthen the term of their mortgages by refinancing. If you've been paying on your current home loan for ten years, you'd have to get a twenty-year mortgage to have a loan that's directly comparable. Don't fool yourself into thinking that you are saving money by cutting the monthly payment if you're paying for a longer period of time.

Also make sure to compare rates *and fees* from at least two lenders—and preferably more—when you consider a refinance. Just as different banks charge different mortgage rates, they also impose varying fees. Some will charge all of the fees listed below. Others will charge just a few. By simply making a few phone calls, you could save yourself hundreds of dollars.

Refinancing

The Costs	***Loan #1***	***Loan #2***
Points	$__________	$__________
Application fee	$__________	$__________
Appraisal fee	$__________	$__________
Attorneys' fees	$__________	$__________
Credit report	$__________	$__________
Hazard insurance	$__________	$__________
Home inspection	$__________	$__________
Loan origination fee	$__________	$__________
Mortgage insurance	$__________	$__________
Recording fee	$__________	$__________
Survey cost	$__________	$__________
Title insurance	$__________	$__________
Underwriting fees	$__________	$__________
Other	$__________	$__________
Total	$__________	$__________

The Payback

1. Current monthly payment $____________ $____________

2. New monthly payment $____________ $____________

3. Monthly savings (subtract old payment from new):

   $____________ $____________

4. Tax cost (multiply the previous number by your combined state and federal tax rate)

   $____________ $____________

5. Net savings (subtract tax cost from monthly savings)

   $____________ $____________

6. Break-even (divide the net savings by the total cost to determine how many months it will take to pay off the costs of refinancing)

   ____________ ____________

7. Estimated number of months you plan to stay in the house:

   ____

This analysis assumes you choose a fixed-rate mortgage. If you refinance into an adjustable, you'll need to estimate your savings, based on how frequently your loan adjusts as well as the index, margin, and the interest-rate caps.

Chapter 12

Insuring Your House

You bought it. Now you've got to protect it by buying some home-owner's insurance.

What the chapter tells you

- Choosing the right amount of coverage can save you hundreds, even thousands, of dollars.
- A standard policy actually insures you for far more than what most people consider to be the policy amount. That's because your home-owner's policy is a package of many coverages.
- With some types of insurance, buying too much coverage is nearly as bad as buying none at all.

What the chapter shows you

- What a standard home-owner's policy covers and what it excludes

Where do I start?

Once you take the plunge and decide to buy a home, you've got to protect it. That means you've got to buy home-owner's insurance.

The single most common error that people make when buying home-owner's coverage is thinking their "policy amount" ought to be the same as the home's purchase price. In fact, there are numerous coverage amounts on your policy. It would be unlikely that any of them would amount to the purchase price of your home.

You don't want to be cavalier about the amount of insurance you purchase, either. The reasons are clear: You buy too little insurance and you leave yourself at risk of losing everything in a natural disaster—some little-known insurance rules kick in and bite you when you're underinsured by a set amount. But, if you buy too much, you could be paying anywhere from $50 to $500 per year too much in premiums—and you get nothing extra for the additional expense. In fact, if you have earthquake coverage, buying too much insurance can effectively *reduce* your coverage.

What a Standard Policy Covers

Before you can contemplate just how much home-owner's coverage you need, you need to understand just what home-owner's insurance covers.

The standard policy protects you from losses caused by fire, theft, windstorms, tornado, hurricane, rain, hail, and falling objects—including planes, trains, and trees.

It does not protect you from losses caused by earthquakes, floods, wars, or nuclear accidents. However, you can buy policy riders or separate policies to cover earthquakes and floods. If you live in a flood zone or an area prone to quakes, these coverages are advisable.

Structure. The standard policy would reimburse you for the cost of rebuilding your home exactly the way it is today—including replacing the wall-to-wall carpets, paint, molding, and wallpaper. To determine the right coverage amount, it's smart to get a guestimate from a local builder (or two) about the per-square-foot rebuilding costs in your area based on your house's construction type and quality. A builder can usually come up with this type of guestimate over the phone in a matter of seconds. Then multiply the per-square-foot price by the number of square feet in your home. That should be the right coverage limit for the structure of your home.

Separate structures. The policy would also cover the cost of replacing separate structures—such as detached garages, tool sheds, and outhouses.

Personal property/contents. The contents of your home are also insured up to set limits. The amount of coverage varies based on the policy you buy, but usually the maximum contents limits are equivalent to 50 percent of the structure limit.

Most policies pay replacement costs—the cost of getting another five-year-old couch, rather than a brand-new one, unless you buy guaranteed replacement cost coverage. If you have replacement-cost coverage, you should be able to buy the same couch new and be reimbursed for the full cost.

In addition, most policies limit reimbursements for certain expensive items in your house to set limits, too. Specifically:

Cash/coins/securities. Most policies limit recovery of cash, bank notes, precious metals, and coins stored at home to $100 to $250, unless you have purchased a separate insurance rider to provide higher limits.

Passports/tickets/stamps. You commonly get up to $1,000 in coverage for securities, deeds, financial documents, manuscripts, passports, tickets, and stamp collections lost as the result of an insured peril.

Watercraft. Up to $1,000 in coverage for jet skis, windsurfers, trailers, outboard motors, and other watercraft.

Jewelry/furs/firearms. Costly items, including jewelry, furs, gems, and firearms, are usually covered to a maximum of $2,500, unless you buy a separate insurance rider.

Silverware. Pricey eating utensils, whether made from silver, gold, or pewter, are usually covered to a maximum of $2,500.

Computers/data-processing equipment. Usually covered to a maximum of $5,000.

Artwork/rugs. Costly artwork, rugs, and carpets are usually covered to a maximum of $2,500.

In addition, your basic policy provides reimbursement for "loss of use" of your home, cleanup and removal of debris from your property, and for replacement of trees, shrubs, and landscaping. These coverages usually come into play when there is a complete loss, such as when a house is consumed by fire or destroyed in a tornado or hurricane.

However, it is also common to have limits on these additional coverages. Specifically:

Loss of use. Your insurance also pays for you to live in a hotel or rental property while your personal residence is getting repaired. The amount of this coverage is usually limited by either a specific dollar amount, or a percentage of your structure coverage, or by a set number of months that it will pay for your loss of use. Some policies, for instance, will pay to rent a comparable residence for up to two years. Others will pay only for twelve months. Others will pay an amount equivalent to 25 percent of the structure limit.

Debris removal. Most policies also pay to remove debris left by a covered peril. However, the most the policy would pay would be 5 percent of the structure amount.

Emergency repair. The policy will pay to make emergency repairs aimed at protecting the property from further damage—such as boarding up broken windows and patching leaky roofs.

Landscaping. Trees, shrubs, plants, and lawns are covered usually to a maximum of 5 percent of the dwelling limits. In addition, most policies won't pay more than $500 to replace any single plant.

Liability/medical payments. If someone hurts himself on your property, your home-owner's insurance will pay to patch him up, defend you if you're sued, and pay damages if you lose in court. You set the limit on the liability coverage when you buy the policy. The more assets you have to protect, the higher the limit ought to be.

Not Covered

- Cars (If your car is consumed by fire while parked in the garage, you'd be reimbursed by your auto insurer, not your home-owner's insurance.)
- Aircraft
- Boats
- Pets
- Business property, except computers (as listed above)
- Business liability
- Liability for transmission of a communicable disease
- Liability for illegal and purposeful acts (If you get angry and push somebody down the stairs, your home-owner's insurance will not cover your losses if you are sued as a result.)

Deductibles

You usually have a deductible—commonly between $250 and $1,000—which is the amount that you, rather than your insurer, pay each time you have a loss. You can lower your annual premium by raising your deductible. But, of course, that means you pay more of the cost if you are unlucky enough to have a loss.

Insured loss:	$2,000
Deductible:	– $500
Insurance reimbursement:	$1,500

Optional and Supplemental Coverages

Most home owners have the ability, but not the obligation, to buy coverage for some non-covered perils, such as earthquakes and floods. Normally, you'd do this with a policy rider or a separate policy.

These policies will generally mimic your basic home-owner's coverage. However, they'd have separate deductibles, separate premiums, and sometimes some separate coverage limits.

It is important to note that the deductible on most earthquake coverage is set as a percentage of your structure coverage. In other words, if you have a $100,000 limit on structure reimbursements and a 10 percent earthquake deductible, you would pay $10,000 out of your own pocket before the insurer would reimburse you for an earthquake-related loss.

Coverage Tips and Traps

Too much insurance. Some people are tempted to overinsure their residence, in order to be certain that they'll be fully reimbursed in the event of a loss. You obviously pay for overinsurance through higher premiums. However, if you don't mind paying a little extra for additional piece of mind, it usually doesn't cause any significant problem.

But there's one exception. If you have earthquake coverage, you could pay dearly for overinsuring your residence. That's because earthquake deductibles are set as a percentage—usually 10 to 15 percent—of the structure coverage limits. In other words, if the coverage limit on the structure of the house is $100,000, the insurance pays once your loss exceeds $10,000. If your structure limit is $200,000, the insurance pays only when the loss exceeds $20,000.

Guaranteed replacement cost. A better alternative to buying too much insurance is to buy so-called "guaranteed replacement cost coverage." Often, this coverage will pay what it takes to replace your home, regardless of the coverage limits. However, in recent years, insurers have become increasingly careful about selling guaranteed replacement-cost coverage to people who appear to be significantly underestimating the cost of replacing their home. If your insurer thinks is the case, the company may require higher coverage limits on your standard insurance or it may limit the guarantee to a set percentage over your coverage limit. In other words, if you have a $100,000 policy, the insurer may say they guarantee to pay up to 20 percent more than that limit to replace your residence. If the actual cost of replacing the residence is higher, you're on your own for the excess amount.

Too little insurance. If you buy far too little home-owner's coverage—as you might be tempted to do to reduce your premiums and the deductible on your earthquake coverage—you may run into one of the least-understood and most dangerous snags in home-owner's insurance: "implied co-insurance." The way this works is this: If you buy insurance with limits that are less than 80 to 85 percent of the actual cost of replacing your home, your policy may say that you have implicitly taken on some of the risk of insuring the house yourself. In such cases, the insurer will only pay the pro-rata share of the loss.

For instance, if the structure limit on your house is $60,000 and it would actually cost $100,000 to rebuild your residence, implied co-insurance says, you're taking on 40 percent of the risk. If you then suffer a $60,000 loss, the insurer will pay just $36,000. You're on the hook for the other $24,000.

Law and ordinance changes. If you live in an older home, it's possible that your house was built prior to numerous changes in local building codes, forcing people to build with more support beams, for example. If these changes could significantly increase the cost of replacing your home, you ought to consider getting a law-and-ordinance rider. What this does is ensure that your coverage will pay to replace your residence based on today's building standards, rather than the standards when your house was built. Otherwise, your insurance policy stipulates that it will pay only to replace the structure precisely the way it's now constructed.

Your insurance agent or a contractor could give you a good idea of whether you need a law-and-ordinance insurance rider.

Chapter 13

Home Inventory

A thorough home inventory can be invaluable if you ever suffer a disaster that damages or destroys your home or its contents.

What the chapter tells you

- Why you want an inventory
- Where to put it

What the chapter shows you

- Different ways to do a inventory
- Where to get additional help for a hand-written record

Where do I start?

Victims of fires, floods, hurricanes, earthquakes, tornadoes, and other natural disasters have learned firsthand what few others have ever considered. It's incredibly difficult—if not impossible—to reconstruct a list of all the things you had once they're lost.

A complete inventory of what is in your home—as well as an accurate description of the home's construction type and quality—can be invaluable if you ever suffer a catastrophic loss.

The Benefits of an Inventory

Ideally, you'll never have to use this. However, if you do suffer a major loss, it will help you in two ways.

First, it will make it faster and easier to file an insurance claim because you won't spend weeks trying to remember just how many pairs of shoes you had in the closet and whether you had the six-pan or the eight-pan set of Revere Ware. You're also likely to get substantially more money for your claim because your description of what you lost will simply be more complete than what a home owner without an inventory could possibly provide.

Secondly, if all or part of your loss is not covered by insurance, this record will help you claim a tax deduction for your casualty losses. Casualty losses are deductible when the uninsured portion exceeds 10 percent of your income, plus $100. That's a high hurdle to clear, so it's unlikely you'll be able to claim this deduction for a theft or anything that's covered by insurance.

Nonetheless, many people are not insured for losses caused by earthquakes and floods. The tax breaks won't make you whole if you suffer such a devastating loss, but they certainly help.

If you do suffer a deductible casualty loss, consult a tax adviser about how best to claim it. There are numerous tricks to filing these claims. A seasoned adviser should be able to help you avoid the pitfalls and get the most out of your tax deductions.

How to Do the Inventory

There are essentially two ways to do the inventory: Write it or videotape it. If you have your own video camera—or can borrow or rent one—you'd be wise to choose the video option.

A video record will take you a fraction of the time a written inventory will take. It's also more accurate because a picture can better describe the condition and construction type of your personal residence and possessions than you can in narrative—no matter how good a writer you are.

Written Record

If there is absolutely no way you can get your hands on a video camera, you can hand-write the record. Be prepared for an arduous evening, however. Completing a thorough list will take you several hours at least. In fact, once you get a few hours into this job and realize how unpleasant it is, you might just find a way to get that video camera after all.

There's no set formula for doing this. However, you're best advised to keep things as simple and direct as possible. For instance, you might start the page with the current date and wording along the lines of:

> Home inventory for Jane and John Doe, at 100 Pumpkin Patch Lane, Greensborough, VA, as of 8/25/95.
>
> Description of residence: Craftsman bungalow, built in 1929. Wood construction; French windows and doors throughout. 1200 square feet; two bedrooms; one bath; family room, modern kitchen, sun porch. Shake roof.
>
> Lot is surrounded by a white picket fence. House is flanked by a detached one-car garage. A 200-sq. ft. tool shed is located in the northeast corner of the property.

You then write your way into the house and describe each room's significant construction details—things like crown molding, French windows, wallpaper or paneling, flooring, fireplaces, and so on. Then detail every item in the room, starting with the furniture and working your way down to the debris in the closets and drawers.

Whenever possible, note how much you paid for the item and when it was purchased. If you have receipts, particularly for big-ticket items such as sofas, beds, refrigerators, tables, chests, and computer equipment, stick them in an envelope with your completed home inventory.

When you start recording what's in the closets and drawers, save yourself some time by grouping similar items. For instance, instead of listing each item of clothing, you might list: Four Brooks Brothers business suits, $1,000; seven wool sweaters, $300; three pairs blue jeans, $75; fourteen pair cordovan loafers, $2,000.

One more tip: Before you start, figure out a routine that you'll follow in every room, such as starting with items in the northwest corner, and working around the room in a clockwise fashion. Start with the big items, then do a second circle to pick up the details, such as what you've got lurking in the closets and drawers.

Following a set routine will help you do a more thorough job, and that's pivotal if you want to get the most from your insurance or casualty-loss tax deductions.

Additional Help

If you need further direction with a handwritten inventory, you can get a free booklet called *Taking Inventory* from the Insurance Information Institute by calling them at 212-669-9200.

The booklet, which is mainly a graphic aimed at reminding you to list specific items, their prices, and approximate purchase dates, is not long enough to accommodate everything you've got in your home. But it may help you organize your listing and remind you about items you otherwise may have missed.

Video Inventory

To do a video inventory, you are going to follow the same basic procedure as the person who does the written inventory. But, thanks to the wonders of technology, you'll be able to avoid the writer's cramp.

To start, take your video camera to the street in front of your home. Make sure you start far enough away to pick up neighbor's homes and a general impression of the street; your flora and fauna; and nonresidential structures such as detached garages, sheds, and fencing. Turn on the camera; slowly sweep from one side to the other, pulling all these items into the camera's gaze.

Narrate as you film, starting with something along the lines of: "This is a home inventory for Jane and John Doe at 100 Pumpkin Patch Lane, in Greensborough, Virginia. The date is: ———. I'm John, your handsome and talented narrator." (You're going to sound like a geek on the tape no matter what you say, so you might as well make it official.)

Now approach the house, talking as you go about when the house was built and the construction type—wood, stucco, brick, stone, steel. The type of roofing. The type of windows. Any significant items of interest. Walk slowly around the residence, getting all sides, if possible. Then return to the front.

Enter the house through the front door and systematically film and narrate your way through the entire residence, making sure to open every closet door, cupboard, cabinet, and drawer. Rifle through the contents enough to feel comfortable that you've caught most everything—even items buried in the back, on the floor, or shelves—on film.

When you are finished, stick the tape in an envelope with any receipts you may have saved for major purchases (computers, furniture, or appliances, for example). Seal the envelope and label it as your home inventory. Date it and give it to a trusted friend or relative, or, if you have one, put it in your safe-deposit box for storage.

Inventory Don'ts

- Don't hand your home inventory to a neighbor or friend who lives so near you that they're likely to be wiped out in the same natural disaster.

- Don't give this inventory to someone you are not certain to know in two years or to someone you don't completely trust. Remember, this record spells out what you've got, what's valuable, and where it is. That's not exactly information that you'd want to have fall into larcenous hands.

- Don't give it to an honest, well-meaning flake, either. An inventory that's lost is the same as no inventory at all.

Updates

You will occasionally want to update the inventory—particularly if you remodel or buy new and expensive property.

Unless your remodeling project is massive—you gut the structure or completely refurnish your home—you should be able to update this record by simply filling an envelope with receipts and photographs of what's new.

You can then file the update with the holder of your original inventory—be that a safe-deposit box, friend, or relative.

Part Four

BENEFITS AND INSURANCE

If you are lucky, your employer will offer all of the benefits listed in the following four chapters to you—at a subsidized price—through work. If not, you'll have to go it alone or go without. Either way, you ought to think a bit about what you've got and what you need.

Chapter 14: Employee Benefits

If you've got a job with a big or mid-sized company, there's a good chance that you are collecting a host of freebies, from paid time off to retirement accounts. Savvy Americans know what they've got—which saves them a fortune when determining what else they need to buy. Learn the ropes, page 136.

Chapter 15: Life Insurance

Are you a parent of small children? Does someone rely on you for financial support? Then you need life insurance. The only trick is figuring out how much you need and determining how to buy that amount at a reasonable price. Sharpen your pencils, page 150.

Chapter 16: Disability Insurance

Although most Americans have at least some life insurance, few think about disability coverage. But you're much more likely to be disabled when you're young and working than to die. Here's what you need to know about disability insurance to figure out how much, if any, you need. See page 161.

Chapter 17: Health Insurance

The rocketing cost of health care means that most Americans would be financially devastated by a single severe ailment if they didn't have health insurance. But health insurance isn't the simple product it once was. Now it comes in varieties—FFS, HMO, and PPO. Here's how to negotiate the maze, page 169.

Chapter 14
Employee Benefits

Employee benefits can boost your standard of living and reduce your income taxes—if you know enough to use them wisely.

What the chapter tells you

- What benefits are commonly offered and how to use them
- How to keep your vacation time from expiring
- Certain child-care benefits can save you tax money.
- The basics on company-offered disability and life insurance

What the chapter shows you

- Where to record what you've got

Where do I start?

You saw the chapter heading and already you're feeling sleepy, s-l-e-e-p-y. . . . Yes, employee benefits are boring. But they can be worth their weight in gold. It behooves you to know about them because:

- Knowing what's provided in your employee benefits package can help you decide whether to buy costly supplemental life insurance or disability insurance.
- They can make your child-care costs more manageable.
- They may allow you to collect occasional cash "bonuses."
- They can save you a fortune in taxes.
- They can vastly reduce your health-care costs.

In fact, a nice employee benefits package is better than a raise. Workers just *think* benefits are boring because most major employers drop a benefit handbook that is roughly as large—and as enjoyable to read—as the Manhattan telephone directory in your lap the day you are hired for a new job. Chances are, you're too busy spending your first paycheck to read it.

After that, you think about reading it. You know you should. You might even leave the book out for a few weeks, saying you'll get around to it eventually. It becomes a fixture on the coffee table. Then a coaster. Then you toss it. After all, you've been with the company for years now. What wouldn't you know?

It's time to find out.

Determine What You Have

If you still have your employee benefits handbook, pull it out. If you burned it, lost it, or otherwise can't get your hands on it, ask for a new one.

Your company doesn't put out benefits handbooks? They keep all their benefits information on the back of a matchbook? Not to worry. Pull out a notebook and, as you read through this chapter, write down questions to ask your benefits representative.

The questions will become obvious. They'll be about benefits you want and are not sure whether or not you have. Or they may be about optional features allowed in some plans that may or may not be available in yours. Once you know the right questions to ask, you're likely to be less confused by the answers.

At the end of each section there's a place to record whether you have the particular benefit mentioned and, where applicable, the type and the cash value.

These listings are for your own reference. They are designed to serve as reminders of amounts, terms, or details that you may forget. If you're certain you'll have no trouble remembering something, there's no need to write it down.

Just jot down the numbers or terms that you might have to look up later. Realize, however, that certain numbers are worth writing down, such as the death benefit of a company-sponsored life-insurance plan, the estimated value of your company pension, and the amount and type of disability insurance that you may already have.

The reason you want these numbers handy is because they'll help you later when you have to decide whether or not to buy more insurance—or how much more you might need to save for retirement.

Begging for Benefits

Realize as you read through this chapter that employee benefits vary from company to company. There is no standard package that's available to all. The vast majority of employee benefits are voluntary—not mandated by any federal or state law.

Companies determine what benefits to offer based on a wide range of criteria, including how much they can afford, the makeup of their workforce, and whether anyone is complaining.

Don't expect your company to offer everything that's listed here. However, if there are benefits that are important to you and your coworkers, you may want to approach management and ask if they can be established at your firm.

It's worth knowing that some benefits cost the company very little to provide. However, having a company sponsor a 401(k) plan or a disability insurance program, for example, can be tremendously advantageous to workers—even when the company does not contribute any cash to the program. (More on why later.)

If you can convince company managers that a desired benefit will be inexpensive to add and yet an advantage to both workers and the company—giving the company an edge when trying to recruit top-notch workers, for instance—you may well make a deal.

However, successful arguments are likely to require a great deal of homework on your part. You may have to research how the particular program works, what it takes to administer the plan, what it could cost the company, and whether other companies like yours offer the benefit. The more compelling your presentation, the more likely you are to win—and that's likely to result in a real boost to your standard of living.

That said, here are some of the benefits you should look for when taking a new job—or find out about in your current job—starting with the simplest things first.

Paid Holidays

Most employers pay full-time workers *not* to work a half dozen days each year—often on Labor Day, Independence Day, Memorial Day, Presidents' Day, Christmas, and Thanksgiving. If your company is open on those days—and offers paid holidays—you'll usually get overtime or holiday pay that can amount to between one-and-a-half and two times your regular hourly wages if you do work that day.

Alternately, the company could simply allow you to take off work on another day, with pay.

Part-time, hourly, and temporary workers are less likely to rate paid holidays. Usually, if you're a part-time or hourly worker, you get paid when you work, period. If you're lucky, the company will boost your hourly rate when you work on recognized holidays, though.

Don't you have the *right* to a paid day off on a so-called federal holiday? Nope. The term *federal holiday* means the federal government isn't operating on that date. Nothing in the nation's labor laws requires your employer to follow suit.

Personal Days

Personal days are a deviation of paid holidays. You may get one or two days a year that you can take off without being sick—without any good excuse at all—and still get paid.

These days are often provided to help workers handle religious holidays and personal emergencies, such as a death in the family, that may otherwise exhaust your vacation time.

However, when it's possible, company managers will expect you to arrange to take personal days in advance—just as you would with vacation time. That allows them to schedule other employees to work your shift.

Vacation Time

You may take it for granted, but paid vacation time is one of the most expensive employee benefits that U.S. companies commonly provide. Offering an average of ten to twenty days of paid vacation time to salaried workers costs companies an amount equal to about 10 percent of company payroll, according to Hewitt Associates, a national benefits consulting firm.

How much vacation time you get usually hinges on how long you've been with the company. Most companies offer two weeks—ten work days—after one year but increase the allowed number of vacation days after you've been with the company for five years or more.

You'll usually accrue your vacation time "ratably" during the year. In other words, there are 260 days in the average work year and you may get ten of those days off. So for every day you work, you could earn about thirty minutes of vacation. After twenty-six days, you would have earned a full day off.

Some companies are sticklers about not allowing you to take time off until you've earned it. Others will credit you with the vacation time right away and allow you to take it whenever you want—as long as you don't take more than you've earned in the year.

Use It, Lose It, or Cash It In

Old-style vacation programs are fairly inflexible. You get two weeks per year. If you don't use the time within a set period—often within six months to one year of earning the full two weeks—you start losing the time. In other words, "Use it or lose it."

Do you always simply lose vacation time that you didn't use? No. Some companies will pay you cool cash to give up your vacation days.

Generally, vacation pay is set at your normal hourly rate, multiplied by the number of vacation hours you didn't use. In other words, someone who earns $10 per hour and who gives up two weeks—eighty hours—of vacation would get $800 in before-tax vacation pay. This comes on top of your ordinary pay—which includes pay for vacation time—so, in effect, you could get paid for fifty-four weeks of work in one fifty-two-week year.

The catch? Vacation time turned into bonus-style pay is fully taxable. That means the actual amount you get will be reduced by employment taxes—the 7.65% of your wages that you pay into the Social Security and Medicare systems—and both state and federal income taxes. The tax bite can easily reduce the amount you get by 20 percent or much, much more.

Moreover, your company may allow vacation payoffs only when it's particularly swamped and wants to keep everybody working. Or it may allow them only at specific points in the year, such as at the end of the fiscal year, when vacation hours are set to expire.

In other words, you probably can't just sell your vacation hours because you went crazy at the mall and don't know how you're going to pay the bills.

What happens to your vacation time when you quit your job or are fired? It depends on where you live, and, sometimes, on company policy.

In California, state law requires that companies compute vacation time ratably and pay you for every unused vacation hour at termination.

However, that's fairly rare. In most states, you only get paid for unused vacation time when the company's policy is to pay workers for unused vacation days when they leave. If that's the company policy, they can't deny you vacation pay because they're mad at you. But they also can't pay you for unused vacation hours if they don't normally, just because company managers especially like you. What's done for one must be done for all.

Vacation Banking

You love vacation time? Wouldn't consider giving it up for something as incidental as money? In fact, your only concern is finding a way to earn more days off? Find out if your prospective or current employer offers something called "vacation banking."

Vacation banks are still relatively rare, but where they're instituted, they usually work like this:

Instead of getting a set number of holidays, vacation days, personal days, and sick days, you get a block of time—maybe thirty days—that you can use for any reason—vacation, illness, school or federal holidays, disability, or anything else you want.

In some cases, workers are able to save banked hours for future use—or contribute overtime hours to the bank. How many hours you can store in a bank—and how long they can be saved—depends on the company.

In addition, some companies will actually *require* you to take vacation hours after a certain period, simply because they believe workers need some time off to be productive.

When company policy stipulates that unused vacation time can be cashed in at termination, vacation banks can also effectively serve as an emergency fund that can be tapped if you are disabled or lose your job. If you have two months of time "in the bank," you have sixty days *at full pay* to recuperate or find new employment. That's a valuable safety net.

Your Vacation

Do you know how much vacation time you've earned and whether you are at risk of losing time if it's not used within a set period? If not, find out and record the answers here.

Accrued vacation hours:	____________
Hours that will expire if not used/when they expire:	______/______
Cash value, if any, of accrued and unused vacation time:	____________
Access to vacation bank?	Yes______ No______
If yes, number of banked hours:	____________

Overtime

There aren't a lot of areas where hourly employees actually have an edge over managers and professionals, but when it comes to overtime, they do.

If you are paid on an hourly basis and you work more than forty hours in a week, federal laws require that you get paid overtime. If you're a salaried worker or professional, you don't get overtime pay.

Overtime pay is usually set at one and a half times your normal hourly rate, but some companies will actually pay more—up to three times your regular hourly wages.

Some states impose stricter overtime rules than federal law mandates. For instance, some require that you get paid overtime if you work more than eight hours in a day—regardless of whether or not you work more than forty hours in the week.

However, companies can usually get waivers of these rules when the longer hours are dictated by so-called "flexible scheduling" plans that are usually for the benefit of the employee.

Sick Leave

Your employer may also allow a limited number of paid sick days. In some cases, unused sick days can be converted into extra vacation time. In other instances, they can be carried over and used in the following year—which can come in handy if you get a serious illness and require a lot of time off.

On occasion, "convertible" sick leave can also be taken in cash—in lieu of days off.

However, in most cases, paid sick days simply keep you from being docked for a lost day of work. If you don't get sick, you can't use them.

Do you know how many days you get? Do you know whether those days can be converted into extra vacation time—or pay? You should. If nothing else, it could help you decide whether or not to stay home an extra day nursing a nasty cold.

Do you get sick leave?	Yes__________	No_____________
Number of paid sick days?	_____________	
Days taken/remaining:	Taken________	Remaining_______

Disability

If you get sick for a long period, there's a good chance that you'll run out of sick time, blow through your paid vacation time, and end up wondering where the income is going to come from to pay your bills.

The good news is many companies offer disability-insurance programs that will provide you with a portion of your regular monthly income to tide you over when you are seriously ill.

It's important to note that these programs are a supplement to federal and, possibly, state programs that you may also be entitled to. You can learn more about those programs in the chapter on disability insurance.

About 78 percent of the nation's largest companies offer so-called "salary continuation" plans, which provide full or partial pay for temporary disabilities.

The duration of these plans varies. They can last for just a few months—usually at least three—or they can last for a year, two years, or more. Promised payment amounts also vary. Some plans pay up to 60 percent of your wages; others will pay up to 100 percent.

A smaller percentage of companies also offer long-term disability programs, which can pay benefits for years.

Workers may be given a minimum amount of disability insurance for free and then be asked to pay a monthly premium for any amount over the minimum. Or, they may be expected to pay all or part of the premium from the get-go.

It's worth mentioning that if you pay 100 percent of the premium, your disability benefits will not be taxable when you receive them—they'll then be considered nontaxable insurance benefits.

If you do not pay the premium—your company pays it for you—the proceeds are taxable income. The bottom line: You need comparatively less insurance when you pay the premium because you won't have to give 20 or 30 percent to the government.

It is also worth mentioning that disability insurance coverage is usually *vastly* less expensive when purchased through a company plan than it would be if you purchased it on your own. It's not unusual, for instance, for premiums to be two to four times higher when disability insurance is purchased individually than when purchased through a company plan. Make sure you buy what you need while under the corporate umbrella.

Your Disability Benefits

If you have disability insurance through work, record the details—the number of months it covers you, the percentage of your salary it would replace, and whether you pay the premiums.

Short-term disability coverage	_____Yes ____No
Term (months) it promises to pay	______________
Percentage of income it replaces	______________%
Estimated monthly benefit amount, based on current salary	$______________
I pay the premiums	_____Yes ____No
Long-term disability coverage	_____Yes ____No
Term (months) it promises to pay	______________
Percentage of income it replaces	______________%
Estimated monthly benefit amount, based on current salary	$______________
I pay the premiums	_____Yes ____No

Life Insurance

Most big employers offer their workers group life-insurance policies, too.

By and large, these policies are "term" insurance, meaning your policy will pay a death benefit as long as you pay the premium and die while the policy is in force.

Usually you get a minimum amount of life insurance—often enough to pay a death benefit of one to two times your salary—for free. In other words, your employer pays 100 percent of the premium. If you want more, you'll have to pay all or a portion of any additional premiums required.

In some instances, you'll have the ability to buy insurance on your spouse through the company plan, too. These programs almost always require that you pay all or most of the premium.

Unlike disability policies, life insurance purchased through work isn't necessarily less expensive than similar insurance purchased on your own. It does have its benefits, though.

One of the main benefits of getting life insurance through work is that you usually aren't required to take a physical exam to get a policy—at least if you sign up at the point when you are hired. You simply fill out a medical history form and you're insured. If you decline the insurance at first, but decide you want it later, you may be required to take a physical exam then, however.

The disadvantage of a work-based policy is that you lose the insurance if you lose—or change—jobs. At that point you would have to buy another policy, go to work for another company that offered insurance, or simply accept the risk of being uninsured for a while.

You know that term life insurance generally pays off only if you die. However, you should know that you may be able to cash out a policy if you're terminally ill. It doesn't matter whether you bought the policy on your own or if you got it through your employer. For more details, refer to the "Viatical Settlements" section on page 159 in Chapter 15, "Life Insurance."

Your Group Life Insurance

If your employer pays the premium for you, simply record how much insurance you have.

However, if you need to pay all or part of the premium yourself, you'd be wise to determine whether or not you need insurance and roughly how much you need. Refer to Chapter 15, "Life Insurance," page 150, if you need help.

Death benefit amount, your policy $____________________
Death benefit, your spouse's policy $____________________
Insurer ______________________________________
Number to call if you have a claim ______-______-________

Health Insurance

Health insurance is widely offered to full-time employees of large and medium-sized companies. Like disability insurance, workers usually get a substantial break on the price when they buy health insurance through a group plan. In addition, employers typically pay the lion's share of the premium for their workers.

However, increasingly, employers are offering more health insurance choices and are passing on a greater portion of the cost—particularly when workers choose the "Cadillac" programs that allow you to choose your own doctors and direct your own care.

Because health-care choices have become so complex, we've devoted an entire chapter to discussing what you should look for and how to make a reasoned choice between plans offered at work. In addition, there are guidelines on how to appeal when your insurer denies coverage for your medical bills. Refer to Chapter 17, "Health Insurance," starting on page 169.

Child-Care Programs

Employers sometimes help workers solve child-care problems by either providing referral services, on-site care, or child-care subsidies.

However, by far and away the most common program—and the most valuable child-care benefit for most families—is the dependent-care account.

Dependent-Care Accounts

If you have small children—under the age of thirteen—and child-care expenses incurred so that both parents can work, you should find out if your employer offers a dependent-care account.

Dependent-care accounts are offered by about half of the nation's biggest employers, benefit consultants say. Yet only a tiny fraction of those who have access to them use them.

Why? Most workers haven't the foggiest notion what they are, what they do, why they'd want one, or what makes them so valuable. The same answer applies to all questions: They don't change how much you pay out in child-care expenses, but they can save you a fortune in federal tax.

To be specific: A dependent-care account could save a dual-earner, middle-income family $1,400 in federal income taxes plus another $383 in so-called employment taxes. Employment taxes are your contributions to the Social Security and Medicare systems.

That can go a long way toward subsidizing your child-care bills.

However, to understand this benefit, you've got to start at the beginning.

Dependent-care accounts are set up by employers and offered as an option at work. If your employer offers one, you can choose to have your employer deduct a set amount from each paycheck and put the money into a dependent-care account.

The maximum you can put in a dependent-care account is the *lesser of* $5,000 annually; an amount equal to the wages of the lowest-earning spouse; or the amount of your work-related child-care expenses.

The money is taken out of your paycheck "ratably"—or proportionally—throughout the year. So if you were able to contribute the maximum, you would have about $417 withheld from each monthly check (or $192 per check, if you are paid every two weeks).

Your contributions accumulate in a dedicated savings account, which is tapped to pay your child-care expenses as they come up. Typically the day-care provider submits a bill, you pay it, and you submit it to the administrator of the dependent-care account, who reimburses you from the money you've saved.

Your contributions are taken out of your wages *before* taxes are computed. As far as the federal government is concerned, you never earned the money. As a result, your contributions to the account reduce your federal tax bill.

If you are in the 28 percent federal income tax bracket—and most middle-income Americans are—that means you'll save $1,400 in federal income taxes by contributing the maximum to the dependent-care account. Moreover, you pay 7.65 percent of your wages in federal employment taxes too. So by effectively "reducing" your income by contributing $5,000 to the dependent care account, you save another $383 in employment taxes. The bottom line: This couple would save a healthy $1,783 annually by using the dependent-care account.

Naturally, if you are in a higher tax bracket, your tax savings are more. If you're in a lower bracket, they're not as substantial.

The Catch

There's only one catch—but it's the one that scares away many parents.

Any money that's left unspent at the end of the year is lost. You can't get a refund. You usually can't adjust your regular contribution levels midyear, either. As a general rule, you set your contribution level just once, at the beginning of the plan year. Then, you use the money that you've accumulated in the account or you lose it.

Still, child-care expenses are fairly easy to predict accurately. If you have a regular babysitter, day-care facility, or after-school care provider, you know how much you spend every year for child care. Just make sure you don't contribute more to the account than you're likely to spend.

Other Child-Care Tax Breaks

It is worth mentioning that you get tax breaks for child care even if you don't have a dependent-care account. That's because the government gives child-care credits to dual-income families that must pay child-care expenses to work. These credits are noted on federal income tax form 1040 and calculated by filling out a separate tax schedule, form 2441.

You can't take both a child-care credit and use a dependent-care account. You have to choose one or the other.

You may be tempted to simply go for the credit, since there's no up-front cost or risk of losing your contributions. But you should know that the dependent-care account is almost always more lucrative for middle- and higher-income parents. That's simply because the credit amount is capped at 20 percent of child-care expenses of up to $2,400 per child ($4,800 maximum) for families earning more than $28,000 annually.

To put it more simply, the family noted above can save a maximum of $960 in taxes by using the child-care credit—that's $823 less than they get if they use the dependent-care account.

Family Medical Leave

Federal law now requires that employers provide up to twelve weeks of unpaid leave to workers who have (or adopt) a baby, or need to attend to their own serious illness or the serious illness of a child, spouse, or parent. The crux of the law is that your employer cannot force you to quit or demote you if you take time off in these instances.

But because some positions cannot be left untended for three months, you are not guaranteed to get precisely the same job you had before you left. You're only guaranteed a similar job, with similar pay and benefits. Most employers comply with the law without a hitch. If yours doesn't, call the Department of Labor in your area and see whether you have an actionable complaint. Local labor department offices are listed in the government section of the phone book.

Flexible Scheduling

It's hard to put a dollar value on it, but flexible scheduling can also be a worthwhile benefit to many working parents. More than half of large employers offer some sort of flexible scheduling arrangements either on a formal or informal basis.

There is no formula for these programs. They can take the form of compressed work schedules, in which you work forty hours in four days instead of five; job sharing, where two workers share one job—or a job and a half; working from home; part-time work; or simply an informal arrangement in which your boss allows you to work an irregular schedule so that you can better balance your job with your home life.

The two most common flexible scheduling arrangements are "flextime"—the informal irregular schedule—and part-time work. Big companies often have formal programs allowing part-time and flexible schedules. However, many companies that don't have any such program do allow flexible scheduling on a case-by-case basis. The trick is approaching your manager, explaining what you want, and detailing why it would benefit the company as well as you.

Retirement Plans

Almost all large and mid-sized employers now offer some sort of retirement savings program to their workers. Some of these programs involve company contributions only. Others require workers to contribute their own money to the program.

If your company offers a so-called "defined benefit plan," and nothing else, you can simply look up your years of service and your income level on a chart. The chart will tell you what to expect in monthly (or annual) retirement income from your employer.

However, companies are increasingly offering so-called "defined contribution" plans, such as profit-sharing programs and 401(k) plans. It's a bit more complicated to figure out how much retirement income you're likely to receive from these plans because the answers will depend on how much you contribute, how long you contribute, and how sagely the money is invested.

Because these programs are varied and complex, retirement plans and programs also warrant their own chapter—Chapter 22, "Saving for Retirement," starts on page 239.

If you are trying to decide whether or not to contribute to a 401(k) plan, be sure to read the 401(k) section in the retirement chapter right away. These defined contribution plans are among the most worthwhile of all employee benefits. They can literally make you rich by doing nothing fancier than socking away fairly modest amounts regularly from an early age.

Your Retirement Account

If you have a defined benefit plan, record the estimated amount you expect to collect at retirement in the spaces below. If you also have a defined contribution plan, such as a 401(k) or profit-sharing program, record today's value in the spaces provided too. In the retirement chapter, you'll learn how to use these numbers to determine whether or not you'll have enough money to live comfortably when you're no longer working.

Defined benefit, estimated monthly payment:	$__________
Defined contribution, current value:	$__________
Profit-sharing, current value	$__________
Savings/thrift plan, current value:	$__________
Other work-related retirement plan:	$__________

Miscellaneous Perks

There are hundreds of little miscellaneous benefits and perquisites that your company might offer that aren't noted here.

Some perks have no real market value, but you may like them anyway. For instance, some companies offer "Christmas clubs," which are simply automatic savings programs that deduct a set amount from your after-tax wages. For people who have a tough time saving, Christmas clubs are helpful. But financially, there's very little difference between having a Christmas club and having a savings account.

However, others are very valuable—company-paid cars and stock options, for example.

Others are valuable to some workers and not to others. If you work for a retailer, there's a good chance that you'll get discounts on merchandise, for example. But those discounts are only worthwhile if you buy the merchandise. If you work for a bank, you'll probably get free checking. If you work for a software company, you may get free upgrades.

If your company offers valuable perks, record what they are and the approximate amount you'd have to spend to replace them. Then, if you're offered another job, you'll be able to quickly determine whether a higher salary will fully compensate you for the potential loss of these benefits and perks.

Miscellaneous Benefits	***Approx. Replacement Cost***
____________________	$________________
____________________	$________________
____________________	$________________
____________________	$________________
____________________	$________________

Chapter 15

Life Insurance

If you have small children, you need life insurance. The only questions are: What kind? And, how much?

What the chapter tells you

- There are two basic types of life insurance, but one type is better at protecting a young family.
- Some people should not have life insurance—unless they get it for free.
- Your life-insurance needs change as you mature.
- A few companies and insurance agents will lie or exaggerate to sell you a policy. But a handful of pointed questions can help you keep your agent honest.
- You generally have to die to collect on your policy. But, if you're deathly ill and need cash, you may be able to get it through something called an accelerated benefit or a viatical settlement.

What the chapter shows you

- How to estimate how much life insurance you need
- How to save hundreds of dollars on a policy
- What to look for before you buy

Where do I start?

Do you need life insurance? The answer depends on whether or not you have dependents—children, a spouse, or other people who rely on you for financial support. If you do, and you want to protect their financial health after you die, the answer is yes. If you don't, life insurance is an unnecessary expense. It's that simple.

Now, a few people—many of them insurance agents—will quibble with that assessment. They'll say you could need insurance before you have dependents. They may tell you that life insurance is an investment. They may argue that even your children need insurance. Not to protect their income—most kids don't support their families—but to protect their "insurability" in case they develop a dread disease and can't get insurance later.

Should you buy insurance as an investment? Probably not. Should you buy it just to make sure you can later? Ditto. There is a risk that you won't be able to buy insurance when you actually need it. There is also a chance that you'll be struck by lightning—or, on the bright side, that you'll win the lottery.

But all of these are very slight risks. Unless there's something unusual in your family medical history that makes you think your personal chance of becoming uninsurable is higher than average, you're probably wasting your money.

Generally speaking, you should buy insurance when you need it. Not before. Not after.

What Is It?

Life insurance is simply a legal contract between you and an insurer. You agree to pay a premium. The insurer agrees to pay a death benefit to your heirs if you die while the contract is in effect. Life-insurance contracts, or policies, come in a wide variety. But, in the end, they all aim to provide financial support to your heirs when you die.

About 70 percent of American adults have some sort of life insurance that they either purchased on their own or received as a company-paid employee benefit.

When Do I Need It?

Usually, you don't need insurance until you marry and have children.

For most families, this is when you have lots of financial obligations and few assets. Although there is only a minuscule chance that you'll die when you're young, the consequences if you do die can be devastating to your family—assuming you provide all or an important part of the family's financial support.

You buy insurance simply to fill the gap between the income your family would have without you and the amount they'd need to survive. That gap usually yawns widest when you've got small children and modest assets. As your children age and become more financially independent—and as you accumulate assets that they could sell to pay the bills in an emergency—your insurance needs diminish.

How Much Is Enough?

Years ago somebody came up with a rule of thumb that said that the death benefit on your life-insurance policy ought to equal two to three times your annual earnings. That figure has been rising ever since. Now agents are likely to tell you that you ought to buy a policy that gives survivors a death benefit of five to six times your annual earnings.

Where do these rules of thumb come from? Thin air.

In reality, the only way to determine how much insurance you need is to take a hard look at your assets and obligations—both tangible and intangible—and have a long, frank talk with your spouse (or dependents) about what would happen if you or your spouse died suddenly.

How would the survivor pay the rent? Who would care for the children? How much income would the survivor need? How long would they need it? And where would the money come from?

Back in Chapter 3, you went through the painful process of listing your assets and obligations. In Chapter 4, you compiled a household budget—another onerous task. Here's where that work begins to pay off.

Flip back to those chapters and take a look at what you've got and how much money it takes to run your household today.

From your list of assets, consider: What tangible assets could you liquidate—sell for cash—if necessary? What assets are you willing to liquidate? What current obligations—debts—could be paid off with the proceeds? Are the debts bigger than the anticipated proceeds or would the proceeds be sufficient to pay off the debts?

(If your calculations include the sale of a home, be sure to estimate the home's value conservatively—especially if you think you would need to sell quickly. And remember that even in the best of circumstances, houses can't be sold overnight. At the very least, they'll have to go through escrow, which almost always takes more than a month.)

From your budget, consider: What expenses would evaporate if one of you died? What continuing expenses would you be willing and able to cut?

What additional expenses might you face if one of you died? Would you be forced to hire a baby-sitter or pay for housekeeping services, for example?

Under normal circumstances you would expect that certain expenditures—food, clothing, and transportation—are likely to decline somewhat if one member of a household dies. However, others are not. Chances are your rent (or mortgage) expenses will stay the same. Your child-care bills are likely to go up.

As unpleasant as it may be to think about, imagining exactly how your life would change if you lost your spouse is necessary to properly estimate your insurance needs. You need to consider the question separately for both spouses—even if one spouse doesn't earn outside income. That's because a stay-at-home spouse is providing valuable services, such as child care, food preparation, and cleaning, that the other might have to buy in the event of a sudden death.

Also consider:

- Roughly how many years would the surviving members of your family need your financial support?
- If necessary, would the surviving spouse be able to pick up some of the slack, earning more than he or she does now?
- How would one spouse's death affect the retirement plans of the other?

The answers are pivotal in determining how much life insurance you need. To put it simply, some families will be able to spend down the principal of their life-insurance settlement without jeopardizing their future. That means they'll need less.

Others will need more so that they can live off the income for a longer—or even an indefinite—time.

Calculating the Appropriate Death Benefit

Let's say you've looked at your budget and you've decided that your family will need $50,000 annually to live on in your absence. But they'll only need that amount for five to ten years, because you both have good earning potential and would only need additional income until the kids were in school. After that the surviving spouse would be able to work more and earn more, and wouldn't have to worry too much about staggering day-care expenses.

Both spouses feel fairly comfortable that they could invest whatever life-insurance proceeds they got and earn 7 percent annually on the money.

How big a death benefit do they need? About $360,000.

Where did that number come from? The present-value calculator. (I told you that thing was useful.) Specifically:

1. You know that the income you want is $50,000 divided by 12 (months), or $4,166.67 per month. Hit: "4166.67, PMT."
2. You know that you'll need this payment for a maximum of ten years, or 120 months. Hit: "120, N."
3. Since the survivor doesn't need support after the ten-year period, you can spend the insurance proceeds to zero. That's the "future value" of the life-insurance account. Hit: "0, FV."

4. You figure that the insurance proceeds can be invested earning 7 percent annually, or 0.58 percent per month. Hit: "0.58, %I."
5. Final step: Punch "compute present value"—the "CPT" and "PV" keys on the calculator—so that the calculator will compute the death benefit you would want if you died today. The result: $359,498.07—or about $360,000.

Other Permutations

What if this family needed support for a longer period—or wanted to save some of the proceeds? For example, what happens if they wanted to keep $250,000 of the proceeds to serve as a retirement account for the survivor? They'd need a death benefit of about $485,000.

You get that by using the same formula as noted above. But you would substitute $250,000 for the projected future value that was previously estimated at zero. In other words, in the previous calculation, you hit "0, FV" in step 3. Now you'd hit all the same keys in steps 1, 2, 4, and 5. But in step 3, you'd punch "250,000, FV" instead.

- What if the survivor doesn't want remaining cash, but thinks he'd have trouble earning 7 percent on his investments? He'd stick to bank accounts, for example, that could pay only 6 percent annually. In step 4, substitute "0.5, %I"—0.5 is what you get if you divide 6 percent interest by 12 months—for the "0.58, %I" you had before.

  This family needs $375,306.

- The interest rate is okay, but your family will only need $30,000 annually for five years instead of ten? In step 1, substitute $2,500—$30,000 divided by 12 months—for the monthly payment. (It was previously $4,166.67.) And, in step 2, substitute 60 months—5 years times 12 months—for the number of periods, or "N." The result: You'd need a death benefit of just $126,255.

Changing Needs

One last note on calculating the amount of insurance you need. Realize that, to some degree at least, you're guessing. You are making assumptions about your spouse's life at some unpredictable point in the future. Because you're doing it carefully and mathematically, you should be close. But don't hesitate to round numbers to the nearest $25,000 or $50,000. And remember that there's no sin in guessing a bit on the high side.

However, also realize that as every year passes without disaster, your insurance needs change. In many cases, they will diminish. That's because you'll build up assets, and those assets can be used to protect your family in place of life insurance. In other words, if this family already had $100,000 in salable assets, they could reduce the death benefit on their life insurance by that amount.

At some point, your need for insurance may evaporate completely. That's when you either cancel your policies or "annuitize" them so that they can start paying you monthly income.

Whether you cancel or annuitize will depend on what kind of insurance you bought.

What Does It Cost?

Now that you know how to figure your life-insurance needs, you probably want to know how much life insurance is going to cost you.

The answer depends on your age and health when applying; your hobbies (skydivers, rock climbers, scuba divers, bungee jumpers, and smokers pay more); the company you choose; and the state you live in. But, most important of all, your rate will depend on whether you want term or cash-value life insurance.

A healthy thirty-five-year-old California male who wants a $250,000 death benefit would pay about $260 annually for a term policy. This same guy might pay $1,000—almost four times more—if he bought universal life, a form of cash-value policy.

For this reason alone, many experts maintain that term is the best choice when you're trying to protect a young family.

What's the difference between cash-value and term? Read on.

Term Insurance

Term insurance is easy to understand.

As the name implies, it provides coverage for a set term, or period of time, which is usually a year. You have to renew the policy, possibly at a different premium, each year that you want the policy to remain in force.

You have the option of renewing with the same company or shopping around for a better rate—assuming you're young and healthy.

As you get older, term insurance starts to get more costly. However, this is also when you're likely to need less insurance because you've built up other assets that can be sold to help support your survivors. And your children are now older, so they're less dependent on you for financial support.

What if you get sick? Your rate could rise before your insurance needs diminish. If you don't like taking that risk, you can look into something called "level-premium term."

With level-premium term, you lock in a rate for a period ranging from five years to twenty-five years. How long you lock the premium is up to you. But realize that you will probably pay a bit extra for the privilege.

Consequently, if you aren't worried about paying a rising premium if you become ill, buying an ordinary term policy will save you a bit of money—at least in the first few years.

How much money? That depends on who writes the policy and market conditions when you apply. However, at the time of this writing, a simple annual-renewable policy for a healthy, thirty-six-year-old male who wanted a $250,000 death benefit was $260 annually, according to InsuranceQuote Services in Chandler, Arizona.

- If this same guy bought a term policy that promised five years of level premiums, he would pay $268 per year.
- A ten-year level premium policy would cost him $263 per year.
- A twenty-year level premium policy would cost $365 per year.

One Contractual Necessity

Regardless of whether or not you go for a level-premium policy, one thing every buyer of term insurance should get is a promise of "guaranteed renewability." That ensures that you'll be able to buy a policy, even when you are sick or old.

Cash Value Insurance

Cash-value insurance is harder to explain. That's because it comes in greater variety and insurers are remarkably reluctant to give out important details of how the policies work and what they cost—even to their policyholders.

What's common to all these policies is:

- They all charge some sort of fee for "mortality"—that's the death benefit, and it's the component of the policy that's similar to the term life policy mentioned before.
- They all are designed to accumulate a cash value that can be tapped by you or your heirs at some point in the future.
- They all promise to pay at least a minimum "guaranteed rate" of interest on the cash accumulation in the policy. And, in reality, they usually pay a better rate of interest than the rate they guarantee. (That's not because insurers are such nice guys. It's because the guaranteed rate is so low that it's not difficult to pay more.)
- They almost all levy hefty "surrender" fees against those who cash out too early—that's usually within seven to ten years.
- Pivotal to their sale are so-called "illustrations," which show what the policy could be worth in the future, how much might be available to borrow, and how much could be left to your heirs. However, what too few buyers realize is these illustrations are based on assumptions—guesses about what may happen in the future based on what's

happening today. All too often these guesses are dead wrong. That could leave you with far less—or, if you're lucky, more—than you anticipated going in.

Confessions About Cash Value

Before we go further, let me just tell you that most financial writers—including me—hate cash-value insurance.

The reason: It's impossible to evaluate whether cash-value insurance is a good deal going in. And if you try to get out—because you realize that it wasn't such a good deal—you pay through the nose.

To be specific, let's say the thirty-six-year-old mentioned above chose the cash-value policy instead of term insurance. He pays $1,000 a year for five years. Then, suddenly, he realizes his policy value is growing slower than he anticipated. He wants out.

How much can he cash out of his cash-value policy? Nothing. Mortality, brokerage, and surrender fees leave him with absolutely no cash value in his cash-value policy at the end of this five-year period. He didn't lose absolutely everything, though.

He did actually buy—and own—life insurance for those five years. And that's worth something. However, if he bought the five-year level-premium term policy, he would have spent $1,340 over that same period for the same death benefit that cost him $5,000. So you can certainly argue that he wasted $3,660.

It's worth mentioning that about 17 percent of the people who buy cash-value life insurance cancel their policies within a year of issue.

Evaluating Cash Value

But why can't you evaluate the value of a cash-value policy going in? Because insurers won't let you.

To evaluate the policy, you have to know how much they're going to charge you each year in mortality fees. They generally won't say. "It changes based on our experience," they argue. "You have to wait and see."

To know whether such a policy was a good investment, you'd have to know the interest rate the company would pay on the invested portion of your account—and, of course, how much of your premium was going to be invested rather than spent on fees. But, again, the insurer won't tell you. That, too, is supposed to be based on their experience. "We'll let you know," they tell policyholders. "Trust us."

If you are tenacious and very, very smart, you can estimate these numbers by pouring through an insurance company's financial data going back numerous years. You have to ask for specific numbers in just the right way, says Joseph Belth, a former professor of insurance at Indiana University and the editor of an industry newsletter called *Insurance Forum*.

Belth wrote an entire book on just how to do it. He, incidentally, believes that cash-value policies can be a good deal. You shouldn't write off the entire product line just because insurers are secretive and refuse to give you any information, he says. In case you were wondering, Belth is very smart. And unusually tenacious.

If you are too and you want to try to figure out the cash-value question, get a copy of his book *Life Insurance: A Consumer's Handbook*. It retails for $12.95 and can be purchased through Indiana University Press at Tenth & Morton Streets, Bloomington, IN 47405 (phone: 812-855-8054). You may also be able to find a copy of the book in a public library.

Post-Purchase Decisions

Choosing a Beneficiary

After choosing a policy, you've got to choose a beneficiary. That's the person who gets the money if you die.

You name the beneficiary and, possibly, back-up beneficiaries directly on the policy. It's worth mentioning that life-insurance policies are not subject to probate if you name a beneficiary. But you cannot change the beneficiary in your will unless you specifically name your estate as the beneficiary rather than naming an individual.

If your primary beneficiary dies before you do—or if you want to change the beneficiary for some other reason—notify your insurer and change it on the policy.

Selling a Policy When Terminally Ill

Normally life insurance pays off only if you die. Your heirs get the money, not you.

But over the last several years an industry has sprung up to "cash out" policies for terminally ill individuals—people who have been diagnosed with an incurable disease and who have only a few years—or months—left to live.

It's worth mentioning that virtually any type of life-insurance policy can be sold. It doesn't matter whether it's term, cash-value, group, or individual. However, most companies will not buy policies that are less than two years old and subject to "contestability" periods, which allow coverage to be canceled if there was misrepresentation when buying the policy.

The options for the terminally ill boil down to two: a so-called viatical settlement, which is an outright purchase of your policy or a portion of your policy by a private investor or company; or an "accelerated benefit" from your insurer.

To qualify for either one, you have to be diagnosed with a terminal illness. Your diagnosis also has to state that you have a limited time—whether that's two years or two months—to live. Your anticipated life span will determine how much you can get for your policy. It will also determine whether you can get an accelerated benefit, or if your only choice is a viatical settlement.

Accelerated Benefits

Most big insurers offer accelerated benefits to their policyholders. The way they work is the insurer will usually pay policyholders cash for a portion—usually somewhere between 25 and 50 percent—of the death benefit. The remaining portion of the death benefit would go to the policyholder's heirs at death.

In most cases, this results in a somewhat higher total payout than you could get if you "viaticated" the policy. However, if the policyholder needs as much money as possible up front, this isn't the best option because the insurer insists on saving something for the heirs.

In most cases, accelerated benefits are not offered unless a doctor says you have six months or less to live. Some terminally ill individuals also have complained that their insurers were slow and bureaucratic when considering requests for accelerated benefits. When you're dying and broke, the last thing you need is a bureaucratic delay.

Viatical Settlements

Viatical settlements are done between policyholders and private companies that are not related to your insurer in any way.

Viatical-settlement companies pay terminally ill individuals between 50 cents and 95 cents on the dollar for valid life-insurance policies. The percentage payout depends on the company buying the policy and how long the policyholder has to live. The shorter the anticipated life span, the bigger the payout.

These companies are governed by state insurance laws. And, in some cases, those laws provide a framework for what policyholders should expect.

In California, for example, viatical settlement companies are required to be licensed with the state. The state attempts to investigate the backgrounds of company principals and make sure that the companies are providing reasonable payout rates.

The state also publishes guidelines for consumers telling them what they should expect to be paid for a policy, based on their prognosis. If you have been diagnosed with less than three months to live, for example, expect a payment equal to 90 percent of the death benefit. With six months, expect 80 percent; twelve months, 70 percent; twenty-four months, about 60 percent. These payout ratios have become industry standards nationwide.

Your Life-Insurance Policies

Your life-insurance policy does little good if no one knows where it is or who to call to make a claim. And, if you want to be really nice to your heirs, highlight the policy number and the phone number your heirs will have to call to make a claim. Or, if you prefer, write the numbers here.

Insurer: ______________________________
Policy number: ________________________
Death benefit: ________________________
Phone number: ________________________

Insurer: ______________________________
Policy number: ________________________
Death benefit: ________________________
Phone number: ________________________

Insurer: ______________________________
Policy number: ________________________
Death benefit: ________________________
Phone number: ________________________

Chapter 16

Disability Insurance

Your chance of being disabled when you are young is far greater than the chance of dying. But Americans are twice as likely to own a life-insurance policy than a disability policy. Go figure.

What the chapter tells you

- There are two types of disability insurance. And you may have some of both—or at least a reasonable substitute.
- There's no point in buying more disability policies than you need. Usually, an extra policy gives you nothing but premium payment obligations.
- Disability policies are not all alike. Some will cover you for a minor ailment, while others only kick in when you're almost completely incapacitated.

What the chapter shows you

- How to determine how much you need

Where do I start?

Do you need disability insurance? The answer depends on what would happen to you and your family if you were unable to work for a fairly long stretch. If you have lots of savings, a working spouse, and few obligations, you may not need additional insurance coverage. But if you don't, you ought to think about how you would protect your family if you lost your income.

The good news is that most companies offer workers the ability to buy disability insurance at work. The bad news is, you'll probably have to pay 100 percent of the cost of coverage. Still, buying disability insurance through work is usually a lot cheaper than buying it on your own.

But before you buy, you'll need to figure out how much you need and what it's going to cost you.

Determine What You've Got

A key element in determining what you need is knowing what you've got. There's a good chance that you've got more than you think you have.

For instance, most people who have been working for several years qualify for federal disability insurance, which is handled by the Social Security Administration. Social Security disability is a long-term disability program that pays off if you are so seriously ill or injured that you are incapable of virtually any gainful employment.

In addition, workers in a handful of states also contribute to and are covered by state disability funds. These are short-term disability programs that will pay benefits for up to a year. Generally speaking, the standard definition of "qualifying disability" is less strict in the state programs than the standard applied by the Social Security Administration.

To make sense of disability coverage, you have to divide it into its two kinds: short-term and long-term. Then determine how much of each kind you have; consider your options during a short- or long-term disability; think about your personal chances of suffering either; and, finally, consider whether you need to buy additional coverage.

Short-Term Disability

What is a short-term disability? The answer depends on what you do for a living. If you're a roofer, you can be considered disabled if you break a leg. You simply couldn't be expected to climb on top of a roof and do your ordinary job in a cast.

If, on the other hand, you're a journalist or a banker, you could lose motion in the lower half of your body and still be able to handle your job without a hitch. As long as you're able to wheel yourself into the office, pick up the phone, and type—or fill out a form—you're able to work.

Having a baby leaves you disabled for a short time. Stress and other psychological ailments, such as agoraphobia, can cause longer-term disabilities.

When you consider whether you need disability insurance—and how much you might need—you must assess your personal likelihood of disability. To do that, simply consider the physical and emotional demands of your work, as well as your family medical history. If your chance of disability is high, you'd be wise to spend more time and effort determining precisely how much insurance you need and what types of disabilities the insurance you have covers. Insurance plans are not all alike.

Remember that accrued but untaken paid time off can serve as a type of short-term disability plan too. If you have a "vacation bank" at work (see page 140) and have accumulated a significant amount of usable time, your need for short-term disability diminishes.

If you have savings that can be tapped to pay your expenses during a two- or three-month stretch, that can also reduce your need to buy a short-term disability policy.

Finally, if you live in one of five states where disability insurance is provided to most workers, your need to buy a private insurance policy drops even more.

State Disability

A handful of states—California, New York, New Jersey, Hawaii, and Rhode Island—offer short-term disability insurance programs. These programs vary by state in both what it takes to qualify for disability and how much you get when you are disabled. However, payment rates are usually based on a percentage of your working income. Normally, you'd need to work for a minimum amount of time—fifty-two weeks, for example—to qualify for benefits.

If you live in one of these five states, you can find out about your disability benefits by calling your state disability office, which is listed in the government section of the phone book.

They'll need to know how much you earn, whether you pay state disability premiums (if you work in industry, rather than for the government or a nonprofit agency, you probably do), and how long you've been working.

However, your company employee benefits representative can also probably give you a ballpark estimate of whether or not you'd qualify for state disability insurance and roughly how much you'd get if disabled.

Be sure to check on the duration of benefits. Where Social Security can pay indefinitely, state programs usually have limitations on both the dollar amount that can be paid and the amount of weeks that you can claim benefits.

Private Short-Term Disability

If you determine that whatever state disability, savings, and vacation time you have coming would be insufficient to cover your expenses if you were disabled, you need to look at private disability-insurance programs.

The best place to find one is through your company's group plan. That's simply because it is difficult and expensive to buy disability insurance on your own. Why? Several reasons, including the fact that insurers assume that the people who individually seek out coverage are more likely than average to need it.

The reason boils down to the fact that defining a disability can be dicey, particularly when the claimed disability stems from a psychological ailment, such as stress. Insurers fear that some unscrupulous people would claim they were disabled, when in fact they had simply lost a job. Disability insurers don't want to be considered unemployment offices, so they check out applicants fairly carefully before agreeing to sell a policy. And they often charge individual applicants two to four times more than someone who buys disability insurance through a group plan.

Could you pay more for a group policy than you'd pay for an individual policy? Yes. But chances are the group has better benefits. If you price-check and find that an insurer is willing to give you a better annual rate on an individual disability policy than the rate your employer is quoting, start checking the details. There's a good chance that one policy pays more than the other, kicks in quicker, or has a easier standard to define *disabled.*

Long-Term Disability

Long-term disability programs generally kick in only after you have been disabled for a set time. That so-called "waiting period" can be anywhere from three months to two years.

If you need disability insurance, it's important to make sure that there isn't a significant gap between the time that your short-term policy expires and your long-term policy kicks in.

Before you go out and buy long-term insurance, you should also recognize that you probably have some through the Social Security Administration.

Social Security Disability

If you work in the private sector—in other words, for a for-profit company, not a government, school, or nonprofit enterprise—you probably pay so-called FICA taxes.

A portion of those taxes funds your Social Security retirement benefits; a portion pays for Medicare insurance; and a portion pays for disability insurance.

As with Social Security retirement benefits, you have to "earn" disability benefits by working a set number of "quarters"—the four three-month periods that make up a year.

However, unlike Social Security's retirement program, where only those who have accumulated forty quarters—or ten years of work—can apply, the number of quarters required to qualify for disability benefits varies based on your age.

Generally, the younger you are, the fewer quarters of work you need. Indeed, a twenty-four-year-old can qualify for Social Security disability payments after having worked just a year and a half, while a forty-year old needs five years of work to qualify and a sixty-year-old needs ten years.

In addition, at least a portion of that work time has to have been built up in years immediately preceding the disability claim.

There is one huge caveat. Social Security disability only covers you if you are *totally* disabled—unable to do any job that you're adequately trained for. And it only pays if you are disabled for more than six months.

You won't get any Social Security disability payments if your illness lasts for less than six months. You'll get monthly checks if it extends beyond the waiting period and the Social Security Administration determines that you are seriously disabled.

For example, if you happen to be a roofer with a broken leg, you are legitimately disabled—but Social Security disability is probably not going to help you. Surgeon with a broken arm? Same deal. But if you were in a car accident and left paralyzed, Social Security would begin to pay seven months after you were hurt.

Once you can do some job—any job—and earn "substantial wages"—that's $500 a month according to Social Security—your government disability benefits are cut off.

On the bright side, if you are totally disabled, Social Security can pay virtually forever. Many other disability insurance programs have limits on the total amount they'll pay out.

How much does Social Security pay? It varies widely because it is based on your working wages and how long you paid into the system. However, the payouts are staggered to give people with modest incomes a higher percentage of their working wages than people with substantial incomes—the same as Social Security retirement benefits.

Does everybody get Social Security disability? No. If you work for the government (state, federal, or municipal), are a teacher, or work for a nonprofit institution, there's a good chance that you're not paying into the Social Security system. To qualify for disability benefits, you must be paying into the system for a set number of quarters.

You can get a reading on whether you qualify for government disability payments, and an estimate of your Social Security disability benefits (as well as retirement benefits) by filling out a form called the SSA-7004, with the Social Security Administration. If you want one, call the agency at 800-772-1213 or flip to Chapter 22, "Saving for Retirement" (page 239).

Private Long-Term Coverage

Because Social Security is unlikely to provide enough income to live on—and because few people have so much savings that they can afford to go without work for years at a time—it's likely that you need some additional long-term disability insurance.

When you buy such a policy you need to look at these things:

Waiting periods. How long do you have to wait until coverage starts?

Disability definitions. Whether you get paid or not is often determined by how a disability is defined. Are you disabled when you can no longer perform the functions of your job? Are you disabled when you can no longer perform the functions of any job that you are adequately trained for? Or are you disabled only if you have lost one or more of the "basic functions of daily living," which include feeding yourself, bathing, dressing, and walking?

Many insurers tighten the definitions of disability if you have been disabled for a very long time. In other words, some may say a disability is simply when you lose your ability to do your current job. But if it is apparent that you will never be able to do that job again, the insurer will expect you to get trained to do another job. The insurance will pay only until you do. Most insurers do not impose the remarkably strict formula applied by the Social Security Administration, however. They won't expect a surgeon to take work at McDonald's. But they would expect a construction worker with chronic back problems to train for a construction management position that could be performed even with this malady.

Coverage cut-off periods. Some policies limit the amount of time they will pay.

Exclusions. Also check your policy for illnesses that are not covered. Some may specifically exclude stress-related claims, for example.

How Much to Buy

Determining how much disability insurance to buy is similar to determining how much life insurance you ought to have. However, it's a bit simpler, because instead of getting a lump sum, disability insurance promises to pay monthly.

So all you have to do is determine roughly what your monthly expenses would be and buy insurance to meet the portion of the bills that couldn't be handled with your savings and other resources.

There are a few tricks to remember, however.

Disability insurance coverage is usually calculated as a percentage of your income—not a strict dollar amount. Some people may think that they want 100 percent of their current income if they're disabled, but *if you are paying the premiums* you don't need that large a benefit. Why? If you, rather than your employer, have paid the premiums, any benefits that are paid out are considered nontaxable insurance proceeds. Because a middle-income family pays about 28 percent of their income in federal income taxes and another 7.65 percent in employment taxes, that means they need about 35 percent less than their full salaries if they are disabled and have been paying disability premiums.

The other thing to realize is that the amount most private insurers pay accounts for other disability payments you may be receiving.

In other words, if you qualify for both Social Security disability and disability payments from a private insurer, the insurer will subtract the amount that Social Security pays from the monthly check that they pay you. If you don't qualify for Social Security disability, but you do qualify for private disability insurance, the insurer will pay you the full amount. Either way, however, you would get a check or checks equivalent to the same set percentage of your income.

For example, let's say you earn $2,000 a month and you buy a long-term disability policy that ensures you 60 percent of your income—or $1,200 a month—if disabled. You have a serious disability and are unable to work for two years.

Social Security reviews your claim and determines to pay you benefits, which, given your earnings record, will amount to $500 a month. Your insurer would then pay the other $700 to get you to the promised $1,200.

If Social Security turned you down—they decided, for example, that you could do another job, though not the job you were trained for—the private disability insurer would pay the full $1,200.

Your Disability Policies

Divide the disability insurance that you've got into two categories—short-term and long-term—and fill in the blanks.

Short-Term Policies

State disability insurance: Yes__________ No__________

If yes, number of weeks it pays benefits: ____________________

Approximate monthly benefit amount: $ ____________________

Other disability insurance:

Insurer/Policy: ____________________

Number of weeks it pays: ____________________

Approx. monthly benefit: $ ____________________

Long-Term Policies

Social Security disability Yes__________ No __________

Approximate monthly benefit: $ ____________________

Waiting period: six months

Other disability policies:

Insurer/Policy: ____________________

Approximate monthly benefit: $ ____________________

Waiting period: ____________________

Chapter 17

Health Insurance

As medical costs have soared, the need for health insurance has become ever more imperative. Here's what to look for when buying a policy.

What the chapter tells you

- Health insurance now comes in three distinct varieties.
- You have to do more work if you opt for the cheaper plans, if you want to make sure they'll provide adequate care for you and your family.
- If your insurance claim is turned down, you can appeal—no matter what type of insurance you buy.

What the chapter shows you

- The basic structure of the different types of health insurance
- How to choose between plans at work

Where do I start?

Over the past several years, the cost of medical care has soared through the roof. Now even the most perfunctory doctor's visit is likely to cost $50. A full checkup? Between $200 and $500. A day in the hospital can saddle you with a bill of $1,000 or more.

In short, without health insurance, a middle-income family could be financially destroyed by a single serious ailment.

Luckily, most Americans have access to health insurance through work. Better yet, employers commonly subsidize the premiums as part of company benefit packages. All you have to do is choose a plan from one of several that are offered and pay a portion of the monthly premium.

However, if you work part-time, are self-employed, or work for a small company, there's a decent chance that you won't have the option of buying health insurance through work. You've got to decide if you should buy it on your own—probably at an eye-watering cost—or do without. That decision is likely to hinge on how old you are, how healthy you are, your family circumstances, and what you can afford.

But no matter whether you are buying health insurance through work or on your own, you are likely to face an array of complicated and confusing choices. Choose wisely and you're likely to save hundreds—possibly even thousands—of dollars. If you choose poorly, you could end up paying too much and getting too little in return.

It's worth mentioning that most employees who buy health insurance through work face these choices once annually, during so-called "open enrollment" periods. People who buy insurance on their own often pay on a month-to-month basis—making it possible for them to choose a new plan at virtually any time.

If you are not happy with your current plan or think you may be paying too much for health care or health insurance, you'd be wise to read through the following pages to get a clearer picture of what your choices are and how they affect your pocketbook.

How do you choose—or find—a good and affordable health plan?

Recognizing the Alternatives

The first thing consumers need to realize is that there are now three distinctly different types of health plans. Each type of plan has strengths, weaknesses, risks, and rewards. The rundown:

Fee-for-service. The traditional fee-for-service plan is the most familiar and easy to understand.

You choose your doctors. You direct your own care. When you think you need to see someone, you make an appointment and go. It doesn't matter whether you want to see a general practitioner or a specialist. For the most part, your insurance company doesn't question your use of medical services. Once you've satisfied the deductible, the insurance will reimburse you for a portion of medical costs whenever you visit a doctor because you are sick.

What these plans don't usually cover is preventative care. Generally, you cannot be reimbursed for simple checkups. The plan only reimburses you for care when you are sick.

Fee-for-service plans also are often the most costly type of health insurance. It is not uncommon, for example, for a family's out-of-pocket costs to exceed $6,000 annually between premium payments, copayments, and deductibles. The cost for an individual policy is less, of course. However, it could still run $3,000 or more per year.

However, your premium—the only definite cost that you pay—often comprises only a small portion of the total. The other costs, frequently the biggest costs, are from deductibles and copayments.

For instance, lately many companies that offer health insurance to their workers have done away with simple fee-for-service options. Traditionally, this option involved paying a large premium, a deductible that amounts to a few hundred dollars a year and 20 percent copayments when you see a doctor. Instead, many of these companies have substituted "catastrophic care" plans.

These plans work like the old fee-for-service option, but they pay your medical costs only if they exceed high thresholds—often $1,000 or $2,000 per person. Because the deductibles are so high, your monthly premium is fairly low—say $200 or $300 a month. (You pay far less if the premium is subsidized by your company. The typical company pays 70 percent of the cost and has their workers pay about 30 percent.)

If you use the plan a lot in a year, you could pay thousands in costs. But if you stay healthy, your only cost is the premium—at roughly $2,400 to $3,600 per year.

Once you satisfy the deductible, you get reimbursed for a portion of your medical costs. Usually the customer pays 20 percent; the insurer pays 80 percent.

Health maintenance organizations. These so-called "managed care" plans are better known as HMOs. At one time, they were among the lowest-cost programs available. However, today, they're frequently almost as expensive as fee-for-service plans.

But the way you get care and pay for services is vastly different.

On the care side, HMOs require that you choose a primary-care physician. This doctor directs your care and decides when or whether you need a specialist.

Let's say, for example, that you have a mole on your arm. It's ugly. It could be cancerous. Instead of immediately making an appointment with a dermatologist (skin specialist), as you might in a fee-for-service system, you make an appointment with your primary care physician at the HMO. That doctor may remove the mole himself or may refer you to a second doctor—a dermatologist or a cancer specialist. Because of the time it takes to get in to see your primary-care physician and the time required to get a referral sent in and approved, it may be a month before you actually see the specialist.

If you get anxious and "self-refer" to a specialist, it's very likely that you'll be forced to pay for 100 percent of the cost of the visit yourself.

On the bright side, when it comes to out-of-pocket costs for approved visits within the HMO, these programs can't be beat. Usually you pay nothing for a once-annual checkup. You pay $5 or $10 for each doctor's visit when you're sick. You may pay $3 or $5 each time you fill a prescription. Hospital visits are usually fully covered. Diagnostic tests, immunizations, and "well care" for children are also usually covered completely—no copayments, no deductibles.

Premiums for this type of coverage vary based on the plan, where you live, and whether you're single or covering a family. One big company that offered workers the ability to choose among a half-dozen HMOs indicated that the unsubsidized premium payments ranged between $5,000 and $6,600 per year.

Recent studies have indicated that people who have routine medical needs are usually most satisfied with HMO care. However, those who have unusual or serious ailments often complain that the system is too slow and too bureaucratic, and that doctors frequently fail to fully explain a patient's options. Moreover, all the financial incentives for doctors and health-care providers involve keeping you within the parameters of the plan.

If you require a diagnostic test that is not available within the system, or the services of specialists who are not members of the plan, you may get next-best services. You can, of course, go outside the system for care. But when you do, expect to pay the full cost yourself.

Preferred provider organizations. Preferred provider organizations are a hybrid combination of traditional fee-for-service plans and HMOs. They come in a wide variety, which makes them somewhat difficult to explain.

However, in most of these plans, you have a primary-care doctor who is your "gatekeeper," providing you with routine general practice medicine and referring you to someone else when you need more—just like the HMO. When you use the services of your primary-care doctor, and handle the system as if it were an HMO—allowing your primary-care doctor to direct your care and staying within the "network" of plan doctors—your out-of-pocket costs are low.

But you also have the option of going outside the plan and getting reimbursed for a portion of the cost. Usually, the reimbursement rate is lower than it would be in a fee-for-service plan. For instance, where most fee-for-service plans reimburse you for 80 percent of the cost of a medical visit, a PPO will frequently reimburse just 60 percent of the cost of an out-of-plan visit. In some cases, the reimbursement rate is lower—40 to 50 percent. In others, it's higher—up to 70 percent.

As with the HMOs, the premiums vary widely based on what's provided, where you live, and whether you're buying coverage for yourself alone or for an entire family. However, because PPOs can provide the best of both managed care and fee-for-service, they're often expensive. The unsubsidized premium costs often exceed $7,000 and can be as high as $10,000.

Choosing Among Plans

There's no getting around the fact that choosing a health plan wisely is a lot of work.

The best way to do it is to look closely at each plan you're offered at work or are considering on your own. Pull out your health-insurance records from last year—if you have them. Otherwise, do your best to estimate the number of times you and your family will use health services in the coming year, using your best recollection of how you've used these services in the past as your guide.

Then, list the different plans on a sheet of paper for comparison. Vertically—going down the page—list the different ways you would use health services and fill in *your cost* for everything from premiums to doctor's visits. Add up the total to determine which plan costs your family the most and least each year. The worksheet on pages 178–179 should help.

Make sure to account for your personal desires on your worksheet. In other words, don't assume that you'll use only plan doctors when listing your out-of-pocket expenses in HMOs and PPOs if you currently go to out-of-plan doctors who you'd like to keep.

If you think you'll continue to visit a particular out-of-plan doctor, make sure you list what you'd pay under each of the options for those unapproved visits.

At the end of this exercise, you'll have a reasonable projected cost of each plan. If the cost differential is wide enough to encourage you to consider the managed-care plans—the HMO or PPO options—or if you are only choosing between managed-care plans, you need to go one step further.

The reason is simple. With managed care, the cost of your health care hinges on being able to use the system effectively. As a result, you need to know a lot about the system and whether it will adequately address your possible health-care needs.

Managed Care Questionnaire

Before you lock yourself into a managed-care plan, you should ask the plan representatives a series of questions. The specific questions you ask will depend on your—and your family's—medical history. However, they generally fall into three categories: access, convenience, and quality. If the plan representative cannot answer treatment-related questions adequately, ask if you can interview—on the phone or in person—plan doctors who can.

Here are a few of the questions to consider.

Access

- Are there waiting periods of exclusions from coverage for preexisting conditions that you or some member of your family may have?
- Are all the doctors listed in the booklet of medical providers currently accepting new patients? If not, are the doctors you prefer accepting new patients?
- How long does it take to schedule an initial appointment? How long does it take to schedule subsequent appointments? Can you get in within a day or two if you need to see a doctor because you are sick?
- Would your primary-care doctor—or pediatrician—be willing to answer phone calls when not on duty? If not, how do you handle medical questions in a minor emergency—for example, your child has a high fever in the middle of the night but doesn't appear sick enough for the emergency room?
- How does the plan handle real emergencies? If you are a long way from a plan hospital and believe you're suffering a heart attack, will the plan pay for care if you go to the nearest hospital rather than the plan hospital? Does it depend on whether you are admitted? Once the immediate emergency is handled, will the plan require you to transfer to a plan hospital to complete your care?
- How are physician referrals handled? If you have a condition that clearly requires a specialist, do you always need to go to the primary-care doctor first? Or can you self-refer to a plan obstetrician when you're pregnant, for example?
- What happens if your primary-care doctor refuses to pass you on to a specialist when you believe you need one? Can you appeal the decision?
- How long does it take to be referred to a specialist? If you are anxious to see the specialist, is there a way to speed the process?
- Can you switch primary-care doctors midyear, if you decide you're not wild about the doctor you originally picked?

Convenience

- Where are the plan doctors and hospitals located? Are they within a reasonable distance of your home, office, and/or your children's school?
- How long do you normally have to wait in the doctor's office before the doctor will see you? Can you make an appointment and reasonably expect to see the doctor within a few minutes of the scheduled time?
- If the doctor is running very late—thirty minutes or more—will the office call you to let you know in advance? Will they let you know that the doctor is running late when you check in for your appointment?
- Do you need to fill out claim forms or any other paperwork on a regular basis?

Quality

- Does the plan have specialists skilled in treating problems that run in your family, such as diabetes, high blood pressure, cancer, or heart disease?
- If a congenital ailment runs in your family, how does the plan normally handle treatment for that problem? How does the treatment program compare to the treatment you've received elsewhere?
- Does the plan track member satisfaction?
- Does the plan attempt to screen out problem doctors? Does it track litigation and arbitration proceedings filed against plan doctors or facilities? Does it have a way of measuring the skills and success rates of plan physicians?
- Are you able to choose a doctor and see that same doctor every time you get care? Or does the plan operate on a clinic-like basis, where you see whatever doctor is available?
- What type of testing facilities are available within the plan? What happens if the best test to diagnose your ailment is not available within the plan? Are you referred outside the plan, or are you given a next-best test?

Serious Ailments and Managed Care

Although managed care programs are generally praised by patients for the way they handle routine care, there is ample anecdotal evidence to indicate that many managed-care plans fall short when dealing with serious, life-threatening diseases.

An exhaustive study by the *Los Angeles Times* revealed that people who suffered with cancer, diabetes, and several other serious ailments frequently faced denials, delays, and bureaucratic hurdles to receive care within the system. At times, these delays, denials, and hurdles were fatal.

If you have a life-threatening disease—particularly one that requires immediate and rapid attention—you may have to be very aggressive about demanding care and demanding care in a hurry.

If you face insurmountable roadblocks in obtaining that care, seek care outside of the system.

Yes, it's very likely that you will be on the hook financially if you get care outside the HMO or PPO. However, it's better to be alive and broke than be a corpse with a big estate.

In other words, worry about getting well first. You can fight about the bills later.

Appealing a Denied Claim

There are numerous reasons why a claim for insurance reimbursement could be denied. Your health insurer could decide the fees for the service were excessive—beyond the bounds of what's reasonable and customary. It could determine that your treatment was experimental, and therefore not covered by health insurance. If you are part of a managed-care plan, it could simply deny a claim based on where you obtained treatment. If you went to a non-plan emergency room for an apparent heart attack, but in fact were suffering chest pains for other reasons, the plan might deny reimbursement for a nonessential visit.

No matter the reason for the denial, no matter what type of insurance plan you have, all plans offer a procedure to appeal a denied claim.

If you are part of a managed-care plan, the procedure is likely to be spelled out in plan literature that you are given when you sign up. If you are part of a fee-for-service plan, the appeals process is usually spelled out on the back of the form that announces the claim denial.

Generally, the process is simple. It usually involves submitting a form on which you explain why you believe the denial was in error. You send that to the appeals address listed in your booklet or on the form and you wait for a response.

However, to successfully appeal, you need to be thorough, and you may have to do a great deal of research to provide your explanation.

For example, if your fee-for-service plan turns down a claim on the basis that the physician's charges were above what's "reasonable and customary" in your area, you need to do two things. First you need to call the physician and find out if there was some reason why your medical care would cost more than the norm. Were there complications? Is there something unusual about your case that the insurer would not know, but that would account for the charges being higher than average?

If so, you need to indicate that reason in your letter.

Your second step is to call several other physicians in your area and ask what they would charge for the same procedure, given whatever complications or special circumstances you experienced. Record the results.

If these charges are equal to or higher than what your doctor charged, you should include this in your letter to the insurance company. If they are lower than what your doctor charged, you may need to go back to your doctor and get a more thorough explanation of why your charges were higher.

If your doctor is simply the highest-priced specialist in your community—and this doctor's specialized skills were not required for any specific reason—the insurance company's denial may well stand. In this case, you should go back to the doctor to see if he or she will reduce the charges to a more ordinary level. You, however, are on the hook for the unpaid portion of the bill.

However, your appeal is likely to succeed if the evidence points to the fact that the fees where reasonable given the particular circumstances surrounding your care.

Making Cost Comparisons

On the following pages, you'll find a worksheet that's aimed at helping you determine the cost of the different health plans that you may be considering.

Using the plan documents, which describe your out-of-pocket expenses for different treatments, your deductibles, and your copayments, write in the estimated cost you would pay for an average year's worth of health care under each of the plans. Add up the totals to approximate the difference in your out-of-pocket medical expenses with each of the plans you're offered.

Remember to write in only *your cost*. What the plan and your employer pays for the procedure isn't important here.

*Cost Comparison**

Procedure	*Plan*__________	*Plan*__________	*Plan*__________
Check-ups	$__________ (your cost)	$__________ (your cost)	$__________ (your cost)
	$__________	$__________	$__________
	$__________	$__________	$__________
	$__________	$__________	$__________
Immunizations	$__________	$__________	$__________
	$__________	$__________	$__________
	$__________	$__________	$__________
Sick visits	$__________	$__________	$__________
	$__________	$__________	$__________
	$__________	$__________	$__________
	$__________	$__________	$__________

**Remember to account for deductibles when figuring your out-of-pocket cost. When jotting down the cost of a doctor's visit, for example, put in the full cost—not the copayment amount—until your out-of-pocket cost satisfies the deductible. The cost of additional doctors' visits—after the deductible is satisfied—should be listed at the copayment cost only.*

Prescriptions	$________	$________	$________
	$________	$________	$________
	$________	$________	$________
	$________	$________	$________
Inpatient hospital services	$________	$________	$________
Outpatient hospital	$________	$________	$________
Emergency care	$________	$________	$________
Diagnostic tests	$________	$________	$________
Lab fees	$________	$________	$________
Other	$________	$________	$________
Annual premium	$________	$________	$________
Total	$________	$________	$________

Part Five

SAVING AND INVESTING

In order to reach any long-term financial goal, you've got to save a little and invest a little. It does take discipline, but it doesn't require a truckload of skill. Here's what you need to know to do it quickly and relatively painlessly.

Chapter 18: Investing Basics

Are you confused by investing? No need to be. All you've got to do is apply a few of the lessons you learned when reading classic fables and fairy tales: Learn about the importance of getting started from an ant; about diversification from a milkmaid. Gather around, friends—the fabled lessons of finance start on page 182.

Chapter 19: Diversification

It's easy to divide milk into several different pails; it's a little harder to divide assets into different investment classes. But if you apply simple tags to the investment classes—"safety," "growth," "income," and "inflation protection"—it gets a bit simpler to pick a pail. Page 189.

Chapter 20: Mutual Funds

If you want to invest, but you don't want to spend a lifetime poring over such sedatives as price-earnings ratios and dividend yields, you need to know about mutual funds. They are arguably the easiest and most efficient way to invest. Page 211.

Chapter 21: Saving for College

Got kids with ambition? Then you probably hope someday to send them to college. Here's how to determine what it will cost and how you can swing it. Page 222.

Chapter 22: Saving for Retirement

Everybody's heard the horror stories: Social Security is collapsing. Private pensions are drying up. Without adequate savings, future retirees are destined for the poorhouse. Here's how to gild your golden years and how to know when you've saved enough. Page 239.

Chapter 18

Investing Basics

The very word investing *strikes fear—or confusion—into many an American's heart. It doesn't have to. You can learn everything you need to know about saving and investing through classic fables and fairy tales.*

What the chapter tells you

- Why you need to plan ahead
- The lesson of diversification
- Falling for a financial fraud is the best way to derail your financial plan. But it's tough not to get taken—particularly because today's cons often involve someone you know or have reason to trust.
- There's no free lunch. So if you need help getting your finances together, don't hesitate to pay up front. Sometimes that's cheaper than looking for "free" advice.

What the chapter shows you

- How to invest wisely

Where do I start?

Nothing can strike up feelings of fear and loathing quite as quickly and effectively as *investing*. The very word confuses some people, bores others, and intimidates most of us. In reality, investing wisely is easy. It can even be fun. All you have to do is remember the lessons you learned at your mother's knee when she read classic fables and fairy tales.

And, then, of course, you have to learn a little about the things you might want to invest in. But fairy tales first.

The Ant and the Grasshopper: Plan Ahead . . . the Earlier the Better

Doubtless, you know the story: An ant and a grasshopper run into each other on a summer's day. The ant is working hard, storing up food for the winter. The grasshopper is enjoying the sunshine. There's plenty of time to plan later when the day isn't so sweet, he says.

When the weather turns, the grasshopper searches mightily—and in vain—for food. The ant, of course, is cozy, warm, and well-fed—he was the sower, the investor who was able to continue living comfortably even in lean times.

Starting to save early is probably the most important lesson of finance. That's because it does two important things: First, it gets you into a healthy habit of deferring gratification, which is necessary to have enough money to save. That habit will allow you to live on less in hard times, which can keep you financially healthy in the long run. Second, unlike food stored for winter, money saved wisely tends to grow. The longer the season, the better the harvest. In finance, that's called the power of compound returns.

Consider Andy and George, two twenty-five-year-olds who are out of school and working at full-time jobs. Andy starts saving for retirement immediately through a 401(k) plan at work. George says he'll save later. Maybe when he makes more money. Or after he pays off his new big-screen TV. Or maybe when he's older and not trying to impress girls with fancy dinners and flashy clothes.

Andy sets aside $200 a month. He earns 8 percent annually on his money. When he turns sixty-five, he has $698,202 socked away. That's enough to pay him about $5,000 per month, every month for the next thirty years—until he's age ninety-five. That may sound impressive, but what is really rewarding is that Andy saved just $96,000 of his own money over that period. The rest—a tidy $602,202—was the reward of compound investment earnings!

George, on the other hand, wakes up to the need for retirement saving when he's forty-five. He figures that he can simply save double what Andy saves—$400 a month—and land a similar-sized retirement account. After all, at the end of twenty years, he would have contributed the same amount—$96,000. But he's sadly mistaken. If he saves $400 a month and earns 8 percent annually on his money, like Andy, he'll have just $235,608 at retirement. (That's enough to pay just $1,729 per month over thirty years.)

To accumulate the same nest egg as Andy, George would have to save $1,185 per month for twenty years—a total of $284,487. That's simply because he gave compound interest less time to work for him. As a result, he has to do more of the work himself.

What if it's too late to start early? What if you are reading this at age thirty-five or forty? Start now. Every month that you don't save is a month that you lose the value of compound investment returns. So get going.

The Milkmaid and Her Pail: The Lesson of Diversification

Patty, the milkmaid, was balancing a pail of milk on her head while walking to market. Daydreaming as she walked, she thought she'd sell the milk and use the proceeds to buy a chicken, which would lay eggs, which she would sell to buy a new dress and bonnet. The new dress would make her pretty friend, Polly, jealous.

"But I don't care," said Patty. "I shall just look at Polly and toss my head like *this*." The pail went flying, and so did her dreams of getting a new dress.

Does Patty's story teach us to avoid gesticulating wildly—particularly when walking alone—because it risks what you're carrying and makes you look like an idiot? Perhaps.

But it also should serve as a lesson about keeping all your milk in one pail. Or eggs in one basket. Or money in one kind of investment. Wise investors divvy their money up, investing some in stocks, some in bonds, some in real estate and/or bank deposits. That protects you from losing everything in a single upset.

Of course, when you're dealing with money instead of milk, deciding how much to put in each pail is a little trickier. But in the next chapter ("Diversification," page 189), you'll learn to do it with relative ease.

The Tortoise and the Hare: Get Rich Slowly

Some people approach investing like they approach a diet—or going to the gym. They wake up one day and suddenly feel disgusted about their figure or their balance sheet. They decide to solve the problem. Today.

So they go nuts. They sweat. They deprive themselves. They work harder and faster at obtaining this goal than they ever have before. But pretty soon they get tired. They need a break from all that work and deprivation. They nap. They backslide. And, often, they never get back on track.

A far wiser course is to start slowly and simply continue on at a steady pace. Pretty soon, you'll have the finish line in sight and you won't even have worked up a sweat. This is particularly easy to do if you have access to a 401(k) plan at work. With these plans, you elect to have your employer deduct a set amount from each paycheck. That money goes into a retirement account for your eventual use. 401(k)s offer some additional benefits, too, which you can learn about in Chapter 22, "Saving for Retirement" (page 239).

If you don't have access to a 401(k), or you simply want to save for a shorter-term goal, you can set up an automatic savings plan with a bank or a mutual fund. These plans work almost as simply as the 401(k); however, the money comes out of your checking account rather than your paycheck (but if you have direct deposit of your paycheck then this is virtually the same as taking it out of your pay). You simply authorize the fund company to take out a set amount every month. It puts your investment program on automatic pilot.

But where can you start slow and steady? See Chapter 20, "Mutual Funds," page 211.

Little Red Riding Hood: Watch for Wolves

A wise investor was once asked how to make a fortune. He replied, "Save a lot of money and don't lose any."

Simplistic? Sure. But also true. The best way to derail a good financial plan is to risk money you're not prepared to lose—or to get taken in a financial con, where you lose every dollar you invested.

Financial cons—which frequently involve some seemingly complex investment "opportunity"—are more prevalent today than ever. And what's even more insidious about today's scams is they often involve somebody you know—a member of your fraternity or sorority; a member of your church; someone who is involved in a business, professional, or social group with you. These are called "affinity frauds." They work roughly like this true story:

The minister of a small evangelical church was offered an investment that allowed him to earn 22 percent on his money—"guaranteed." The minister jumped at the chance to buy this "complicated insurance product" because the person peddling the investment was a popular parishioner. The minister later acknowledged that he really didn't understand how the investment worked, but the parishioner was so charming and appeared so honest, the minister simply believed what he had been told.

News of the investment program spread like wildfire. Parishioners begged to be "let in." Pretty soon, half the church's members were investing and getting returns that were roughly 10 percentage points higher than they could have earned on any other type of traditional investment at the time. Then, one day, the "interest payments" stopped. The broker was arrested. Members of this church found out that the investment program was a scam—a ponzi scheme where the money from new investors was paying interest to the old investors—and, of course, paying for the broker's opulent life-style.

In fact, today's con artists are a lot like the wolf in "Little Red Riding Hood." They're friendly, well-dressed, and smooth. It's hard not to be taken in, especially when they say: "I know your grandmother. She just loves flowers . . . ." With an affinity fraud, the con man will use just enough truth and familiarity to get your guard down, causing you to ask fewer questions and to evaluate the deal with less skepticism. The con artist tells the victims that all their friends are investing and, as one securities regulator laments, "everybody else falls like dominoes."

Before you start out, map out your route to grandmother's house—or to your financial goal. Stick with the route that you've carefully chosen. Don't let someone lead you down another path, no matter how enamored you become with his big, toothy grin.

The Pied Piper: Pay for Help When You Need It

If, after reading through this and the next two chapters, you don't feel comfortable making your own investment decisions, look for a financial planner to help you.

However, choose your planner carefully. Get recommendations; look for important professional designations; and, when applicable, check the planner out with state and federal securities regulators to make sure he or she doesn't have a criminal record or a history freckled with investor lawsuits.

Before you start looking, however, it's important to know how financial planners make their money. There are three different ways to pay a planner: Commissions, fees, or a combination of both. Commission-based planners are usually paid out of what you invest. For example, if you invest $10,000 in a mutual fund with a 5 percent "load" (commission paid to a planner), only $9,500 goes to work for you. Meanwhile, insurance commissions are often invisible, but they also significantly impact your investment returns. Many people are drawn to commission-only planners because it seems as if their advice is free. They don't charge a percentage of your profits or an up-front fee to draw up a plan for you. They only get paid through commissions on products that they convince you to buy.

The problem with this method of payment is that it can encourage the planner to recommend products that may be less attractive for you but that pay big commissions to the planner. Cash-value life insurance, for example, is frequently peddled to young couples as an investment that protects their families by paying a death benefit if the insured person dies. However, it is often a rotten buy. (See Chapter 15, page 150.) Why, then, do so many planners sell it? The commission paid to the planner or insurance broker who sells the policy can amount to 100 percent of the first year's premium—an amount that often exceeds $1,000, even on a modest-sized policy.

It's worth noting that these commissions are often invisible to the consumer. Nowhere on your life-insurance policy, for example, do you see a line stating: "Commission paid to agent, $1,000," but it costs you, nonetheless. You'll notice on your cash-value policy that if you want to cancel the policy—cash out, so to speak—in the first year, you get nothing back. Cash out in year two? Likely the same deal. In fact, with most policies, only after five years of paying premiums do consumers actually start to build up a modest amount of cash in their cash-value policy.

Limited partnerships are also an iffy investment—and largely unsuitable for unsophisticated investors. Yet some planners peddle them with vigor. The commission rate frequently amounts to between 15 and 25 percent of the amount you invest.

Meanwhile, so called "load" mutual funds—the type that charge an up-front fee—can be good long-term investments. But industry studies indicate that, over time, they perform no better than funds that don't charge an up-front fee. If you go to a commission-only planner, you will be presented with funds that charge a fee—which can amount to as much as 8.5 percent of the amount you invest—because the fee is paid to the planner. And the planner has to eat.

If, on the other hand, you go to a fee-only planner, you will pay to have a plan drawn up for you. For a comprehensive plan, it's not unusual to be charged between $1,000 and $2,000 for the service. However, a fee-only planner has no financial incentive to steer you toward a product that pays the planner, rather than you.

A planner that gets paid through both fees and commissions usually charges less up front, but will recommend some products that will pay the planner a commission. Commissions are usually computed as a percentage of what you spend.

The point is, it makes little sense to scrimp on visible costs, because, if you seek financial advice, you will be paying for it one way or another. If you hire a planner, make sure you know, and are comfortable with, how the planner is paid. Don't kid yourself into thinking you can get valuable advice for free.

How do you find out how a planner is paid? Ask. Registered financial advisers are required to fill out an extensive form called an ADV-Advisors form. This form is provided to securities regulators, and regulators expect planners to make the second part of it—which discusses how the planner is paid, the type of business he or she specializes in, and other facts about the financial-planning firm—available to their clients. Ask for this form. Read it. Make sure you understand the pertinent sections before you entrust your financial life to the planner.

How do you find a financial planner in the first place? You can get referrals from friends and relatives, as well as professional organizations. The Institute of Certified Financial Planners—800-282-7526—will provide names, phone numbers, and biographical sketches of three certified financial planners in your area. Again, all you have to do is ask. Certified Financial Planners must adhere to strict educational and ethical guidelines laid down by the ICFP.

If you specifically want a fee-only planner, you can get referrals by calling the National Association of Personal Financial Advisors—800-366-2732—which is the trade association that represents financial planners who shun commissions in favor of visible, upfront fees.

Specific Investments

Now that you know the basic concepts of investing, you need to learn a bit about your investment options. Turn to the next chapter, "Diversification," to learn about what different investments are and what they do.

Chapter 19

Diversification

The hard part of investing is determining just where to invest. The spectrum of complicated choices can boggle the mind. But if you break the choices into categories, it suddenly becomes a lot simpler.

What the chapter tells you

- Where to find growth; where to find income; where to find safety or protection from the ravages of inflation
- How to evaluate the risk of an investment
- How to build a diversified portfolio

What the chapter shows you

- How various investments have fared over time
- What happens to your savings based on how you invest

Where do I start?

The hardest part about investing is deciding where to invest—the vast number of complex choices can boggle the mind.

There are nearly 7,000 publicly traded stocks to choose from. There are almost as many equity mutual funds. There are bonds issued by the U.S. Treasury and federal agencies; bonds issued by state and local governments; and bonds issued by literally thousands of corporations, not to mention a seemingly endless array of bond funds. There are bank deposits; money market mutual funds; limited partnerships; Real Estate Investment Trusts; commodities; options; and a myriad of so-called "derivative" securities, including "strips," "spiders," "CMOs," and "reverse floaters." If you try to analyze it all, there's a good chance that you'll end up paralyzed by a combination of fear, confusion, and intense boredom.

But you can negotiate the investing morass once you understand that all investments fall into five broad categories. Each category has a purpose, and there's a time for every purpose in your investment portfolio:

1. Investments that provide access and *safety* for your principal
2. Investments that promise *growth* for your capital
3. Investments that provide current *income*
4. Investments that protect you from the long-term ravages of *inflation* or political upheaval
5. Securities that allow you to gamble or *speculate*

If you are an average investor, you'll probably want to divide your money among specific investments in the first three or four categories—that's to diversify your investments, so you don't end up like Patty the milkmaid in the previous chapter. How much money you put into each "pail" will depend on your personal situation, including your age, your goals, your income, and your personal preferences, especially your ability to tolerate risk. If you have lots of money—some of which you can afford to lose—you can play in the fifth category too.

The different classes of assets have varying potentials, risks, and rewards. For an overview of the historic returns and volatility of investments, see the graph, "Stocks, Bond, Bills, and Inflation." Here then is a pail-by-pail introduction to specific investments.

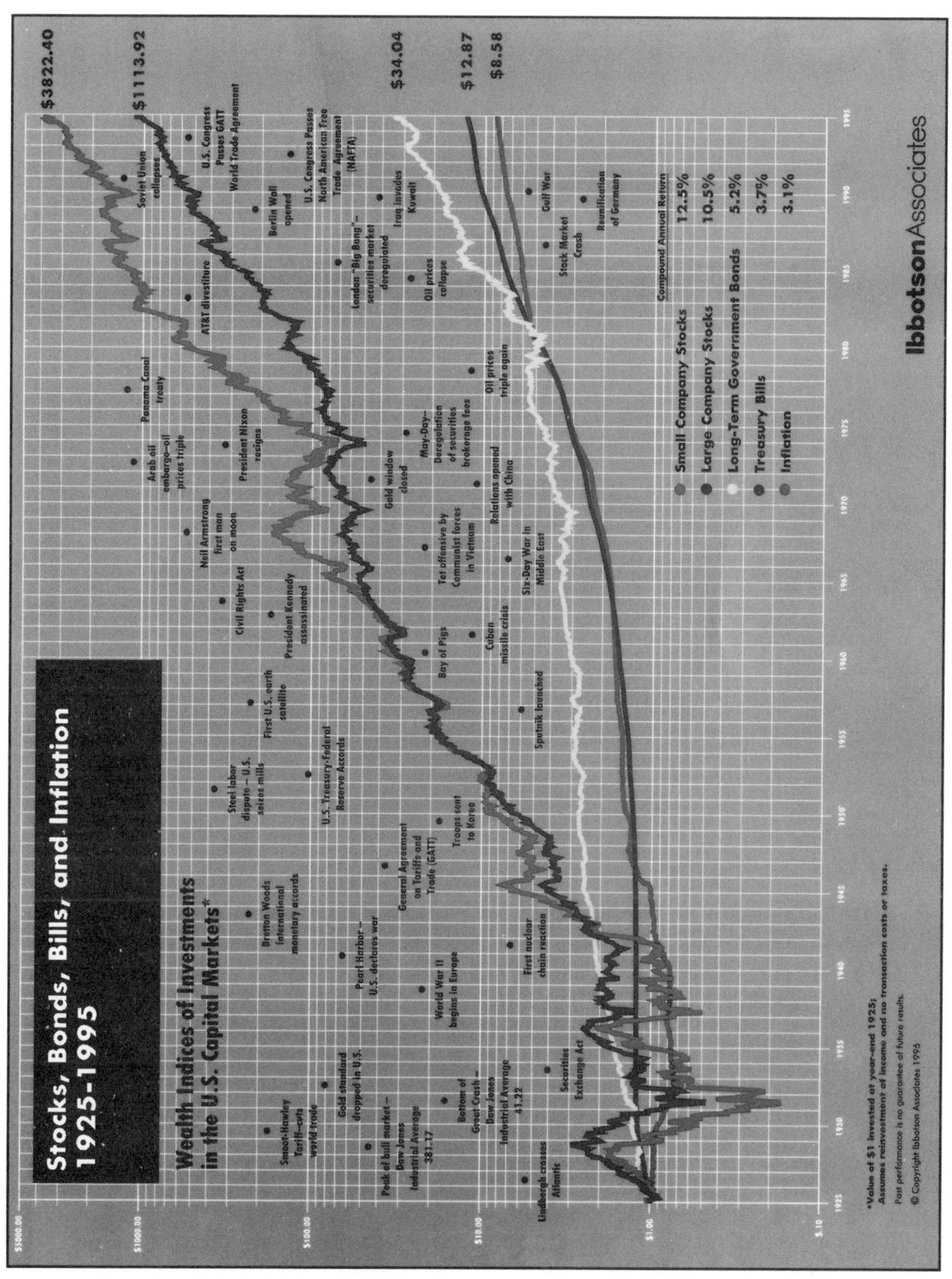

Copyright © 1996 by Ibbotson Associates. Reprinted by permission.

Safety Bucket

One of the first goals of many investors is to create an emergency fund—money that can be tapped if you ever lose your job, are disabled, or face a financial crisis, from uninsured medical expenses to major car repairs.

Because you never know when something like this might happen, the funds you save for emergencies must be easily accessible—what's known on Wall Street as being "liquid"—and your principal can't fluctuate too much in value, either.

That limits your investment choices to just a few, namely:

Bank deposits. Whether your money is in a checking account, passbook savings account, money market account, or a short-term certificate of deposit, deposits in your local bank or savings and loan have the dual advantage of being available at nearly a moment's notice and being federally insured up to $100,000.

The downside is you earn very little interest on these super-safe, super-liquid investments. Money held in a standard checking account usually earns no interest at all. Dollars in interest-bearing accounts frequently earn just 1 to 2 percent per year.

Short-term certificates of deposit pay a bit more, but you lose the immediate access to your money. If your emergency hits two months prior to the date when your CD matures, you're likely to face an early-withdrawal penalty. These penalties frequently amount to one month's interest earnings on a short-term CD. However, in some instances, they can be more. (For details see Chapter 6, "Bargain Banking.") If you use a CD for emergency funds, make sure you inquire about early-withdrawal penalties in advance and feel comfortable that the penalty won't prove devastating.

Short-term treasuries. Every week the U.S. government borrows money by issuing short-term IOUs that pay set rates of interest. These IOUs are called Treasury bills and they are held by literally millions of Americans.

Treasury bills technically don't pay interest. Instead, they're sold at a discount of their face value. In other words, a $10,000 fifty-two-week bill may sell for $9,500. At maturity, the buyer gets back the $10,000 face value—$500 more than paid—which generates an effective yield of 5.26 percent.

You can buy Treasuries that mature—or pay off—in thirteen weeks, twenty-six weeks, or fifty-two weeks. They are sold in minimum denominations of $10,000. If you have more than $10,000 to invest, you can buy additional bills in multiples of $1,000.

Treasury bills can be purchased through a broker or directly from the Treasury. If you buy them from a broker, you will pay a commission that simply reduces the rate of return you earn on the bill. If you buy them from the Treasury, you don't pay a commission. But you'll have to find a local Federal Reserve branch to get started. (Turn to page 210.)

"Treasuries," like bank deposits, are backed by the full faith and credit of the U.S. government. Treasury yields vary based on interest rates at the time they're sold.

Money market mutual funds. When you invest in money market mutual funds, you are essentially buying into a pool of short-term bank deposits, Treasury bills, and corporate IOUs. Your interest rate will vary daily, but unless your fund manager is doing something funky, the yield will roughly correspond to the current yield on bank deposits and Treasury bills.

These investment pools are sold by way of a prospectus, which spells out the rules, risks, rewards, and fees charged by that particular fund. Never buy a mutual fund without reading the prospectus. (You'll find out why in the next chapter, "Mutual Funds," which begins on page 211.)

Access to your cash is often as easy as writing a check. But, usually, there are limitations on how many checks you can write each year and the minimum amount you can withdraw with each check.

Growth Pail

The second reason people save is because there is something that they want in the future that they can't afford today—a new car, a new house, or a comfortable retirement, for example.

The faster their money grows, the sooner and more effectively they can reach the goal. The hot spot to look for rapid growth of your savings is the stock market, both domestic and foreign.

Domestic stocks. When you buy a share of stock, you are buying a piece of the issuing company. Admittedly, it's probably a small piece, but that share you purchased gives you the right to participate in the company's wealth (or fiscal decline) and vote on matters of some importance—directors, company auditors, and some shifts in corporate policy.

In some cases, you will also be entitled to dividends—payments of cash or stock to shareholders. Some companies also provide their shareholders with perquisites, such as tickets to the company's theme parks or discounts on its merchandise.

Because companies tend to grow and prosper over time—and because a share of stock allows you to participate in the prosperity—stock prices, in the aggregate, tend to appreciate over long periods of time. However, individually, some companies prosper. Others fail. If you buy a share in a loser, you could lose all, or a significant portion, of your initial investment.

In other words, when you invest in stocks, you risk losing your initial investment, but because you are taking a bigger risk, you get the opportunity to earn far better rewards.

How big a reward? A Chicago-based company called Ibbotson Associates has been tracking the performance of U.S. stocks from 1926 to the present. That period includes the Great Depression, the New Deal, World War II, the Korean conflict, the Vietnam War, the Kennedy assassination, Reaganomics, and the Gulf War, not to mention when the first man landed on the moon, the breakup of Ma Bell, the Watergate scandal, and the dismantling of the Iron Curtain.

In other words, it is a fairly diverse period that has had its share of ups and downs just like any period in history. However, between 1926 and 1995, the average annual return on small-company U.S. stocks was about 12.2 percent. The average annual return on big-company stocks was 10.5 percent. Over the same period, inflation rose 3.1 percent per year and the return on U.S. Treasury bills was 3.7 percent.

To put it another way: If you invested in large company stocks during that period, the value of your investment portfolio rose 7.1 percentage points faster than the rate of inflation. For every $100 you put in the market, you hiked your buying power by $7.10 each year. At the end of twenty years, that means your real—inflation-adjusted—buying power nearly quadrupled to $394 from $100, without any additional payments from you.

Although investing is as much an art as a science, it's reasonable to expect that future investment returns will mirror historic returns over long periods. In other words, it's reasonable to assume that stocks will continue to appreciate faster than the rate of inflation and other types of traditional investments.

The downside: It is also reasonable to assume that stocks could repeat their short-term historic performance over shorter periods too. And that's been far less illustrious than the long-term performance.

To be specific: The market crash of 1929 so depressed stock prices that investors who put $100 in the market then saw the value of their securities fall to less than $20 at the market's nadir in 1932. It took roughly eight years before securities prices rose back to ground zero, where $100 invested in 1929 was worth $100 again. And then the market took another sickening slide, from which it didn't recover until after World War II had ended. From start to finish, it was a full fifteen years of pain for stockmarket investors.

The market also took a sharp, decade-long dive in 1969. And it experienced short-term "crashes" in 1987, 1989, and 1990. But its performance in 1995 was enough to make an investor beam. Stock values as measured by the Standard & Poor's 500 index were up more than 37 percent.

Incidentally, although investors in small companies have done better than investors in large companies over the long haul (average annual return of 12.2 percent versus 10.5 percent, respectively), in bad times, small-company stocks do worse than big-company stocks. They fall farther and faster, and they stay depressed longer.

These heady climbs and sickening slumps are called "volatility." When an investment is as volatile as the stock market it is unwise to invest unless you have a fairly long time horizon that allows you to wait out the price swings and go for the long-term price appreciation.

How long is a "fairly long" time horizon? That depends on you and why you are investing. Let's say you want to buy a house in five years and you're trying to determine where to invest the down-payment money. The stock market would be a good place for all or part of that money, if you wouldn't be crushed if your home-buying plans had to be put off because of a market slump that depressed the value of your investment portfolio—and thus reduced the amount you had saved for the down payment.

Stocks are also ideal to have in your retirement portfolio. The younger and farther from retirement you are, the more stocks you can handle. And they're a good choice for college funds for young children.

Foreign stocks. Just as U.S. companies issue ownership interests in the form of stock, so do foreign companies.

The risks and rewards of foreign stock markets are similar to those in the U.S. stock market, but they are frequently magnified. There are a variety of reasons that can sometimes include political instability and the fact that many foreign markets are smaller and more thinly traded than the U.S. market. That tends to make them subject to wider price swings, both up and down. That's simply because of supply and demand. When supply is short, a boost in demand can rapidly drive prices higher. And a sharp drop in demand can send prices plunging.

In addition, U.S. investors who buy foreign equities face something called currency risk.

Here's why. When you buy stock in a foreign country, you buy the shares with that country's currency. When you sell them, you get paid in that country's currency too. Before you can spend the proceeds in the United States, you have to convert the foreign currency into U.S. dollars at the going exchange rate. And exchange rates vary day to day based on the relative strength of any given country's balance sheet and the interest rates that country is paying on government securities. (That's the equivalent of Treasury bills.)

If currency values in the foreign land have risen since you purchased your foreign stocks, you win when you exchange the currency. If they fall, however, you lose.

Jane Smith of Anytown, U.S.A., decides she wants to get into the foreign stock markets. She buys $1,000 in Mexican stocks and $1,000 in German stocks at a time when each U.S. dollar buys one Mexican peso and one German mark. The value of the shares she purchased rise 10 percent over the course of the year.

Jane decides to sell and invest the proceeds in the U.S. market. How much does she have to invest? The answer depends on what happened to currency prices during the year. In this case, let's say the value of the Mexican peso dropped, so it now takes 1.3 pesos to "buy" a dollar. Meanwhile, the value of the German mark rose, so it takes just 0.9 marks to buy a dollar. Here's how the money works out.

	Mexican investment	German investment
Purchase price	$1,000	$1,000
Appreciation	+$100	+$100
Proceeds from sale (in foreign currency)	$1,100	$1,100
Divided by the cost of a U.S. dollar	1.3	.90
Net proceeds, U.S. dollars	$846	$1,222

In some cases, the currency swings can be more significant to your total return than the actual appreciation or depreciation of the particular stocks you purchased. (See the box, above.)

On the bright side, there are years when a foreign country's stock market can nearly double in value. And, if currency swings are working in your favor at the same time, your returns can be stunning.

Equity mutual funds. Mutual funds are investment companies that pool the money of many investors and buy securities in bulk. The securities that your fund buys will be determined by the fund's investment objectives—they're spelled out in the prospectus—and by the fund manager, who makes the investment decisions.

When you buy a piece of an equity fund, you're actually buying an interest in all of the different stocks held by that fund. That gives you the benefit of broad diversification. Diversification reduces the risk that your investment portfolio will be savaged by a single bad stock.

There are lots of other benefits and tricks to buying mutual funds. However, the entire next chapter is devoted to explaining this topic, so there's no need to go into the details here. For now, let it suffice to say that buying equity mutual funds is an alternative to buying individual domestic stocks.

Global/international mutual funds. Just as buying shares in a domestic equity mutual fund is similar to buying domestic stocks, buying shares in global and international mutual funds is similar to buying shares in foreign stocks.

The big benefit to buying foreign stocks through a fund is that global mutual funds not only spread your money among numerous stocks, they also can spread the investments among numerous countries. That reduces currency risk too.

Income Basket

At some point in your life—perhaps after you retire, perhaps sooner—you'll want at least a portion of your investments to generate income. That income can be used to supplement your wages, Social Security, or pension, making your life more comfortable. There are numerous investments that can provide that income, including bank certificates of deposit, bonds, and dividend-paying stocks.

Didn't we talk about CDs in the "safety" category? And, aren't stocks listed under "growth"? Yes. But the CDs and stocks mentioned here are significantly different than those discussed above. That's because the CDs purchased for income are the longer-term variety that will pay higher rates of interest in exchange for your promise to leave your principal alone for a while. If you break your promise, you'll pay for it—sometimes dearly.

Meanwhile, although many growth stocks pay dividends, these dividends usually account for just a tiny fraction of the total return on a growth stock investment. On the other hand, some "mature" companies have reached a point where they are unlikely to grow quickly, if at all.

At that stage, instead of plowing profits back into the business to help it grow, these companies pay out a large portion of their profits to investors in the form of quarterly cash dividends. These companies are considered "income" stocks.

What are the risks and rewards of different income-oriented investments?

Certificates of deposit. Certificates of deposit are bank deposits, like any other. They're insured by the federal government to $100,000, which means you can't lose any principal—and usually can't lose any of the promised interest—unless you pull your money out of the bank before the end of the contracted period. (Or unless the principal and interest you have in one institution exceeds $100,000 when the bank fails.)

If you pull your money out early, you are likely to face an early withdrawal penalty that can amount to six months of interest payments or more. If your savings have not generated enough interest to pay the penalty, the bank has the right to take the penalty out of your principal.

How much would the early-withdrawal penalty be on your CD? It varies based on the maturity and the bank. On a six-month CD, it's common to be charged one month's interest. On a five-year CD, the penalty can amount to between six months and one year's worth of interest. If there's any chance that you'll need your funds before the end of the contracted period, ask your banker about the early withdrawal penalties and under what circumstances these penalties can be waived.

Treasury notes. Treasury notes are a lot like Treasury bills—they're issued and backed by the full faith and credit of the U.S. government. That government backing means that Uncle Sam promises to pay back the principal and interest on your note, as long as you hold the note to maturity.

The difference between Treasury notes and Treasury bills is when they mature. Where Treasury bills are short-term investments, with maturities of one year or less, Treasury notes can be purchased with two-year, three-year, five-year, or ten-year maturities. Remember, the maturity date is when the government pays back your principal, but generally you would receive interest payments at regular intervals during the years that you hold the note.

However, Treasury notes are often sold before maturity. If you sell the note before maturity, you could make money or lose money on the sale. Generally speaking, when interest rates fall, the market value of old high-interest notes will rise (because you have an investment that guarantees a higher rate of return than the market currently offers). Conversely, when market interest rates rise, the value of old, relatively low-interest notes will fall.

Treasury notes are sold in denominations of $1,000 or more. They can be purchased directly from the government through the Treasury's noncompetitive bidding process or they can be purchased through brokers. Under normal circumstances, Treasury notes pay higher interest rates than Treasury bills.

Treasury bonds. Treasury bonds are the same as Treasury notes, but they're issued with even longer maturities. You can buy Treasury bonds that mature thirty or forty years from the date they are issued. Again, as long as you hold the bonds to maturity, the U.S. government promises to pay back your principal, plus interest at a set rate. Similarly, if you sell before maturity, the amount of money you make or lose is based on the prevailing interest rates and market conditions at the time of the sale.

It's important to note that although the value of Treasury notes varies somewhat when interest rates climb or fall, the value of Treasury bonds varies much more. That's simply because your money is locked up at a set interest rate for a longer period of time. That makes Treasury bonds more "volatile" than the shorter-term Treasury notes and far more volatile than the very short-term Treasury bills.

But, since volatility is a type of risk, and you usually get rewarded for taking increased risks in the financial markets, Treasury bonds typically pay more—often 1 or 2 percentage points more—than ten-year Treasury notes.

Ginnie Maes. Ginnie Maes are the best known of a variety of so-called "mortgage-backed securities." What's a mortgage-backed security? Let's look at an example:

John and Jane Doe buy a house and finance it with a $100,000, 9 percent fixed-rate loan. Their bank then sells the Does' mortgage to a third party. It may be to another bank or financial institution, but usually it is to one of several quasi-governmental agencies such as the Government National Mortgage Association (Ginnie Mae); the Federal National Mortgage Association (Fannie Mae); or the Federal Home Loan Mortgage Corporation (Freddie Mac).

Despite their cutesy names, Ginnie, Freddie, and Fannie are major corporations with some U.S. government backing. They take the Does' mortgage and put it into a "pool" of similar mortgages that pay like amounts of interest and are expected to pay off at the same time. They then sell interests in this pool of mortgages to investors. What investors get when they buy a Ginnie Mae, for instance, is a bond that pays somewhat less than what the Does are paying on their loan. (If the Does pay 9 percent, for example, the investors may get 8 percent; the 1 percent difference is eaten up in fees and charges.) Because Ginnie, Fannie, and Freddie are government backed, these organizations will make up for any losses if the Does stop paying on their loan.

There's only one problem with the securities sold by Ginnie, Freddie, and Fannie: the Does.

John and Jane may never default on their loan but, when interest rates fall, they are going to refinance their mortgage to get a lower rate. So instead of getting comparatively high rates of interest for thirty years, investors in mortgage-backed securities are likely to get back only their principal. In marketspeak, that's called "prepayment risk."

If rates rise, the Does will hang on to their mortgage, and investors will be stuck with comparatively low-yielding securities for thirty years. That's called "interest-rate risk."

CMOs. Otherwise known as Collateralized Mortgage Obligations, CMOs started life as mortgage-backed securities. But then, some smart investment bankers thought about the problem with the Does. They know that can't change the Does' behavior, but they can find ways to "restructure" the average mortgage-backed security to shift around some of the prepayment risk and interest-rate risk.

How do they do that? They take the Does' mortgage (and thousands of other mortgages like it) and slice them into pieces. Each piece includes an element of the original mortgage. For instance, one slice may give investors the right to half of the interest payments made by the Does, plus the first repayment of principal. The next piece may give the investor the right to the second repayment of principal, plus another half of the interest. A final piece may be structured like a zero-coupon bond, where the investor doesn't get anything until the bond matures, at which time he's repaid an amount that works out to what he paid for the bond, plus some. (In reality, CMOs are usually cut into more slices, but you get the idea.)

Of course, investors who buy the first type of CMOs have the greatest prepayment risk while investors in the final category have the greatest interest-rate risk. Investment bankers assess the risks of each slice—or "tranch," as they like to say on Wall Street—and they price the securities with that in mind. Thus some CMOs, which usually sell in minimum denominations ranging between $1,000 and $25,000, sell for less than their face value, while others sell for more.

Corporate bonds. Some companies finance growth by selling debt—IOUs—to investors. These formal IOUs are called bonds and, in many ways, they're like the bonds issued by the U.S. Treasury. They have stated interest rates and maturity dates and they're sold through brokers.

However, because individual companies are presumably less financially secure than the U.S. government, which can exercise its taxing authority if it ever runs short of cash, corporations typically pay higher rates of interest than the U.S. Treasury pays on bonds with similar maturity dates.

The less financially secure the corporation, the higher the interest rate. You're taking a bigger risk that the company will default, failing to pay back your principal and interest, so you get a higher return. When the bonds are especially high-risk and high-yield, they're called "junk bonds."

Conversely, bonds issued by healthy companies—or backed by bond insurance—pay comparatively less interest, but pose far less default risk to investors. High-quality bonds are frequently termed "investment quality," "triple-A," "double-A" or simply "A-rated" bonds.

Properly chosen, this type of bond can increase the yield on the income portion of your investment portfolio, without dramatically increasing the risks.

Municipal bonds. These bonds, issued by state and local governments and some government agencies, pay relatively low interest rates, but the interest you earn is usually tax free. That can make these bonds attractive to investors who are in high tax brackets and who would otherwise have to pay a large portion of their interest earnings to Uncle Sam (and, perhaps, Aunt California or New York).

Like corporate bonds, municipal bonds are graded. Some are good quality; some poor. Some are backed by private insurance companies that promise to pay bondholders the principal and interest that they're due, if the issuer fails to pay.

Income stocks. What kind of company would accept growth prospects that are so lackluster that the company simply gives most of its income away to shareholders? Utilities.

Utility companies are regulated and often restricted to doing business in a set geographic area. They sell a commodity—such as water, electric power, or gas—that is not likely to see a big upsurge—or drop—in demand. (Your need and desire for water is dictated by thirst—and landscaping. Unless there's dramatic growth in a community—lots of thirsty people move there and plant lawns—the community's demand for water doesn't change much from year to year. And a community's growth is limited by the available amount of real estate.)

So when a utility completes its expansion—has the majority of its power plants built and its infrastructure solid—it becomes a cash cow for investors. Dividend yields at utility companies often can range between 5 and 8 percent.

What's a dividend yield? It's a ratio that indicates how much money the company pays out in annual dividends, compared to what you originally paid for the stock.

Let's say, for example, that you bought 100 shares of a company for $10 a share and that company pays dividends of 15 cents per share each quarter, or 60 cents each year. Your $1,000 investment pays $60 annually. That's a 6 percent dividend yield because $60 divided by $1,000 is 0.06 or 6 percent.

The benefit of income stocks is that you get current income and you get the chance to participate in the company's stock price appreciation, if the company happens to have a good year that's reflected in its stock price. The bad side is you also would participate in the company's stock price depreciation, if the company had an unusually bad year.

Worse still, there's no law requiring a company to continue paying regular cash dividends. If the company decides it can no longer afford to pay you that $60 annually, they can unilaterally announce that the dividends will stop. There's little, if anything, you can do about it, except lick your wounds.

Bucket o' Inflation/Disaster Protection

For some people, the goal of investing is not so much getting ahead as it is not falling behind. Because inflation marches forward each and every year, the fear is that you will fall behind if your investments don't rise as quickly as the cost of buying necessary goods and services.

There is also a group of investors who fear that the U.S. dollar could become worthless someday. At that point, the only way to buy things you need would be to trade "hard assets," such as precious metals and gems, or barter something you have, like food, for something they have, like shelter.

There are two types of investments that are widely considered inflation hedges: Precious metals and real estate.

Precious metals. If you talk to a "gold bug," he'll tell you that gold—the bellwether of precious metal investments—holds its value over time. An ounce of gold would buy you a suit of clothes in the days of Henry VIII; and it will still buy you a suit of clothes today.

What they won't tell you is that while inflation has risen 3.1 percent per year since 1925, the value of gold—which only became publicly available in the U.S. in the late 1970s—has fallen from about $800 per ounce to less than $400 today. In other words, where it would buy you a marvelous suit—and plenty of accessories—in 1980, it would buy you a merely adequate suit and, perhaps, an inexpensive pair of socks in 1995.

There are other disadvantages to buying gold, too.

Namely, if you buy gold bullion or coins, you have to store them somewhere—like a bank safe deposit box. And a safe deposit box is likely to run you $40 or $50 a year. In addition, gold doesn't pay dividends; it doesn't pay interest. It just sits there. In a box. In the bank. In the dark.

It's tough to justify buying bullion with a reasonable argument that doesn't include some kind of doomsday scenario.

However, there have been times when you could make a small fortune merely by speculating in the gold market, buying shares in gold mining companies. When inflation fears are high, for example, the value of gold tends to rise. When per-ounce prices rise a nudge, the value of gold-mining shares often soars. If you are quick on your feet—or, actually the phone, calling your broker—you can make a tidy sum. But, this is less protecting yourself from inflation than it is speculating—rolling the dice and hoping you'll hit sevens.

Residential real estate. Residential real estate—in other words, your home—can provide a real hedge against inflation *no matter what happens to the price of your house in the future*. How so? By buying a home that you can live in, you eliminate the need to pay rent. That protects you from possible rental rate increases that could come down the road. You also get some tax benefits when you buy residential real estate, so your actual out-of-pocket cost—or after-tax cost—may be less than the sum total of your down payment and total monthly payments. (See Chapter 11, "Home Sweet Home," page 100, for details.)

National statistics that indicate changes in the price of residential real estate are somewhat dubious because they track only sales prices without attempting to determine the size and quality of the residences sold in any given period. However, average real estate prices do appear to rise over long periods of time, seemingly somewhat faster than the rate of inflation.

Prices don't rise in lockstep with inflation. In fact, when inflation is high, real-estate prices are likely to fall (because when inflation is high interest rates go up, and when interest rates go up so do mortgage rates—which means people can't afford as much). But later, home prices catch up by taking dramatic leaps in value when inflation and interest rates drop.

If you're a subscriber to the doomsday theory—the idea that inflation will be so high that U.S. currency will become worthless and we'll all be driven to barter to survive—whose proponents usually advocate gold as an investment, you should be aware that you can't eat gold. But you can grow vegetables in your backyard.

Speculation: The Gambling Pail

There are a wide array of speculative investments that range from limited partnerships to commodities contracts to derivative securities. And there are trading strategies, such as short-selling and buying "puts" and "calls," that can occasionally supercharge—or decimate—the value of your investment portfolio.

Unless you are both wealthy and highly sophisticated about investing, you should avoid this type of speculation. Not only is there a good chance that you will lose all, or a significant part, of your money, in some cases you can actually lose *more* than you originally invested.

If you want to gamble, go to Las Vegas. You'll probably lose less money, and they'll serve you free drinks while you play.

Risk

Investing and risk go hand in hand. To invest, you have to accept that you are taking a measure of risk.

If you invest in stocks or bonds that offer no guarantee about the safety of your original investment, you are taking a risk that you could lose a portion of your principal. If you invest in bank deposits and Treasuries, where your principal is guaranteed, you are taking a risk that your savings will grow slower than inflation—which means you lose buying power over time.

There is no risk-free investment.

But you also know that you take risks all the time. When you drive your car to the market, you're taking a risk that you'll run into a tree on the way or that another car could hit you. When you go outside for your newspaper on a frosty morning, you're taking a risk that you might catch a cold.

You don't stop driving—or picking up your paper—because of these risks. You simply recognize the risks and take whatever precautions you deem necessary to cope with them realistically. In other words, you may put on a robe and slippers before you venture out for the paper. You probably wear your seat belt in the car, and try to avoid people who drive erratically.

Dealing with risks in investing is no different.

You simply have to look for the risks and make sure you are comfortable with the specific risks you are taking.

The Treasury Test

How do you know how great the risks are? Take a look at the return—or the expected return—on the investment. Under normal circumstances, you can expect that the higher the anticipated return, the higher the risk. It's that simple.

However, because actual returns vary based on market conditions, you can't simply pick a number and say "returns over 12 percent are very risky" or "returns of just 5 percent are risk free." Instead, with traditional—nonspeculative—investments, you can use the Treasury test.

Treasury bills are as close as you can come to a risk benchmark, because they're believed to be devoid of principal risk—the chance that you'll lose your initial investment if the borrower (U.S. government) defaults. As a result, you can measure other risks by how much the return would deviate from the return on Treasury bills, notes, and bonds.

To do the Treasury test, match your investment up against the Treasury that has the closest maturity date.

For instance, if you're looking at six-month certificates of deposit, see how the yield on the CD compares to the yield on six-month Treasuries. In this case, the yields are likely to be very close, because both investments offer similar security—U.S. government backing—and similar access to your money.

If you're considering a bond, match its maturity to a Treasury bond. In other words, you are thinking about buying a ten-year corporate bond. You look at the current yields on ten-year Treasuries. You would expect an investment-grade company to pay somewhat more—one to three percentage points more annually—than the federal government. However, if the company is paying more than that, there's a very good chance that the bond-issuing company is in tenuous financial condition. If that's the case, there's a real risk that the issuer will default and leave you with a loss.

What about municipal bonds that pay *less* than Treasuries with like maturities? Because the income earned on municipal bonds is free of both state and federal income taxes, the yield on a muni is calculated on a "taxable equivalent" basis.

For the purpose of assessing risk, divide the bond's yield by .6. The result is the taxable equivalent yield for someone who pays 40 percent of their income in tax. (Your actual taxable equivalent yield may be different. To find out your taxable equivalent yield, subtract your tax rate from 1 and divide the bond's yield by the result.) For example, at a time when thirty-year Treasuries are paying 7 percent, a good-quality municipal bond might be paying 5 percent. However, a 5 percent nontaxable yield is equivalent to an 8.33 percent taxable yield for someone in the 40 percent tax bracket. (5 divided by .6 equals 8.33.) That taxable equivalent yield would help signal that this bond is riskier—but not far riskier—than a Treasury. If the taxable equivalent yield was in the 10 percent range, that's a tip-off that you're taking a bigger risk with your money.

How do you do the Treasury test when the investment you're buying has no stated yield and no stated maturity date—such as a company stock or equity mutual fund? You do the test based on history, rather than current data—because, frankly, you don't have any current data.

However, there's lots of historic data for guidance.

Based on data compiled by Ibbotson Associates, long-term government bonds have posted an average annual return of 5.2 percent, while big-company stocks have posted a 10.5 percent average annual return. That indicates that stocks are about twice as risky as long-term government bonds. What makes them riskier? There is no guarantee that you get back your principal; market prices swing wildly in short periods; and investors have no guarantee of current income.

(Although you can buy or sell stocks at any time, you compare them to long-term investments because you should expect to hold on to them for long periods of time—five to ten years, or more.)

And small-company stocks have historically posted even higher average returns—12.2 percent—so you should expect that they're even riskier than big-company stocks.

What if someone presents you with a "safe" investment that returns 18 percent at a time when Treasury bond yields are 8 percent? Keep tight hold to your pocketbook and flee. The investment this person is promoting is either highly speculative, a fluke, or a scam. You simply cannot earn 10 percent more than Treasury yields without taking a very big risk.

Still, you say, the promoter is very convincing. How do you know that what he's saying isn't true? Give it the smell test.

Why is this fabulous investment being offered to you? Are you this person's best friend, son, daughter, grandmother, father? If not, it doesn't make sense that you'd be singled out to participate in such a fabulous "opportunity."

But the salesman insists this is "perfectly safe, fully guaranteed"? Ask why the salesman doesn't borrow money from a bank and buy the stuff himself. Stock answer: "The bank doesn't understand it" or "they don't like to loan money to entrepreneurs like me."

In reality, banks make a living by loaning money to entrepreneurs, and bankers are pretty smart about money. If the bank is turning it down, you'd be wise to pass up the opportunity too.

A high relative yield is like a flashing red light. It should tell you to look a little closer. Make sure you haven't missed something. If you are not certain whether or not you've missed something, and the investment is too complicated for you to understand, turn it down.

Now, you might be wondering, does a low yield always indicate you're taking little or no risk? No.

It's similar to driving. When there's no red light—or a green light—you can go. But do you race through intersections, without looking, and risk that some other driver breaks the rules and hits you? Probably not. Clearly you don't have to scrutinize the road as carefully, but you keep your eyes peeled and give at least a cursory glance at opposing traffic before you hit the gas.

You should exercise the same caution when investing. Look at what you're doing. Feel comfortable that you've looked closely enough to determine the risks and then proceed with reasonable caution.

Building a Diversified Portfolio

Now it's time to apply what you know about individual investments to your own portfolio. There are a million ways to do that—some of them complicated, some easy.

However, because no one has ever been able to show that the complex approach makes more money than the simple one, I say go with the easy way.

To wit: Separate out whatever amount of money you decide that you need in cash and inflation protection. These aren't really "investments"—they're financial safety nets that can keep you from falling into poverty, or simply from worrying too much about your money.

Then, divide the rest of your assets among stocks and bonds. If you want to get fancy, throw an international mutual fund or two into the mix.

A tip: You may have numerous goals—some short-term, like buying a car; others long-term, like saving for retirement. But you have just one investment portfolio. You diversify the whole portfolio—not necessarily the pieces. In other words, don't worry about diversifying the investments in the "college fund," investing part of it in stocks, part in bonds, and then do the same thing with the retirement portfolio.

Instead, look at your entire savings/investment portfolio and diversify it in a way that makes sense and cuts down on the number of accounts you need to own. There's nothing wrong with having the entire college fund in bonds, if you have your entire retirement account in stocks. Certainly, rebalance your portfolio occasionally. But the fewer investment accounts you open, the fewer you need to keep track of. At tax time, particularly, less is better.

You're considering an investment that's not listed in this chapter and you don't know how to evaluate the risk? Borrow or buy a copy of Andrew Tobias's *The Only Investment Guide You'll Ever Need.* It goes through numerous investments with greater depth—and it's remarkably fun to read. Tobias even includes a chapter of financial quips for cocktail parties and tips on what to do if you ever win (or inherit) a million dollars.

But otherwise you can consider stocks, bonds, and cash the chocolate, strawberry, and vanilla of the investing world. You can't go wrong sticking with these three, although the longer you stay in the market, the more likely you are to yearn for a little variety.

Your Portfolio

Just how much should you have in cash, inflation hedges, stocks, and bonds?

Cash. The purpose of safety-oriented investments is provide you with emergency money. You have to determine just how much emergency money you are likely to need.

To do that, ask yourself a few questions: What's the worst thing that could happen to you financially? Chances are the answer is that you could lose your job and have a hard time finding a new one, or you could become disabled and unable to work for an extended period of time. How much do you need to protect yourself against that type of serious disaster?

The answer depends on three things:

- Do you have disability insurance, an "income continuation" plan at work, or a "vacation bank" that's full of unused vacation days? Or, if you lost your job, would you qualify for unemployment insurance benefits? (If you don't know, call your local unemployment office and ask. People in a handful of industries are not covered, but most employees do qualify for unemployment insurance benefits that could replace a portion of your pay.)
- Do you have a working spouse who can pick up part of the slack?
- Do you have untapped credit that you could use to tide you over for a while? In other words, do you have a credit card or other unsecured credit line with a substantial borrowing limit that you aren't using already? Borrowing power can be as effective at handling an emergency as money in the bank.

If you have all these things, your need for emergency savings is minimal—perhaps the sum total of your need equates to the minimum balance you're keeping in your checking account.

But if you don't have any of these things, you need an emergency fund that probably amounts to between three months' and six months' worth of wages.

How much do you need? Enter it here: $____________

Inflation. Do you have a house? If you do, you've already got a healthy chunk of your assets tied up in this category. Chances are, this portion of your portfolio is going to grow until you've paid off the mortgage, too.

If you don't have a house, but you want one, see Chapter 11 (page 100) for buying and financing strategies.

Otherwise, simply ask yourself if inflation is one of your greatest fears. If it is, do you want an inflation-hedging investment—something that's likely to appreciate over long periods of time by about 3.1 percent annually? Or would you feel more comfortable with growth and income investments that are likely to appreciate faster than the rate of inflation?

If you prefer growth and income, skip to the next section. If inflation concerns you enough to want to address it head on, determine how much of your assets you want to devote to protecting yourself from it. Enter it here: $______________

Stocks and bonds. The rest of your investable assets ought to be divided among growth and income investments—in other words, stocks and bonds. How much you'd put in each category depends on your age, your assets, how you feel about risk, and your tax situation. (There are some tax benefits to "growth" investments, such as stocks, because you pay less tax on long-term capital gains than you pay on income from taxable bonds.)

However, the rule of thumb is you subtract your age from 100. The result is the percentage of your investment assets that you ought to put in stocks. The rest should be invested in bonds.

In other words, if you're twenty, you'd put 80 percent of your investment assets—not counting your emergency fund and your home—into stocks and 20 percent into bonds; If you're sixty, you'd put 40 percent in stocks and 60 percent in bonds; If you're eighty, you'd put 80 percent in bonds and 20 percent in stocks.

That formula isn't bad for a rule of thumb. It increases the income portion of your portfolio as you get older and are more likely to want to tap it. At the same time, it allows you to reap the very substantial rewards of long-term stock market investing.

When should you deviate from the rule of thumb? When it makes you nervous. If investing in the stock market makes you so nervous that you'll lose sleep, you should avoid it. Look at the range of cash and income-oriented investments above and see if those better suit your personality.

However, before you succumb to a mild fear, pull out your present-value calculator and play the what-if game for a minute.

Plug in the current value of your savings, the time you have until retirement (or any other goal where you expect to tap your savings), and the average return you'd expect to earn on the type of investment you're considering.

What are reasonable returns to use? Rounded versions of the historic figures. In other words, if you are investing over long periods of time, use 3 percent for inflation; 4 percent for the average annual return on cash investments; 5 percent for the average annual return on bonds; and 10 percent for the average annual return on stocks. For a blended portfolio, which includes stocks, bonds and cash, you can use returns ranging between 6 and 8 percent, depending on the mix.

If you have a shorter time horizon, refer to the chart on page 191 to see what you can expect in terms of return and volatility.

Now do the what-if game: What if I saved $200 per month in a tax-deferred retirement account, such as a 401(k), every month from now until retirement—and retirement is thirty years away?

- If all the money were invested in stocks, I'd have: $452,098.
- If I diversified, and earned 8 percent annually, I'd have: $298,072.
- If all the money were in bonds, I'd have: $166,452.
- If all the money were in cash, I'd have: $138,810.
- If all the money were in inflation hedges, I'd have: $116,547.

Think about what percentage of your assets you'd like in stocks and what percentage in bonds. Enter the result here:

Percentage in stock: ____________%
Percentage in bonds: ____________%

If you'd like to diversify your assets overseas—which can be advisable—shave a touch off both of the previous numbers—say take 5 to 15 percent of the stock money and 5 to 15 percent of the bond money—and devote it to international mutual funds.

The next chapter, "Mutual Funds," shows you how to invest without really trying.

Buying Treasury Securities Direct

Do you want to buy U.S. Treasuries direct from the Treasury, thus bypassing brokers and brokerage fees? Contact the Federal Reserve office nearest you and ask for information about their policies and procedures. Or write to the Consumer Information Center, P.O. Box 100, Pueblo, CO 81002, and ask for publication 566B—"Buying Treasury Securities." It's free.

Here are phone numbers of the various Federal Reserve Banks, for your reference.

Atlanta: 404-521-8673
Baltimore: 301-576-3300
Birmingham: 205-731-8708
Boston: 617-973-3810
Buffalo: 716-849-5030
Charlotte: 704-358-2100
Chicago: 312-322-5369
Cincinnati: 513-721-4787
Cleveland: 216-579-2490
Dallas: 214-651-6362
Denver: 303-572-2470
Detroit: 313-964-6157
Houston: 713-659-4433
Jacksonville: 904-632-1179
Kansas City: 816-881-2409
Little Rock: 501-372-545, ext. 272
Los Angeles: 213-624-7398
Louisville: 502-568-9236
Memphis: 901-523-7171
Miami: 305-591-2065
Minneapolis: 612-340-2075
Nashville: 615-251-7100
New Orleans: 504-586-1505, ext. 293
New York: 212-720-6619
Oklahoma City: 405-270-8652
Omaha: 402-221-5636
Philadelphia: 215-574-6680
Pittsburgh: 412-261-7863
Portland: 503-221-5932
Richmond: 804-697-8000
St. Louis: 314-444-8665
Salt Lake City: 801-322-7900
San Antonio: 512-224-2141, ext. 303
San Francisco: 415-974-2330
Seattle: 206-343-3605
Washington, DC: 202-287-4113

Chapter 20

Mutual Funds

The easiest way to handle nonretirement savings is to invest through a mutual fund. Here's what you need to know to choose one—or more—that suits your goals.

What the chapter tells you

- How mutual funds work—and how to make them work for you
- Most require minimum investments, but you can invest less if you set up an automatic savings program.

What the chapter shows you

- Where to find the key elements in a mutual fund prospectus
- Where to go to get more information about your choices
- Phone numbers for some top-notch mutual fund families

Where do I start?

If you read the last two chapters, you know the timeless rules of investing. You've got a passing familiarity with risk-reward relationships. You know about a dozen different types of investments. And you've thought about how you should divide your investing dollars among stocks, bonds, cash, and, possibly, real estate.

Now all you have to do is get started.

For nonretirement savings, the easiest way to do that is through an automatic savings program offered by a mutual fund. (For retirement savings, see Chapter 22, "Saving for Retirement.")

These plans allow you to have a fund company take a set amount of money out of your checking or savings account each month and invest the money in a fund that you've preselected. It puts your savings program on automatic pilot, which is a great way to go if you normally have trouble saving.

The only part of the process that most people find difficult is choosing a fund—or funds—to invest in. But before you try to pick a mutual fund, you need to know a little about what mutual-fund companies are and what they do.

What Is a Mutual Fund?

A mutual fund is an investment company that pools the money of many investors who have similar goals. The fund then simply takes that money and buys securities in bulk.

Each shareholder of the fund owns a share of the dividends and profits—or losses—earned on these investments.

The specific investments purchased by the fund are determined by a fund manager. However, the types of things the manager can buy are spelled out in the company's prospectus, which is the primary investment guidebook for the fund.

There are two significant benefits to buying a mutual fund rather than purchasing stocks and bonds on your own.

First of all, you get professional money management. Each fund has a fund manager whose job is to watch the financial markets all day and determine what stocks or bonds the fund ought to buy and which ones it should sell. You don't have to study price-earnings ratios, dividend yields, and the relative attractiveness of stocks over bonds or bonds over cash. When you buy a mutual fund, you are hiring somebody to make those decisions for you.

The second benefit is broad diversification. Unless you're rich, you are not going to be able to buy shares in dozens of different companies on your own—it's simply too expensive. However, because you're buying with a group when you're buying through a mutual fund, you can—and usually do—own pieces of dozens of different companies through the investments of the fund.

That ultimately makes your portfolio safer, because you're less likely to be savaged by a single bad investment choice.

The Prospectus

However, the precise risks you are taking are spelled out in a long, boring legal document called the prospectus. With no-load funds—those sold without the help of a broker or commission-based financial planner—the fund company must provide you with a prospectus before you invest.

There are six key points you should examine when reading the prospectus.

Objectives. Skim the section that details the fund's investment objectives and strategies to make sure that these objectives mesh with your own.

A great deal of the information is boilerplate. A stock fund is likely to say its "objective is to provide rapid growth of capital through investments in common stocks with strong appreciation potential"—which means little.

However, if you had decided to invest in small-company domestic stocks, you simply want to make sure that's what the fund is doing. Every once in a while, you'll find a fund that's mislabeled—a "growth" fund that ought to be investing in a wide range of stocks but is actually a "sector" fund, investing in just one or two industry groups. In such a case, the fund's description may say its objectives are to "provide rapid growth of capital through investments in technology-oriented stocks with strong appreciation potential."

If the fund is clearly focused on one specific area and you're not, look for another fund.

Risks. In many cases, this section is also boilerplate. With an average stock or bond fund, the disclosure will say that financial markets are volatile. In other words, prices rise and prices fall. Because the value of your initial investment is not guaranteed when you invest in stocks and bonds, you could make money or lose money by investing in the fund. That's the type of risk you should expect.

What are the red flags? "The fund uses leverage" or "derivative securities" to boost short-term returns. What that means is that the fund is taking unusual risks. Unless you're up to unusual volatility—price swings and possible losses—look for another fund.

Fees. Every fund charges some fees in order to pay administrative costs. These fees are deducted from the total return, so they're usually indicated as a percentage of your investment. For instance, the fund may set its annual management fee at 1 percent. In effect, that means that if the fund earns 11 percent on its money, it will deduct a 1 percent management fee and pass 10 percent returns on to investors.

There's nothing wrong with fees. This is how you pay that professional money manager to make all those investing decisions for you. However, the bigger the fees, the lower the return to investors. So make sure the fees don't get excessive.

There are three different types of fees you could pay—a "load," a 12(b)1 fee, and a management fee. While all funds charge management fees, only some charge loads and 12(b)1 fees. What are they?

Loads are lump-sum "marketing" fees that you'll pay when you buy or when you sell the fund. A front-end load is taken out of your initial investment. For example, let's say you have $100 to invest and you want to buy a fund that charges an 8 percent front-end load. You pay your $100, but only $92 is invested for you. The other $8 pays the load, which is essentially a commission paid to the broker or financial planner that sells the fund to you.

A back-end load is deducted from your proceeds when you sell. So let's say you bought the fund for $100 and over several years, the value increased to $150. You sell and the fund deducts a 8 percent back-end load, so you get $138 instead of $150. The other $12 pays the load.

All things being equal, it's better not to pay a load than to pay a load. But you generally must pay a load when you buy a fund through a commission-based financial planner. And if that planner is giving you good advice that you need to help you invest, the load is worth paying.

12(b)1 fees are also marketing fees, but they're paid in small increments over time. A fund that charges 12(b)1 fees, for example, may deduct an extra 1 percentage point from your total return each year to pay this fee. If you invest over long periods of time, 12(b)1 fees can end up costing you more than a load.

What do 12(b)1 fees get you? When I find a good answer, I'll let you know. As far as I can tell, they're simply another fee. If you get something good as the result of paying them, I've yet to discover what it is.

All the fees charged on any given fund are spelled out in a chart near the front of the prospectus.

Performance. The fund company also will disclose its performance over short and long periods. Look for two things: Is the fund performing well compared to the index that measures its performance? Most funds measure their performance against a market index. A so-called "small cap" fund may measure itself against the Russell 2,000, for instance, which is a gauge of how the stock prices of relatively small-growth companies have fared. A good fund manager will track, and occasionally beat, the performance of the index over time.

The second thing you should be looking for is volatility. Do the fund shares swing wildly in price, posting double-digit gains in some years and double-digit losses in others? Can you handle big swings like that, or would you be more comfortable with a fund that's a bit more stable?

Management. Look to see how long the fund manager has been at the helm. If he or she is new, the historic performance data may mean little because it doesn't indicate this manager's success or failures in picking investments. If, on the other hand, the manager has been with the fund for a long time, you can expect that the past performance is indicative of the manager's skills.

It's worth mentioning that some managers are new to a particular fund, but they have extensive track records managing other funds. If this is the case, the prospectus will normally mention what funds this manager has directed in the past. You can then look at the performance of that fund to determine how comfortable you are with your fund manager's skills.

Rules. The prospectus—and investing documents sent with it—will also spell out the rules of investing in that particular fund, such as: What's the minimum amount you can invest initially? And what's the minimum amount you can add to your account at any given time? Will the fund allow you to set up an automatic savings program, where your investments are taken out of your checking or savings account each month, or do you have to physically write and send a check to add to your savings?

Do you have instant access to your money, or are there specific times when you cash out? (A few funds might restrict "redemptions" to once a quarter, for example. And money market funds often limit the number of checks you write against the fund's assets in any given year.)

If you have paid an up-front load, will the fund allow you to switch into another load fund, operated by the same fund family, without paying a second load? If the fund charges a back-end load, does the percentage amount decrease over time?

Does the fund offer twenty-four-hour telephone service? Does it have a toll-free phone number that investors can call to ask questions or make changes to their accounts?

Minimum Investments and Automatic Savings Programs

When you open a bank account, you can usually deposit whatever amount of money you wish. And, if you want to add to your savings, you can add $100 or $10 at a time and nobody cares.

Mutual funds don't work that way. For the most part, they expect you to invest a minimum amount to start. Then, if you want to add to your account, there are minimum "subsequent" investments too.

The initial minimums vary from fund to fund. They can go as low as $250 for funds that want to attract a lot of small depositors to as high as $1 million for funds that want to discourage all but the wealthiest investors. Subsequent investment minimums usually start at $25 or $50.

However, if you don't have a big pile of cash ready to throw into a mutual fund at a moment's notice, don't be discouraged. If you are willing to invest relatively small amounts—about $50—every month, dozens of funds will set up an automatic savings/investment program for you that will get you started and keep you going.

What is an automatic investment program? It's where you authorize the fund company to take a set amount of money out of your checking or savings account each and every month. The fund company invests your contributions in a fund that you've preselected. When you decide that you want to withdraw the money—or shift into a different fund—you simply call the company and let them know.

These programs do two good things for you. First of all, they impose discipline in your investment program. One of the things that makes it hard to save money is that it's so much more fun to spend. You're on your way to the bank or the broker, determined to invest your modest savings, and you pass a display window at Nordstroms. They're having a big sale, and that pair of shoes you've been lusting after is half price. What are you going to do? Buy the shoes, of course. You'll invest next month, you tell yourself.

When you set up an automatic savings or investment program, you don't have to physically wander over to the bank or brokerage. It's done for you. As a result, you don't pass the display window. You don't know about the sale. You only buy the shoes when you've got enough in your checking account—after making your automatic savings contributions—to buy without bouncing a check. After a while, you forget you even earn that $50 a month. It's squirreled away for you, earning compound investment returns.

The other thing automatic savings plans do for you is allow you to "dollar-cost average." That's a fancy way of saying that you invest the same amount every month, without worrying about whether prices are up or down.

Dollar-cost averaging works particularly well when you are investing in stocks. The reason: Over short periods of time, investment values rise and fall, but over the long run, stock values tend to rise.

When you dollar-cost average, you invest the same amount each and every month. When stock prices are rising, your investment buys fewer shares. When stock prices fall, it buys more. Either way, if you keep it up, and stock prices rise over time—as they have in the past—you make money.

Fund Categories

Because there are literally thousands of mutual funds to choose from, you'll want to narrow the field before you start searching for a specific fund.

The first step in that process is to decide what fund category you want. Funds are generally broken into one of a few dozen categories. These categories describe the type of investments the fund buys. The more popular categories are described next.

Stock Funds

Aggressive growth. These funds look for fast appreciation of your principal. They do that by taking greater risks—buying shares in relatively young, untested companies that pay little or no dividends. Additionally, managers of aggressive-growth funds may employ sophisticated and speculative investment techniques such as writing options and using leverage to boost total returns. Because these funds frequently buy shares in smaller, more speculative firms, they can also sometimes be called "small cap" funds. They're high risk and potentially high return.

Growth. Growth funds generally invest in the shares of well-established firms that may or may not pay dividends. They pose moderate risks to long-term investors.

Growth and income funds. These funds buy stock in firms that have a solid record of paying dividends and in companies that are expected to continue to grow and appreciate in value. Risk level: moderate, for long-term investors.

Equity income. These funds look for current income by investing in stocks that boast high dividend yields. Risk: moderate, for both short- and long-term investors.

Equity index funds. If you like the performance of the overall stock market and want to participate without a lot of fuss, equity index funds may be just the ticket. These funds buy shares in every stock that's included in a particular index—most commonly the Standard & Poor's index of five hundred U.S. common stocks. The fund holds those same stocks until and unless a company is dropped from the index. In addition to broad diversification, these funds provide the benefit of very low management and trading fees. Where the normal equity fund charges about 1.5 percent of assets in fees and charges, index funds often charge between 0.2 and 0.5 percent annually. That means more of the total return is passed on to investors. But when the market does poorly, so do index funds. Risk: moderate, for long-term investors.

Global/international and foreign equity. These funds can invest in overseas or domestic stock markets. Some invest primarily overseas; others may have the bulk of their investments in the U.S. Some of the funds look for big, established companies to invest in; others invest in smaller, less established firms. Because the normal risks of stock-market investing are coupled with currency risk (see Chapter 19, "Diversification," page 189), these funds are considered high risk. However, how high the risks are will depend on the fund and will generally be spelled out in the "Risks" section of each fund's prospectus.

Sector funds. These funds concentrate their investments in a single industry. For instance, a technology-sector fund would buy stock in only technology companies, while a financial-services fund would buy shares in just banks, savings and loans, and insurance companies. As a result, the price of these funds' shares can be buffeted by investing fads—the financial world's equivalent of pet rocks, hula hoops, and bell bottoms. At times, they're hot. Sometimes, they're not. If you invest in a sector fund, you've got to be prepared for a rocky ride. Risk: high.

Income Funds

Taxable money market mutual funds. These funds seek to maintain a stable net asset value by investing in high-quality, short-term, interest-bearing securities, such as certificates of deposit, Treasury bills, and short-term corporate debt. Risk: low.

Tax-exempt money market mutual funds. These funds invest in short-term municipal securities that are not subject to federal tax—and may also be exempt from state taxes. Risk: low.

Medium-term income. These funds invest in a mixture of government and corporate bonds with average maturities that can range from two to twenty-five years. Risk: moderate.

Ginnie Mae funds. Ginnie Maes invest in mortgage-backed securities that are packaged and sold by quasi-governmental operations such as the Government National Mortgage Association and the Federal National Mortgage Association. (See page 199.) Risk: moderate.

Long-term government bond funds. These funds invest in long-term government bonds—those with maturities of twenty years or more. These securities don't present a lot of default risk, but the market value of long-term bonds can be buffeted by interest-rate changes. When interest rates rise, per-share values of bond funds fall. When interest rates fall, bond fund share values rise. However, the movements—both up and down—are mitigated a bit by the income earned on the bonds that the fund holds. When interest rates rise, any new bonds that the fund buys pay higher rates of interest. So the fund pays you more income on your investment, even though the value of your principal may have fallen. Risk: moderate.

Long-term income funds. These funds seek to pay high current yields by investing in a mixture of corporate and government bonds. These funds present the same risks as the long-term government funds, but because companies are arguably less financially sound than the U.S. government, this type of fund presents a little more default risk too. Risk: moderate.

High-yield corporate funds. Often called "junk bond funds," these funds buy debt from companies that are heavily indebted and are considered poor credit risks. These bonds can pay healthy rates of interest, but investors are taking a serious risk that the borrowers will default. In addition, prices of these bonds are also affected by interest rates. Risk: high.

International bond funds. These funds buy the debt of foreign countries and companies. Because you are taking on default risk, interest-rate risk, and currency risk, these funds are considered high risk to both long- and short-term investors.

Blended Funds

Balanced funds. Balanced funds aim for current income, stock-price appreciation, and security of your principal—a tall order. They do that by investing in a wide variety of stocks and bonds. Risk: moderate.

Asset allocation funds. These are perfectly suited to investors who really want somebody else to be making the investment decisions for them. These funds allow managers to pick what percentage of your investment portfolio should be in stocks; what percentage in bonds; and what percentage in cash. The manager then buys an array of investments to round out your investment pie—all in one fund. Risk: moderate.

Finding a Fund

Once you figure out what kind of fund you want to buy, your only challenge is finding a specific fund in the category that suits your needs. Thanks to a plethora of newspaper and magazine articles that highlight strong-performing funds in various investment categories, that may be easy to do.

If you need more guidance than you can pick up in the most recent issue of *Money*, *Worth*, *Smart Money*, or *Kiplinger's Personal Finance*, consider picking up a mutual-fund directory. There are roughly a dozen on the market that can be purchased by mail for between $5 and $15. They may also be available in your local public library.

One worth mentioning is the *Investors Guide to Low-Cost Mutual Funds*, which costs $15 and can be ordered from The Mutual Fund Education Alliance at 100 NW Englewood Road, Suite 130, Kansas City, MO 64118.

What makes this directory worth noting? It gives lots of important detail about many of the nation's top funds. Importantly, it includes historic performance data for every fund listed, including the fund's one-year, five-year, and ten-year average annual returns. (When the fund hasn't been in business long enough for the longer-term figures, the guide lists the return since inception.) If you are planning to buy a no-load fund, it is probably the easiest way to weed through the pack without requesting dozens of prospectuses.

Funds That Accept Small Investments

How do you find funds that will take small, regular investments—like $50 a month?

If you are investing through a broker or a commission-based financial planner, you simply ask. Load funds—those that charge up-front fees and are sold by brokers and planners—are almost all willing to let you start small.

Fewer no-load funds allow small, regular investments, but a number of large, well-respected fund "families" do. What's a fund family? It's a fund company that offers numerous different funds.

Fund families provide convenience for investors because they make it easy to switch your money from one type of fund to another. For instance, you may have all your discretionary investments in stock funds, then decide you want to switch into bond funds. If you invest with a fund family that offers both, you don't have to cash out, wait for your check, and then reinvest. You simply call the fund's investor service line. Within a matter of hours, your money is switched from the stock fund into the bond fund. No delays. No hassles. In fact, you usually don't even have to pay toll charges. Most fund families offer toll-free phone numbers for investors.

Here's some well-established fund families that offer a broad array of investment options, including both stock and bond funds—and their toll-free phone numbers.

If you're interested in getting started, all you have to do is select a handful of these companies and ask them to send you information about the company and the funds that suit your investment objectives (growth, income, etc.).

You then simply choose the fund or funds that you like the best by comparing the details—investment objectives, strategies, performance, fees, and rules.

How will you know if you have chosen the "best" fund? You won't. And, in fact, you shouldn't worry too much about hitting the investment world's equivalent of a home run. What you want is a solid fund—one that has a good record of hitting singles and doubles. Too often, the home-run hitters have stretches when they're striking out. Happy hunting!

AIM Funds	800-626-1919
Benham Group	800-472-3389
Berger Associates	800-333-1001
Dreyfus Corporation	800-645-6561
Founders Funds	800-525-2440
Invesco Funds	800-525-8085
Janus Funds	800-525-8983
Neuberger & Berman	800-877-9700
Scudder, Stevens & Clark	800-225-2470
SteinRoe	800-338-2550
Strong Funds	800-368-1030
T. Rowe Price	800-638-5660
Twentieth Century	800-345-2021
United Services	800-873-8637
Value Line	800-223-0818
Vanguard	800-523-0857

Chapter 21

Saving for College

The good news is your children are smart and ambitious. The bad news is you've got to find a way to send them to college.

What the chapter tells you

- Sometimes saving isn't the best alternative.
- Saving in your child's name could cost you when it comes time to apply for financial aid.
- What savings strategies suit your child's age
- Starting early pays big.
- What to do when college is looming and you haven't got the dough

What the chapter shows you

- How to approximate the cost
- How to figure out how much you ought to save
- What you'll have when you save what you can afford

Where do I start?

College-tuition horror stories often start before the baby is delivered: "You'll have to refinance your house to send him to college," one friend warns. "$100,000 minimum to get her through school," nods another. "Scholarships," a third whispers. "Teach him to bowl. Myrna's kid got a full ride."

Unfortunately, the warnings have a grain of truth. Over the past several years, the cost of a college education has risen significantly faster than the rate of inflation. To be specific, at a time when inflation is averaging 3 percent per year, college expenses are rising between 6 and 10 percent on average, depending on the type of school you choose.

Many project that tuition for four years of private school will exceed $100,000 by the year 2000—and could exceed $200,000 when today's newborns graduate high school.

For most middle-income families, saving $100,000 for each child is a pipe dream.

In dollars and cents, the parents of a ten-year-old would have to set aside $747 *per month* from now until the child's eighteenth birthday—and earn 8 percent annually on the money—to produce that nest egg.

Impossible?

The good news is saving 100 percent of your child's anticipated college expenses is foolish. You don't have to do it. You shouldn't do it.

Why? The simple answer is federal income taxes.

As you scrimp and save to create this stunning savings account, you will be building up a federal income tax obligation that could make your eyes water.

Let's say, for example's sake, that you do put $8,965 per year, $747 per month, into a college account and you earn 8 percent annually on your money. Over the eight-year period, you'd owe an extra $8,769 in income taxes—assuming you pay 31 percent of your income in taxes—on the investment earnings accumulated in the account.

These taxes would be incidental if you truly needed the money saved and there was no better alternative to a simple college fund. But for millions of Americans there are much better alternatives.

Things to Do Before You Save

Before you start flipping dollars into a college fund, you should look at the size of your mortgage and at your retirement fund. Then, you should consider throwing that $747 per month into paying down your mortgage loan or pushing up your 401(k) contributions.

Either option will save you thousands of dollars, improve your overall financial picture, and make it easier to finance the college bill—no matter what the cost.

The House Account

Consider what happens if you make the $747 payment to your mortgage lender instead of the college fund. Assuming you have a $150,000 thirty-year, fixed-rate mortgage with an

8 percent interest rate, your payments work out to roughly $1,100 per month. You boost that by the $747 and pay a total of $1,847 per month.

You will pay off the loan in under ten years. And, because you've saved twenty years of interest payments that you would otherwise have paid, you will have saved a stunning $179,504.65 in mortgage interest expenses.

When the child starts college in 2003, your loan balance is about $40,000. You can then return to paying $1,100 per month on the mortgage and give the $747 per month to the child. Or, you can refinance the home—or get a home equity loan—that will allow you to tap the $100,000 of equity you've built up whenever you want it.

It's worth mentioning that a slightly higher monthly payment will allow you to have the house paid off completely by the time your child is in college. Specifically, if you made monthly payments of $2,120.50—an extra $273.50 per month—the loan would be paid off in eight years. Then, with the mortgage out of the way, you would have significantly more cash to pay your child's college bills as you go.

Obviously, few people have an extra $800 a month hanging around that they can kick into their mortgage. But, even if the amount is $50 or $100 a month, the point remains. Assuming your house doesn't decline in value faster than you're building up equity, extra money paid into the mortgage can be tapped later, whether it's to pay for college, a wedding, or a car.

What about the tax implications? Doesn't that mean you'll eventually lose your mortgage interest deductions? Yes.

If you don't refinance or pull out cash with a home equity loan, you will eventually lose your mortgage tax deduction. You'll also lose your mortgage payments, which is nothing to sob about.

The 401(k) Strategy

Yet the best strategy for college savings may be to forget the kids and save aggressively for your own retirement. Why? Federal aid formulas exclude from consideration the money you have socked away in qualified retirement plans, such as 401(k)s. Yet many 401(k) plans allow you to borrow a portion of the savings to pay for your child's college expenses.

What are the federal tax implications of pumping the $747 per month into the 401(k) instead of the mortgage? Strictly positive.

The money you put into a 401(k) is taken out before tax. As far as the government is concerned, you've never earned it. That means you don't pay income tax on the $8,965 in annual contributions, which saves you $2,779 in federal tax payments—assuming a 31 percent bracket—each year. Over the eight-year period, that's a tidy $22,233 tax benefit.

(Most states also provide state tax deductions for 401(k) contributions. However, the precise benefit varies markedly state to state based on your state's tax rates.)

Better yet, borrowing money out of the 401(k) generally doesn't trigger income tax liability on the amount you've tapped. Until you officially withdraw the money—take it out with no plan to pay it back—you don't pay tax on contributions or the investment earnings the account generates.

You will have to pay yourself back, of course. But, if the college money was simply additional dollars that you would not have contributed otherwise, you can stop making new contributions while you are paying back the loan.

The one caveat: 401(k) plans vary somewhat from employer to employer. Some plans do not allow borrowing. You need to check the provisions of your plan—assuming you have access to one—to see if this is a viable college saving strategy for your family. In addition, even plans that do allow borrowing have limitations on how much you can borrow. Typically, you can borrow no more than the *lesser of* half of your account value or $50,000.

Saving in Your Name vs. Junior's: A Question of Tax vs. Aid

If you are a renter or don't have access to a 401(k), your saving strategies will be more traditional. But you've still got to answer one question before you start kicking money into a college savings account: Will you save the money in your name or your child's?

In the past several years, parents have increasingly opted to save in their child's name because they understand that this strategy will save them money on their income taxes.

It does present some modest tax savings. But you should know that it could also cost you dearly in financial aid.

Here's why.

Before your child goes to college, you'll be asked to fill out a voluminous form to assess the child's eligibility for federal financial aid. The form asks a series of questions about your income, assets, and the income and assets of your child. You'll also be expected to provide financial aid officials with a copy of your most recent tax return, which will help them verify some of the information you've provided on the form.

That information is processed by one of two companies that score your child's "need" based on current financial-aid formulas. Those formulas anticipate that a child will spend 35 percent of their savings on education each year, while their parents will spend a little more than 5 percent of their nonretirement savings annually.

Based on this analysis, the processing firm determines the most your family can afford to spend each year on college. It sends that analysis to the colleges your child chose and the colleges determine the child's need for financial based on the cost of their school vs. the amount your family can afford.

In other words, if your child chose a school that costs $10,000 annually and the aid formula says your family could afford to spend $6,000 annually, your child would need $4,000 in aid.

The college comes up with a financial-aid package built around an array of grants, loans, and work-study programs aimed at filling the $4,000 gap between what you can afford to pay and what it costs.

The real issue here, however, is that 5 percent versus 35 percent.

If you have $10,000 saved in your name, the school will expect you to contribute about $500 of it each year—roughly $2,000 total. The dollar value of the expected contribution falls as the size of the savings account diminishes. (That won't be the sum total of your expected contribution. Aid officials will also expect some money to be paid out of current income. But this is how your savings account works into the formula.)

If your child has saved the same amount, they must spend about $8,300 of it over the four-year period. The result: They get roughly $6,000 less in aid.

Did you save enough in income taxes to make up for the loss of financial aid? The answer will depend on your tax bracket, the size of the college fund, and the age of your child when you start saving.

But unless you're in the very highest tax brackets or you have a very substantial, high-return college fund, the tax savings won't make up for what you lose by saving in the child's name.

The Tax Benefit

Until your child is age fourteen, the first $650 she earns is tax-free. The next $650 is taxed at a 15 percent rate. Investment earnings that exceed $1,300 are taxed at the parents' rate. After age fourteen, your child is taxed at her own rate, no matter how high her earnings.

Parents, on the other hand, would be taxed on 100 percent of the investment earnings at their ordinary income tax rate—either 15, 28, 31, 36, or 39.6 percent. Capital gains are currently taxed at a 20 percent rate.

The disparity between income tax rates is what gives the impression that you'll save a fortune by saving in the child's name. But once you run the numbers, you realize the savings are somewhat illusory—unless you have little chance of qualifying for financial aid.

To illustrate, let's say the parents are in the 28 percent tax bracket and they save $25 per month for their child's college expenses over an eighteen-year period. They earn 8 percent annually on the money. Their college fund is worth $10,795 when junior is college age. About $5,694 of that amount is interest earnings on the savings. The rest are contributions, which are not taxable.

Assuming that the interest earnings would not be taxable at all if the account was in the child's name (which is likely, in this case), the parents would have saved $1,594 in income taxes over the seventeen years by saving in junior's name rather than their own.

But because the student aid formulas anticipate that the child will spend more than $8,214 of his or her $10,000 savings account on college expenses and Mom and Dad will spend just $2,192 of theirs, this child qualifies for $6,022 less in financial aid.

Ultimately, this family is $4,428 poorer (the $1,594 tax savings minus the $6,022 loss of aid eligibility) because they saved in the child's name.

If, however, these parents are in the 39.6 percent bracket, their tax savings are greater. Moreover, unless they suffer some financial reversal before the kids hit college age, the chance that they'll qualify for financial aid is slim. They'd probably save money by saving in the child's name.

The Caveats

There is a chance that student-aid formulas will change before your child starts school in a way that is adverse to a parent saving in their own name. Or that a middle-income family who saves with financial aid in mind will suddenly strike it rich, making it impossible for their child to qualify.

However, the financial-aid formula has favored saving in the parent's names for as long as anyone can remember. And, logically, it ought to. Parents have other financial obligations. Children don't. Consequently, it's reasonable to assume that children can use up nearly all of their savings for college. It isn't reasonable to make the same assumption about parents.

And Then There's the Porsche . . .

There's one other caution about saving in your child's name. As your children's guardian, you control their assets until they reach the "age of majority"—which varies state to state, but is usually either eighteen or twenty-one. At that point, the money is theirs. They can use it to go to college or to go to Europe.

How Much Is Enough?

In a perfect world, we'd all be able to predict how much it would cost to send our kids to college and we'd be able to save that amount in advance.

In the real world, predicting how much college will cost is an imperfect art. Colleges make it difficult by changing tuition and fees by irregular amounts at unpredictable intervals. The federal government exacerbates the problem by periodically changing the rules governing who can qualify for student aid—and how much they'll get. Our kids make it impossible by refusing at birth to make it clear whether or not they're Ivy League material.

The fact is, there are stunning differences between expenses at one university versus another. There's simply no comparison between the current cost of a state college and the cost of a private school. The cost of two-year public colleges is less than the cost of many private grammar schools—which parents typically swing using their current earnings.

By the time it's clear what college is going to cost, it's way too late to start saving.

What do you do?

You make a guess based on historic costs (see chart), what you want for your child, and what you are willing to pay for. If an Ivy League school is very important to you, you should try to save at least three times as much as someone who is content with sending their child to a public college or university.

Also consider your attitude about paying for school. Many parents want their children to contribute to their own education on the theory that the education will mean more to those who've made a few sacrifices to get it.

If that's the case, you can save less. But you'll need to encourage your child to start saving a portion of his or her earnings—or allowance—from the time they're very young. Deferred gratification—what you get when you save rather than spend—is something that you learn. It's much easier to learn it early than when you're under the gun.

Sample Undergraduate Budgets 1995–96

College Type	Tuition/ Fees	Books/ Supplies	Room/ Board	Transport	Other	Total
2-year public resident	$1,387	$577	*	*	*	*
Commuter	$1,387	$577	$1,752	$894	$1,142	$5,752
2-year private resident	$6,350	$567	$4,243	$578	$972	$12,710
Commuter	$6,350	$567	$1,796	$902	$1,220	$10,835
4-year public resident	$2,860	$591	$3,964	$565	$1,306	$9,285
Commuter	$2,860	$591	$1,721	$929	$1,348	$7,449
4-year private resident	$12,432	$601	$5,198	$521	$1,010	$19,762
Commuter	$12,432	$601	$1,845	$863	$1,169	$16,910

**Sample too small to provide meaningful information.*
Source: The College Board.

This table shows artificial budgets, because the number of institutions reporting values in the various budget components vary. Therefore, these sample budgets cannot be presented as "average budgets." But the values are illustrative of the kinds of fixed charges and estimated additional expenditures that students and their families face in the 1995–96 academic year.

The Value of Starting Early

Obviously, you don't *have* to start saving from the moment your child is born. But it's smart.

When you start saving early, you can put your money in "volatile" investments, such as growth stocks. Volatility means you can make a lot of money one year and lose a lot of money the next. It means you are taking more risk with your money.

Why would you want to do that? Because taking reasoned risks allows you to reap higher rewards. (See Chapter 19, "Diversification.") That means the college fund grows faster than it would if you invested the money conservatively.

It's worth mentioning that a reasoned risk is not buying lottery tickets. It's a seasoned investment that should rise in value over time, but could vary in value over shorter periods. Generally speaking, that means corporate stocks and bonds.

Still, many people hesitate to take reasonable risks because they've been told that they shouldn't gamble with their money. That's true if you're investing the rent money.

But a college fund isn't rent money. Many kids have made it through graduate school without a dime in the college coffers. Clearly, that's not ideal. But no one's going to turn the lights out, your kids are not going to sleep in the streets, and the family is not going to have to live on food stamps if you face an investment loss in the college fund.

Starting early and taking a few calculated investment risks allows you to reap the very real and very dramatic rewards of long-term compounded returns.

Consider someone who wants a $10,000 college fund for their child. If the child is a newborn, they can reasonably expect to earn an average annual return of 10 percent by investing the money in domestic stocks. (That's the average annual return of large company stocks from 1926 through 1994; the average return on small company stocks is higher.)

As a result, this family can put away just $17 per month—a total of $3,672—and seventeen years of compounded investment earnings will provide the rest—some $6,328, or nearly twice as much as they saved.

If, on the other hand, the child is fifteen and college costs are looming near on the horizon, this family would be foolish to take as many risks. They will have to invest more conservatively, accept lower average returns, and their money will have less time to work for them.

The procrastinators will invest in short-term Treasuries, bank deposits, and certificates of deposit. In today's market, their expected annual return would amount to less than 7 percent. They'd have to save $250 per month for thirty-six months—a total of $9,016.

In other words, the family that saved early needed to save $5,344 less.

Savings Strategies

Exactly how do you invest the college money? The possibilities boggle the mind. You can invest in any one of more than six thousand listed common stocks. You could put the money into Treasury bills, bonds, notes, or "strips." You could put it in municipal securities, which are issued by virtually every state, county, and special-purpose district on the map. You could buy savings bonds, zero coupon bonds, or international stocks and bonds. Or you could sock the money away in a bank account.

But this variety obscures logic. Your saving strategy should depend on how long you've got until you need the money and on how you feel about risk. If taking some risks with the college money will keep you up at night, you should invest more conservatively—no matter how hard others try to encourage you to take more risks.

If, on other hand, you understand that you're not betting the ranch and you're not going to reach for the antacid pills every time the market takes a dip, you should invest the bulk of the account in corporate stocks. Then, as the child gets closer to college age, gradually decrease the percentage of volatile investments—stocks—and go into safer, shorter-term securities, such as Treasury notes, certificates of deposit, and money market mutual funds.

Sample Plans

If you're looking for ideas on how to invest the college fund, you can get some help from the sections below. However, realize that a college fund that's in the parents' names rather than the child's is just a part of your overall portfolio. You don't need to segregate it. You don't need to do something special with it. You simply fold it into the regular mix of your invested assets.

In other words, make sure you look at your financial life as a whole, rather than as a group of small parts. For help, refer to Chapter 19, "Diversification," which starts on page 189.

If you have a separate college fund, refer to the section that corresponds with your child's age.

But you should realize that investment strategies are somewhat arbitrary. There is no one formula that works for everyone. An advisable strategy for you may not be the right formula for your neighbor. Make sure you understand and feel fairly comfortable with your investment portfolio.

If you don't like the suggested investment mixes here, create your own. Chapter 19 can help you determine what risks and rewards you face with any of these strategies or with a strategy that you create on your own.

You should also know that all of the suggested strategies in this book involve mutual funds. Why? They provide an easy way to diversify a small investment portfolio without significantly eroding your investment return. Diversification reduces the chance that the value of your investment portfolio will be savaged by hard times at any one company. With most mutual funds, you are buying a small stake in literally hundreds of different stocks. Presumably, when one company hits hard times another will just be hitting its stride. Investing in lots of companies makes it safer to invest in an otherwise volatile market.

Besides, it's easy. You can set up an account at a mutual fund and simply have them take $50 out of your paycheck each month. (See Chapter 20, "Mutual Funds.") Then a professional money manager decides which stocks or bonds to buy and sends you regular statements showing how your investments are doing. All you have to do is decide whether you like the fund and the fund manager. It puts your portfolio on automatic pilot.

There are other reasons to like mutual funds, particularly for small regular investments. If you want to get into them in more detail, refer to Chapter 20.

Children Birth to Age Seven

You have lots of time. Use it to take risks that would otherwise make you queasy. Aggressive growth stocks should comprise a substantial chunk of your portfolio, as should international funds and domestic stock funds. Only the seriously risk averse should consider putting a portion of their toddler's college fund in low-risk options such as savings bonds and bank accounts.

If you're starting small, you can contribute to one type of account at a time. For instance, you might set up an automatic investment plan with a big mutual fund company such as T. Rowe Price or Vanguard. In the first year you'd have your contributions sent solely into the international fund. In the second year, you switch and have the new contributions go into the stock fund. In year three, you have new contributions put into a growth-and-income fund.

Or simply find an asset allocation fund or a general-purpose stock fund that you feel comfortable with and just pump your monthly investments into that one fund. (Details in Chapter 20, "Mutual Funds.")

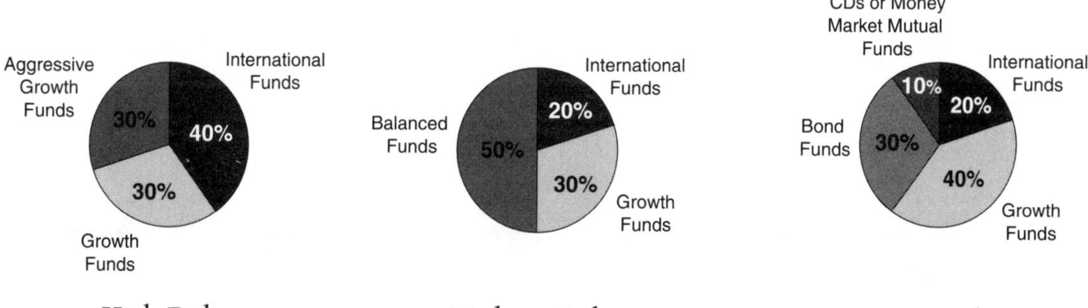

Children Ages Eight to Thirteen

You've still got plenty of time, but as your child gets older, you should start reducing your international investments because they pose both investment risk and currency risk (see Chapter 19, "Diversification"). If you have invested in foreign funds that specialize in a single country, you should also consider shifting the money into domestic stocks or international funds that are more broadly focused. Single-country funds tend to swing widely in price from year to year. Also start weeding out the more volatile domestic mutual funds—those that post the biggest annual gains and losses. You simply have less time to recoup losses generated in a bad year.

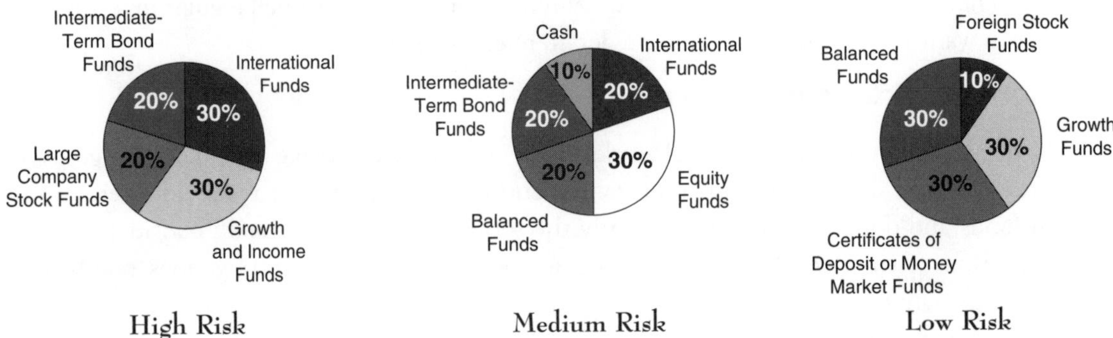

High Risk Medium Risk Low Risk

Children Ages Fourteen and Older

If you are just starting to save, you need to consider financial aid as carefully as you consider savings strategies. Indeed, planning your aid profile may well net you more than even an aggressive savings strategy.

Go to the library or the bookstore and invest in some information before you start saving. Three recommended books: *The Princeton Review Student Access Guide to Paying for College* by Kalman Chany; *The New College Financial Aid System: Making It Work for You* by David Jaffe; and *The College Board College Costs & Financial Aid Handbook.*

The first two books are written by New York financial aid consultants, who spend their days helping parents send their children to Ivy League schools without going bankrupt. They explain how to play the system to get the most financial aid possible.

The College Board's book, on the other hand, details precisely how much you can expect to pay for any given school in the country. The costs include tuition, fees, room, board, books, transportation, and "other." It's helpful guidance if you're trying to choose between schools. Additionally, it suggests ways to cut your costs through practical means—like attending community college for a few years before transferring into a four-year

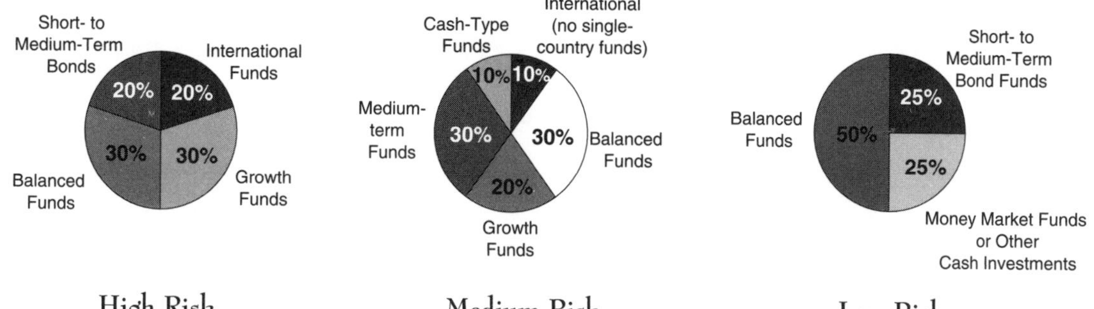

High Risk | Medium Risk | Low Risk

university, or having your child take advanced-placement courses. Either course of action can save your family a small fortune.

One last suggestion: Call 800-4-FED-AID. That's the government's financial aid hot line, which can provide you with free booklets about sources of government aid as well as how and when to apply. These booklets are not as clearly written as the others; they also provide less in the way of practical advice. But they're free and they do go over many of the basics.

If you simply want to know what to do with your child's established college fund: It's time to start shifting a portion of the college account into less volatile investments. The way to do that is to review how each segment of the investment portfolio has fared over time, specifically looking for where you had the biggest percentage losses and biggest percentage gains.

The funds that swung highest and lowest are the most volatile. Those are the ones you want to start selling. Look for good opportunities to get out. For example, when one of these funds completes a banner year—up well over the average—sell. It's always tempting to hang on at that point, hoping for another banner year. But with volatile funds, there's a decent chance that performance will be miserable in the following year instead. So be disciplined and pull the money out.

Put it into something that's unlikely to risk a significant amount of your initial investment, such as a certificate of deposit or short-term government bond that matures in the first year your child attends school.

Realize that you don't need to write a check for four years' worth of tuition on the day your child turns eighteen. Instead, you'll probably be paying tuition costs in four lump sums. Other college expenses—for room, board, books, and fees, for example—will occur monthly or at irregular intervals. But in general it's nice to have about one-quarter of the college fund in safe, easily accessible investments at any given time, once your child is ready to enroll.

As your child gets closer to freshman year, your college portfolio should look increasingly like the low-risk option.

Savings Bonds

Clearly, these are just a few ways you might handle a college savings program. There are hundreds of other options. One option nearly everyone considers—and many people use—are U.S. savings bonds. Why aren't they mentioned here? Because the preceding graphs were compiled on the assumption that you're saving in your child's name, with a dedicated college savings account. Under those circumstances, savings bonds have some serious shortcomings that make them relatively unattractive, except in fairly rare cases. Specifically:

- The interest earnings on savings bonds are not subject to federal tax if a middle-income parent cashes out the bond and uses the proceeds to fund her child's schooling. If the child owns the bond, the built-up earnings are taxable when the bond is cashed in.
- Your rate of return on a newly purchased savings bond is no longer guaranteed. (Bonds purchased before 1995 and held for five years or more paid the higher of a guaranteed rate or a market interest rate. These were a better deal than today's bonds with pay a market interest rate, which is based on the current return on Treasury notes and bonds.)
- Savings bonds pay interest only once every six months, compared to daily or monthly compounding with most ordinary savings accounts. The government doesn't indicate on the bond when it matures, when each semiannual interest payment is paid, or when it can be cashed in for face value.

The bottom line: Under current rules, savings bonds are a lot of trouble and expected rate of interest is paltry. You've got better options.

Other Strategies

Prepay. Prepaid tuition plans are springing up at costly colleges around the country to give parents peace of mind that they'll have enough to pay for college. If you pay in advance, you normally don't have to worry about how much the college costs escalate in the years prior to enrollment. Prepaid tuition is taken as payment in full, no matter how much costs have risen.

There's one big shortcoming to all these plans, though: your kids. Do you really know where they will attend school ten years from now—or five years from now or three? Unless you are willing to force your child to attend a school of your choosing rather than hers—or unless your child is unusually set about her long-term decision making—there's a decent chance that you'll be applying for a tuition refund. If you're lucky, your refund will be the amount you paid plus a minimal amount of interest. If you're not lucky, your refund, minus processing fees, could amount to less than you paid in.

Budget. If college is just around the corner, you've applied for financial aid, and the size of your "expected family contribution" is making you dizzy, don't panic. You may be able to get credit for some of the family contribution, without actually spending the money. How? One of the things many parents don't realize about financial aid is that it's expected to address the total cost of college, including tuition, fees, books, room, board, transportation, and incidentals. Where tuition, fees, and book expenses are fairly inelastic, the cost of a student's housing and transportation can vary. If your child is willing and able to economize on discretionary expenses, the amount he or she saves counts as part of your contribution.

Bargain. Another tip that many parents don't know: Financial aid is negotiable. If your child is a good student and has been accepted at several schools, you can actually play one university's financial aid package against another's, aid counselors say. In other words, Suzie Jr.—a girl of extraordinary academic and personal achievement—has been admitted to both Harvard and Princeton; Princeton is offering more in the way of scholarships and grants, but Suzie really prefers Harvard. Talk to Harvard's financial aid officer and ask if he can restructure the package to look more like Princeton's. Be polite, but direct. After all, cost definitely has an impact on what you choose to buy—be the product a shirt or a school. If, however, Suzie was an average student, she'll have less negotiating power.

Returning students, who are making reasonable academic progress, also have the ability to rejigger their aid packages. If you can't afford what the college says you can afford, march into the financial aid office and explain why. Usually, the college will find a way to help by providing more in the way of grants, scholarships, or loans.

Pay monthly. Also unadvertised, but widely available, are programs in which you pay college costs in monthly installments over the course of the year, instead of in an up-front lump sum. If you don't have the money saved but think you could swing your portion if it was spread out over time, ask about your ability to pay monthly.

Gifts from grandparents. If Grandma and Grandpa are loaded and they want to help with your college expenses, they can pay all your education bills directly without running into estate or gift tax troubles. They should, however, consult a tax or estate-planning professional before they do to make sure they don't mess up their overall financial or estate plan.

College Cost

It's impossible to know precisely how much college is going to cost in the distant future. That's going to depend on where your child goes, if he or she gets scholarships and financial aid, and inflation. But you can make a decent guess at it by figuring out what you want for your child—or, if your child is old enough, what she or he wants. Then adjust that figure for college-cost inflation, which is higher than ordinary inflation. Use the "What Will It Cost?" worksheet for guidance.

Then, if you want to know how much you have to save today to have enough, go to the next worksheet, titled "How Much Must I Save?" Again, this is more art than science, but it should get you fairly close.

What Will It Cost?

		Example
1. Current cost of college*:	$____________(PV)	$40,000
2. Inflation factor:	____________(%I)	6%
3. Years to college:	____________(N)	10
4. Payment:	$0 (PMT)	$0
5. Future cost:	$____________	$71,634

*See college cost table, page 228.

Calculation: Pull out your present-value calculator. Plug in the result of line 1, and hit "PV." That's the present value—or, in this case, the present cost—of the type of college you expect your child to attend.

Enter the result of line 2, hit "%I" because that's how much college costs are likely to rise while you're waiting.

Plug in the result of line 3, hit "N" because that's the number of years you'll be waiting.

Hit "0, PMT" because you're not yet trying to figure out how much to save—you just want to know what it will cost.

Finally, hit "CPT, FV" for compute future value.

Using the above example, you would hit: "40,000, PV"; "6, %I"; "10, N"; "0, PMT"; "CPT, FV." The result: Four years of college that costs $40,000 today will cost $71,634 in ten years, assuming that college costs rise an average of 6 percent per year.

How Much Must I Save?

You obviously don't need to save 100 percent of the future college costs in advance, but if you want to know how much you'd have to save each month to get there, estimate the rate of return you're likely to get on your money. (Use the investment returns chart, page 191, for a ballpark figure, matching historic returns to the type of investments you choose.) Then, again, plug in the figures corresponding to the number of years you have before your child starts college, the future cost (that you just figured out), and the present value of your current college savings account (if any).

		Example
1. Future cost of college:	$______________(FV)	$71,634
2. Expected annual rate of return:	______________(%I)	8%
3. Years to college:	______________(N)	10
4. Present value of savings account:	$______________(PV)	0
5. Annual savings needed:	$______________(PMT)	$4,945
6. Divide the result of line 5 by 12 to get monthly savings amount:	$______________	$412

What Will I Have If I Save What I Can Afford?

Can't save as much as you'd like and want to know how much you'll have if you save less? You can find out the "future value" of your savings account by turning the previous calculations around a bit.

There's one trick to this calculation, though. Many present-value calculators are designed to figure out your monthly payment on a loan. So, if you put in a present value ("PV") and a payment amount ("PMT"), it will assume you are paying off a debt. Unbeknownst to you, your calculator will make the "present value" of your savings account a negative number. If your calculator functions this way, you can fix the problem by making your payment amount negative too. Do that by hitting the "+/–" key on the calculator after you plug in the amount of the payment, but before you hit the "PMT" key.

Additionally, because you're likely to do your savings on a monthly rather than annual basis, this chart will adjust interest rates and number of years you have to save into monthly numbers.

		Example
1. Current value of my savings:	$____________(PV)	$10,000
2 Expected return:______ divided by 12 (months)	____________(%I)	8 = 0.6667
3. Years to save:______ multiplied by 12 (months)	____________(N)	10 = 120
4. Amount I'll save each month:	$____________(PMT)	$50
5. The future value of my savings:	$____________	$31,344

Chapter 22

Saving for Retirement

Saving for retirement has fast become America's number one, long-term financial goal. Here's how to determine if you're saving enough.

What the chapter tells you

- Determining the cost of any future goal is as much art as science, but you can make a reasonable guess with the right information.
- How inflation will affect the amount you need
- Where your income will come from in retirement
- The best tax-favored retirement savings options
- The value of starting early

What the chapter shows you

- How to compile a retirement budget
- How to get a benefit estimate from Social Security
- What your savings will be worth in the future
- How to determine how much more you need to save

Where do I start?

It seems that everywhere you turn these days, somebody is telling you something horrible about your prospects in retirement. Expert after expert warns that Social Security won't be around as long as you are; that your company pension may prove inadequate; and that Americans aren't saving enough to pick up the slack.

Nobody wants to be poor when they're old. (Most people don't even want to be old, but this book does have limitations.) As a result, saving for retirement has become America's number one financial goal.

But how do you know how much to save? How can you tell when you've saved enough? How do you balance the incessant financial demands of everyday life with the need to handle a potentially gigantic long-term obligation? It's not as hard as it sounds. You just need to take it one step at a time.

Step One: Determine What You'll Need

Before you can contemplate how much you need to *save* for retirement, you need to figure out how much you'll need to *spend* in retirement. In other words, you have to compile an estimated retirement budget.

How do you do that? Start with your current budget and then hypothesize about how your financial life would differ in retirement. Subtract out monthly expenses that you don't expect to have at retirement and add back in expenses that you don't have now but probably will have then.

What about inflation? That's step two. For now, don't worry about it. Do everything in current dollars. We'll adjust for inflation later.

To get started, flip back to Chapter 4 (page 30), where you put together your current budget. Take the "average monthly expenses" figure and start subtracting work-related expenses, retirement-savings contributions, and other monthly costs that are not likely to last when you quit work.

For instance, a portion—possibly a large portion—of your clothing budget is work related. So are some of the expenses you pay for transportation—such as parking, gasoline, subway, or train fares. Chances are you won't be eating lunch out as often in retirement either. So subtract the portion of those costs that you can reasonably expect to go.

If part of your budget goes to 401(k), IRA, or Keogh contributions, subtract that.

If you're now paying private school expenses for your kids—and you expect them to graduate before you retire—deduct that cost from your monthly budget too. If you've got a home and expect the mortgage to be paid off, deduct the payment from the total.

Now start adding expenses for things that you want to buy—or expenses you think are going to be necessary—in your golden years.

You may, for example, have grand vacation aspirations. If so, budget in an amount that would pay for that type of vacation today. If you're young and healthy, you should also expect that your medical expenses will be at least somewhat higher in retirement than they are now. If you want to be golfing every day once the workaday world is behind you, start adding up the greens fees and the cost of a cart, and jot it down. Don't forget about taxes, either.

When you're done, you should have a dollar figure that is a rough estimate of how much you'd need each month to live on in retirement.

Record that number here: $__________________

Adjust for Inflation

Pull out your calculator. You now need to adjust this figure for inflation. To do that, you'll need to make a reasonable estimate of what inflation will average in the future. And you'll have to consider how many years you have until retirement.

Inflation has averaged 3.13 percent for the past seventy years, according to Ibbotson Associates, a Chicago-based economic research and consulting firm. It's reasonable to assume that it will continue to average between 3 and 4 percent over long periods of time.

However, if you are retiring within five or ten years, you may want to look at current inflation figures instead. That's simply because the temporary peaks and valleys of the inflation rate won't have time to even out before you'll start to be affected by them.

Now, to adjust your budget for inflation, pull out your present-value calculator or go to the Macmillan Web site at http://www.mcp.com/mgr/macmillan/dollars. Plug in the inflation rate you've estimated and hit "%I"; put in your needed monthly income (noted above) and punch "PV"; enter the number of years before you retire and hit "N"; and then hit "0, PMT". Finally, punch "CPT, FV". The result is your estimated monthly budget, adjusted for inflation.

Enter the result here: $____________________

Step Two: Marshall Your Resources

How are you going to come up with that amount of cash? Chances are, you'll have three sources of income—your company pension, Social Security, and your own savings.

Can you rely on Social Security? Of course, it's impossible to say for sure, but if you're retiring in the fairly near future—anytime within the next ten to fifteen years—you probably can.

There is a great debate raging about what to do about the program in the future. But there are no current plans to dismantle it. If it is eventually revamped, there's a good chance that the changes will be phased in gradually to protect those who relied on Social Security's promise when doing their retirement planning.

However, if you are in your twenties, thirties, or forties, there's a much better chance that massive systemic changes will severely erode your potential to receive substantial Social Security benefits. Although you may get something, many financial planners advise not to count on it.

Getting a Benefit Estimate

To determine how much you're likely to get from Social Security, request an estimate of monthly benefits from the Social Security Administration. How? Call the Social Security Administration at 800-772-1213 from a touch-tone phone. That gives you a twenty-four-hour recording, with several prompts. One allows you to request a "record of your earnings and future Social Security benefits." If you follow the instructions, the agency will send you a short form that you'll fill out, sign, and return. A few weeks later, you'll get a detailed report that estimates how much you'll receive in monthly benefits. The report also explains your benefits; how many quarters of work you need to qualify for Social Security; how much you could receive in Social Security disability benefits if you were severely disabled and unable to work for a long period of time; and how much your spouse or survivors could receive by claiming benefits off your work record too.

But recognize that the younger you are, the more speculative this figure is. There are two reasons why. First of all, you have a limited earnings history. And that earnings history—forty quarters of it, anyway—is used to determine your monthly benefits. If you expect to earn a lot more in the future than you do now, your actual benefits could be higher.

The second reason boils down to political tinkering. Congress can change Social Security rules, regulations, and benefits any year from now until we all die. But legislation—particularly important, controversial legislation—tends to move at glacial speed. So a fifty-year-old who is between twelve and fifteen years away from collecting benefits (you can get reduced benefits at age sixty-two), is at less risk of having benefits ripped out from under him (or her) than a thirty-year-old, who won't be collecting benefits for another thirty-five years.

Still, there's no downside to requesting the estimate. It's fast. It's easy. There's no limit to the number of estimates you can get, so you can request one again later if there are changes to your income or to the rules.

When you get the answer, enter it here.

Monthly Social Security benefit: $____________________

Determining Pension Payouts

If you have a company pension plan, call your employee benefits department and ask whether you're "vested" in the plan and how much you could reasonably expect to collect at retirement.

Chances are the answers will hinge on how long you have been with the company and how long you stay. Many people won't know the answer to the second part of that equation—at least not for a long time. Nonetheless, you make a guess—planning anything far into the future involves a significant amount of reasoned guesswork—and try to guess relatively conservatively, so that your future surprises will mainly be positive ones.

Your employee pension is likely to amount to a set percentage of your wages in the final three to five years of work. The percentage will depend on your income at that point and how many years you worked for the company. However, most company pensions also have Social Security offsets. What these do is reduce your pension amount by a percentage of the Social Security benefit you collect. For instance, if your company pension works out to $2,000 per month and your Social Security is $700 per month, your company's Social Security offset may decrease your monthly pension by half of the Social Security amount. That would reduce your pension payments by $350 per month to $1,650 instead of $2,000.

Ask your employee benefits representative whether your company pension has a Social Security offset and how it could affect your monthly benefits.

Enter your expected monthly pension amount here: $__________

Stipend from Your Savings

If you already have some money socked away for retirement, you need to determine just how much this amount will be worth in the future. To do that, you need a present-value calculator. If you have one, pull it out and follow the steps in the worksheet below. If you don't have one but have a computer with Internet access, you can do the calculation on the Macmillan Web site at http://www.mcp.com/mgr/macmillan/dollars.

You don't know how much you'll earn? Nobody does, really. But if you have a portfolio of both stocks and bonds and a long time horizon, it's reasonable to use an 8 percent average annual rate. If your investments are mostly in bonds and fixed-interest accounts, you should expect to earn less—somewhere between 5 and 6 percent. If they're mainly in stocks, you might earn more. But because stock-market returns are less predictable—particularly over periods of a decade or less—it's better to be conservative in your estimates. Using a rate ranging between 8 and 10 percent is fairly reasonable.

Retirement Savings Worksheet

1. Current amount of your savings $ __________(PV)
2. Estimated annual rate of return __________%
   divided by 12 (months) = __________(%I)
3. Number of years to retirement __________
   multiplied by 12 (months) = __________(N)

4. Amount of monthly payments into savings (For now, enter 0) ______________(PMT)

5. Compute future value ____________(CPT, FV)

6. Approximate amount my savings will be worth at retirement $______________

So, let's say you've got $30,000 saved in a 401(k) plan; have it invested in a mixture of stocks and bonds and figure you'll earn about 8 percent annually on average. You're thirty years from retirement.

Because interest usually accrues monthly, rather than annually, you're going to convert the interest rate and the time the money is invested (number of years) into months.

You divide 8 by 12 months to get a monthly interest rate of 0.6667. Multiply 30 years by 12 to find that your money will be invested for 360 months.

The calculation works like this: "30,000, PV"; "0, PMT" (you're just trying to figure out what this sum will be worth without adding to it, at this point); "0.6667, %I"; "360, N"; then "CPT, FV" for compute future value. You get $328,111.

Now do it with your numbers:

1. $______________(present value of your savings), "PV"

2. ______________(number of months to retirement), "N"

3. ______________(estimated monthly rate of interest), "%I"

4. $______________(amount of monthly payments to the account, if any. In the previous example, we assumed you weren't adding to the account each month. But if you contribute regularly to an IRA or a 401(k) plan, plug in the amount of your monthly contributions—the "payments" you make to your retirement), "PMT"*

5. Compute future value: "CPT, FV." Enter the result here: $______________

**Hit the "+/–" key. With many present-value calculators, when you're adding to savings you'll need to hit the "+/–" key before hitting the "PMT" key. The reason: These calculators are designed to determine the cost of paying off loans. So when you plug in a preset value and a payment, the calculator is likely to assume that you're paying off a debt, making your "present value" figure negative. If your calculator works this way, you can counteract it by making the payment a negative number as well.*

Determine How Much Monthly Income Your Savings Will Generate

What will this savings account provide in monthly income? To answer that you have to first consider whether you want to spend the account down to zero or if you want to live only on the interest income, leaving the principal alone for emergencies or your heirs.

If you want to leave the principal alone, multiply the future value by a reasonable interest rate—the rate you'd earn on fairly conservative income-producing investments that you'd be likely to invest in at retirement.

For example, if your savings account was likely to be worth $300,000 at retirement, you might multiply that by 6 percent to find that the annual income this account would generate would be about $18,000 annually or $1,500 per month. ($300,000 times 6 percent equals $18,000, divided by 12 months, equals $1,500.)

If you plan to spend down the principal, you have to decide how much time you'll take to do that. Let's say you assume you'll live thirty years after retirement—to age ninety-five. So you plan to spend the retirement account to zero over that time. How much do you get monthly?

Assuming you earn 6 percent annually on the money while you're whittling it down, you get roughly $1,799 per month. How do you figure it? Mentally put yourself into retirement with your $300,000 nest egg. Now do the present-value calculation again, this time solving for "payment."

1. $________________ (value of savings at retirement), "PV" (answer #5 from previous worksheet)

2. _______ (estimated monthly interest rate earned on savings while retired = Annual rate divided by 12), "%I"

3. ________ (number of months that payments are needed), "N"

4. $________________ (future value of the account. If you plan to spend the account to zero over the period of time noted in #3 above, plug in "0, FV"), "FV"

5. Compute payment: "CPT, PMT" $________________

Step Three: Add It Up

Your final step to determine your retirement readiness is to add up your estimated monthly Social Security benefits; your expected monthly pension benefits; and the monthly amount of income your retirement savings is likely to generate. Compare that total to the total that you'll need—the inflation-adjusted monthly income amount in step two.

If the anticipated income is higher than your expected expenses, you're in good shape. Just continue doing whatever you're doing, and you should retire comfortably.

Be sure to check in on your retirement plan every few years, though, just to make sure that you remain on track.

If, on the other hand, your anticipated expenses are higher than your anticipated income, you need to boost your savings or learn to live with less.

Step Four: Determine How Much More to Save

Determine the amount of your monthly shortfall by subtracting your expected resources from the amount you believe you'll need at retirement. Then figure out the amount of money you need to save by punching the numbers you put on each blank, followed by the key listed next to the blank, into your present-value calculator.

1. ________________ (monthly shortfall), "PMT"

2. ___________ (expected monthly interest rate during retirement), "%I"

3. ___________ (number of months that you'll need monthly payments from your savings. This should be roughly the number of years you expect to live after retirement multiplied by 12 months.), "N"

4. ____________ (future value of your savings. If you plan to spend the account to zero over retirement, hit "O, FV"), "FV"

5. Compute present value: "CPT, PV" $______________________

6. Enter the result on line 5 and hit "FV" (because that's the amount you need to have in savings at retirement)

7. ____________ (monthly interest rate you expect to earn on your savings prior to retirement), "%I"

8. ______________ (number of months until retirement), "N"

9. $0____________ (present value of your savings. Enter zero here, because you're already using your current savings), "PV"

10. Compute payment: "CPT, PMT" $__________________

Line 10 shows how much you need to save each month from now until your projected retirement date to meet your goal.

Evaluating Your Savings Options

Now that you know how much you'll have to save, consider how you should do it. There are numerous types of tax-favored savings programs that you can use for retirement—specifically, 401(k) plans, Individual Retirement Accounts (IRAs), Keogh plans, and so-called SEP-IRAs. Some experts also recommend variable annuities, although they usually make sense only when you have exhausted all other retirement savings options.

The Best Option: 401(k)s

Each program has its benefits, detriments, limitations, and exclusions. However, if you have a 401(k) plan available to you—they're offered only through employers—you should seriously consider contributing to it. And you should seriously consider contributing the maximum amount possible—even if that means you may have more than you need in retirement.

Why? Most 401(k) plans allow you to borrow from your own account, at a reasonable interest rate, to finance major events—the purchase of a house, a wedding, sending kids through college, major medical expenses, and so on. Few other retirement programs have this flexibility.

If you put money in an IRA, for example, you get penalized if you want to take your money out before you are fifty-nine and a half. The penalty? You pay tax on the amount withdrawn, plus a 10 percent federal tax penalty. Many states assess penalties too, which often results in people paying taxes equal to half of the amount they've withdrawn. In other words, if you pull $10,000 out of an IRA so that you'll have cash for a down payment on a house, you're likely to pay $5,000 in tax, leaving you with just $5,000 for the down payment.

However, if you have a 401(k) and your plan allows borrowing—most do—you can borrow the down-payment money from your plan. You don't pay taxes and penalties, as long as you agree to pay yourself—your 401(k) account, that is—back, and you continue to make the scheduled payments. However, in most plans, the maximum amount you can borrow from the 401(k) is the lower of $50,000 or 50 percent of your account value.

What makes saving through a 401(k) even more compelling is the fact that most employers "match" a portion of worker's contributions. That supercharges your investment returns.

Consider: If you contribute $2,000 a year to an IRA and earn 8 percent annually on your money, you'll have $98,170 saved in twenty years. If you contribute the same amount to a 401(k) and get a 25 percent employer match, which is fairly common, you'll have

$122,772 in twenty years, assuming that you earn the same rate of interest. That's simply the long-term value of the 25 percent, or $500 annual, employer match.

Better yet, the contributions come out of your paycheck before taxes are computed. The government acts as if you've never earned the money. As a result, you save income taxes on your contributions, which makes it easier to contribute.

To be specific, if you contribute $300 a month—10 percent of your $3,000 monthly salary—and pay 28 percent of your income in federal income taxes, your paycheck decreases by just $216 a month. That's simply because the other $84 would have gone to federal income taxes, which you don't need to pay.

IRAs

If you don't have access to a 401(k) and are employed by a company that does not offer a retirement plan, you can contribute up to $2,000 per year to an Individual Retirement Account and deduct the contributions on your income taxes.

If your company does offer a retirement plan, you can only deduct your IRA contributions if you earn less than certain threshold amounts. Specifically, if you earn less than $25,000 and are single, or earn $40,000 and are married (filing jointly), you can deduct IRA contributions regardless of whether or not your employer offers a retirement plan.

You can deduct a portion of your contributions when you earn up to $35,000 and are single, or you are married and earn up to $50,000 in joint income.

If you earn more and are covered by a company plan you can't deduct your contributions. But the investment earnings that accumulate in the account are tax-free until withdrawn at retirement. That gives you the benefit of having interest compound on money that would otherwise have been paid to the government.

Simple Accounts

Last year's minimum-wage bill created a new type of pension plan for companies with up to one hundred employees. The plan, called "simple," for "savings incentive match plan for employees," can be set up to work like traditional Individual Retirement Accounts—where you have virtually limitless investment choices—or like 401(k) plans, where employees' investment options are limited to a relative handful selected by their employers.

Workers can contribute up to $6,000 per year. Employers, meanwhile, are encouraged to kick in an amount equal to about 3 percent of workers' pay.

Keogh Plans

Keogh plans are for people who are self-employed or who operate small businesses. (SEP-IRAs are being eliminated due to newly passed health-care law.) The advantage to a Keogh is you can contribute up to $30,000 a year and deduct the contributions from your business income.

However, you also have to decide whether to set up the plan as a defined contribution-style program—similar to the 401(k)—or as a defined benefit plan that's more like a traditional pension. There are advantages and disadvantages to both.

If you have your own business, you'd be wise to consult a tax adviser to explain your options and determine which type of plan—and plan "elections"—best suit your needs.

Tax-Deferred Annuities

Contributing to a tax-deferred annuity is similar to contributing to a nondeductible IRA. It only makes sense if you don't have access to any tax-deductible plan and you want to contribute more each year than you can contribute to an IRA.

The investment income that accumulates in the annuity is not taxed until retirement because these plans have a life-insurance component that allows them special tax status.

However, the life-insurance element also poses some risks because most insurance companies have restrictions and impose penalties on anyone who tries to withdraw their money early. The insurance company penalties are added on top of the tax penalties, which can make withdrawals remarkably costly.

In addition, the annual costs of an annuity are usually higher than they'd be on a mutual fund. That reduces your investment earnings over the long haul.

If you choose to invest in a tax-deferred annuity make sure you read and understand the fine print—including how much of a penalty you'll pay if you take your money out early.

The Value of Starting Early

One final word of advice. There's no right time to start saving for retirement. But the earlier you start the less it costs you. That's simply because compound interest works for you in dramatic fashion when you give it lots of time.

Consider four future retirees. They all want to have $1 million in savings by the time they quit work at age sixty-five. They all earn 8 percent annually on their savings.

Sam starts at age twenty-five and contributes $286.45 per month for forty years—a total of $137,496.12. The rest—a tidy $862,503.88—is interest that accumulates over the forty years.

Mike starts at age thirty-five. He has to contribute $670.98 per month—$241,552.48 total—to accumulate the same nest egg.

Joe starts at age forty-five. To get $1 million at retirement, he's got to save $1,697.73 each month—a total of $407,456.18.

Tom starts at age fifty-five. To save $1 million, he must contribute a walloping $5,466.09 per month—a total of $655,931.15. Needless to say, it's unlikely that Tom will ever reach this goal.

Part Six

SURE THINGS: DEATH AND TAXES

I know, it was really rotten to lure you into this section with a come-on like "sure things." Since it's right after saving and investing, you probably thought I was going to give you a hot market tip that would ensure 20 percent returns for life.

No such luck.

In my defense, it has often been said that the only sure things in life are death and taxes. And knowing just a few simple things about both subjects can save you money and make your life—and the lives of your heirs—better, too.

Chapter 23: Prepare to Die

It's unpleasant to think about, but eventually you will die. If you go unprepared, your heirs will suffer. Here's everything you ever needed to know about getting prepared for death. Page 252.

Chapter 24: Taxes

A lot of people deal with taxes just once a year. But if you make tax organization an ordinary part of your routine, you'll save yourself time, trouble, and lots and lots of money. Page 271.

Chapter 23

Prepare to Die

Nobody likes to think about it, but the grim reaper eventually comes for us all. For your family's sake, don't go unprepared.

What the chapter tells you

- Why you need a will
- Low-cost will-writing options
- What probate is and who should avoid it and how
- A few simple ways to avoid estate taxes
- How to help ensure that your mind and body check out at the same time
- What funerals cost and how to manage the expenses

What the chapter shows you

- How to write a simple will
- Where to get a copy of a Living Will or Health Care Power of Attorney
- How to price-check funeral expenses

Where do I start?

Ever wish you could live a fairy-tale existence? Well, it may be too late for you. But if you fail to plan for your eventual death, you could arrange a fairy-tale existence for your heirs.

Consider Cinderella—the beautiful and beloved daughter of a wealthy gentleman. He gives her everything when he is alive. But alas, her father proves to be a poor judge of character, marries poorly, and dies without a will. Cinderella is left to the mercy of her wicked stepmother.

Snow White? Same story, different hair color.

Jack, of beanstalk fame, is driven to a life of crime because he and his widowed mother are starving. And Jack, who clearly can't afford a college education, sells the family's last asset—a cow—for a handful of beans.

In fact, most fairy tales start with a parent who has "suffered an untimely death" and left his or her heirs to fend for themselves. If it wasn't for fairy godmothers, magic beans, or the kindness of a house full of dwarfs, these characters would have been in dire straits.

Because fairy godmothers are tough to come by in the twentieth century, do your family a favor and plan to die—someday.

Who Needs to Plan?

Does everyone need to plan? No. If you have no heirs, no assets, and no children who need guardians, there's no reason for you to waste time. Skip this chapter.

But if you have children, you need a will even if you don't have assets. That's simply because if you die "intestate"—without a will—a judge will parcel out your assets and offspring according to state law. State laws vary, but formulas can't accommodate family idiosyncrasies. In other words, if you have a weird relative that you don't want as your child's guardian; if the best guardian for your children isn't a family member at all; or if you want to choose the particular family member that gets your kids in the event of your death—you need a will.

If you have assets, you may also need an estate plan. If you feel strongly about quality-of-life issues—wouldn't want to live as a vegetable—you may want an advance directive too. And, sooner or later, everybody deals with funeral expenses.

Here's a brief guide on death and dying, broken into sections that indicate up front whether you need to read them or not.

Every Parent Needs a Will

Do you need a will if you are married but don't have children? Only if you don't want to leave the bulk of your estate to your spouse. Most state laws assume you will leave the majority of your assets to your surviving spouse, some to your children (if you have any), and, sometimes, they'll stipulate that smaller portions of your assets should go to parents, nieces, and nephews.

If you know how your state divvies up assets when you die "intestate"—without a will—and you like the state-ordered distribution formula and don't have minor children, there's no need to bother with a will.

However, if you are unfamiliar with the state formula or don't like it, you ought to write a brief will even if you don't have children.

If you have children, you need a will. It doesn't matter whether you are sixteen or sixty. Writing a will doesn't mean you think you're going to die. It means you care enough about your family to want them to be taken care of, regardless of whether you live or die.

Preparing a will is the first step in creating a viable plan that will protect your family if something happens to you. It is easy to do.

There are several ways to prepare one: You can hire an attorney; you can write it yourself; you can have an attorney "review" one you've already written yourself.

Clearly the cheapest option is to write your own. The next step up is to have an attorney review the will you've written—approximate cost $100 to $500, depending on your attorney's hourly rate and whether there are any noteworthy problems. If you have any concerns about the validity of the will you've written yourself, you should have it reviewed.

However, you may be able to have a will written for you almost as cheaply, if you present your attorney with a comprehensive listing of your assets, who they should go to and any limitations on your bequests. Most estate planning and probate attorneys have written so many wills that they have all the standard legal formalities in their office word processors. Plugging your information—as long as it's clear and fairly simple—into the formula could be a one- or two-hour job.

Additionally, if you have complicated wishes or a grand estate, you should hire an attorney, which could cost anywhere from a few hundred to several thousand dollars.

Whether you write your own or hire someone to write your will for you should depend on how comfortable you feel about your ability to legally bequeath your assets to the right people; the amount of assets you have; the amiability of your heirs; the complexity of your family tree; and, to some degree, your age.

If you are young, you'll probably rewrite your will several times before you die. That's simply because you need to revise your will if you have a new child, remarry, or move to another state. And there's a decent chance that one of those three things will happen—maybe several times—before you die. For that reason alone, you may want to go with a less expensive option.

However, be realistic both about your ability and your heirs.

If your kids are at each other's throats over who gets the last muffin at the dinner table, it's not likely that they're going to become big-hearted and generous when it comes to

Wired and Willing to Bequest, Anyone?

A company named Legaldocs has set up a Web site at http://www.legaldocs.com where you can fill out a questionnaire about your life and wishes. Hit "Print." You get a will—for free. All you need to do then is sign it in the presence of two witnesses (non-heirs) and have your heirs sign it as well. It'll take 15 minutes—tops.

dividing up the life-insurance proceeds. Issues involving stepchildren, adopted and foster children, second wives, and charitable bequests also get complicated. In such cases, you probably need a lawyer.

If you can't write a personal letter without having your friends wonder what the heck you were talking about, there's a poor chance that you'll write a valid will.

However, if you are fairly articulate, have simple goals, and all the people you plan to leave money to are nice agreeable folks who don't argue with each other about money, there's no reason you can't do it yourself.

If you can't decide whether to do it yourself or hire a lawyer, take the quiz on page 269. Prepared with the help of several leading attorneys, it's designed to ferret out issues that are likely to cause problems if you do it yourself.

Bequeathing Basics

If you decide to write your own, you should realize that every will should do three things: Divide your assets among your heirs; appoint guardians for minor children (and trustees to watch over money left to minors); and appoint an executor to handle—or simply police—the distribution of your estate.

How you actually put this to paper is up to you and to state law. Some states allow so-called "holographic"—or handwritten—wills. Some acknowledge "statutory" wills, which are fill-in-the-blank forms where all the legal language is done for you. Meanwhile, there are "will kits" that are valid in every state. If you are not sure whether a particular type of will is valid in your state, call your state bar association and ask. If you have a will but move to a new state, make sure you revise it so that it complies with the laws in your home state.

The options in more detail:

Holographic wills. These are the simplest. They're handwritten documents, where you simply write your name, the date, and how you want to handle the distribution of your assets and children in the event of your death. Make sure that you state clearly, somewhere on the document, that this is your will.

You sign the document at the end. You are done. There is no reason for witnesses because your handwriting validates the fact that it was, indeed, you who made these bequests.

Make sure, however, that your handwriting is legible and that your wishes are clear. There's no need to be fancy. You can simply state: "I own X, Y, and Z. My wife, Zena, should get X; my son, Zack, should get Y; and my daughter, Zoe, should get Z."

Do not try to revise the will by scratching things out and adding things in. If the will needs revising, do it over. There's no point in having a will if a judge later invalidates it because it looks as if it's been tampered with.

Statutory wills. Like form letters, the legal language in a statutory will—including the heading "My last will and testament"—is written in for you. All you have to do is fill in the date, the names of your heirs, what you've got, and who it goes to; sign it; and get a couple of friends—preferably friends who are not also heirs—to witness your signature and sign it themselves.

However, you cannot personalize these documents by changing the preprinted form. If the form does not suit your desires, get a different form—most states that allow statutory wills have several formulaic options. You can buy them at stationery and some book stores.

Will kits. Available in a wide variety, there are at least a dozen will kits on the market, ranging in price from about $9.95 to $70.

Some are books; some are computer programs. Many are helpful to the average consumer who needs to be reminded about how state intestacy laws could derail your bequeathing plans. In most cases, wills produced by these kits are legal and valid in all the states where they are sold. But make sure to look for an indication that the book, kit, or software you are buying is designed for your state. That may be as obvious as the title: *The California Will Book*. *Writing a Will in Florida*. Those are good clues. But in other instances, you'll need to look on the back of the book or software to see what states are mentioned—or excluded.

One other shopping tip: Make sure the written will kit you buy isn't just a neatly packaged group of "statutory" wills. If you want a statutory will, you can buy one for $1 to $5, depending on the form, the store, and the state. If you're going to spend extra money on a kit, make sure it makes writing the will easier by giving you directions on what to do and how to do it.

The most expensive of the will kits are the computerized ones, such as WillMaker, a software program produced by Nolo Press in Berkeley, California. However, if you've got a computer, this may be the easiest and most effective way to write your own will. That's simply because the software signals when you've got a sticky issue that may cause your will to be invalidated. The only place WillMaker does not work is in the state of Louisiana, where state probate laws deviate significantly from the norms everywhere else.

The good news on the cost front is these programs can usually be purchased at a discount. So even though the so-called "list" price is $60 or $70, the price in a discount software store is more likely to be half that—anywhere from $30 to $40. Additionally, several people can usually use one program. Indeed, one of the coauthors of the WillMaker program, Steven Elias, suggests that friends and relatives set up "will-writing parties," where you can all write wills, serve as witnesses for each other, and then have a few laughs. (Don't serve alcohol at your party, though. You can't write a valid will when you're drunk.)

To Err Is Human . . .

Some attorneys criticize do-it-yourselfers, saying that they can make important errors and end up with a will that isn't valid. There are, indeed, situations when you shouldn't be writing your own. If you are elderly, wealthy, or have complicated family arrangements—or complicated desires—you should hire an attorney.

Otherwise, the errors are fairly standard and fairly easy to avoid. What are they?

Witnesses. You need witnesses to prove that you were sane and not coerced when you wrote your will. Most states require two adult witnesses—a few prefer three. They must sign the will, date it, and be ready to swear you were sane when you wrote it.

But make sure the witnesses you choose are not also heirs. A will can be successfully challenged if your only witnesses are the people who get all the money. Clearly, they are the ones who are most likely to have coerced you.

The only type of will that does not require the signatures of witnesses is a holographic will. However, having more witnesses than you need never hurts. Having fewer does.

Forgotten heirs. Some states will not allow you to disinherit certain people—current spouses and natural children, for example. You may not want to mention them in your will because you don't want to leave them any money. But, by not mentioning them, the will may be subject to a successful challenge when the unnamed individual claims you lost your marbles because you "forgot" you had another heir. The judge doesn't know that this is your lazy, good-for-nothing relative who never calls or writes and doesn't deserve a dime.

If you want to disinherit someone, be sure to mention them. You may also want to leave them a dollar, dime, or trinket, to ensure that you don't run afoul of inheritance laws that require bequests to members of your immediate family.

Bequeathing spoken-for assets. Your will does not control the distribution of every asset. For example, life-insurance proceeds go directly to the beneficiary named on the policy—not to the person named in your will. If you want to change the beneficiary, you must do so on the policy. Likewise, some assets held in joint tenancy—houses and cars held by husband and wife, for example—generally revert to the joint owner on your death. Some bank accounts are set up with named beneficiaries, too, and are not governed by what is said in your will. If you have assets like these, you can mention them—and who gets them—in your will. But you cannot *change* who gets them by writing a will.

Clarity. One reason some do-it-yourself wills are invalidated is simply because the author's wishes were not clear. Use simple declarative sentences. "I leave my house to Suzie." "I leave my retirement account to John." or "My brokerage account at ______, currently worth $100,000, should be divided equally between Suzie and John." If your bequests are contingent on specific things happening—you only want to leave your children money if they graduate from college, for instance—or are simply too complicated for simple declarative sentences, consider hiring an attorney.

Bequeathing for both of us. You die alone. So even if you've been married for forty years and think you know your spouse's wishes as well as your own, bequest solo. You write a will. Your spouse must write a separate will. If you like, your wills can be mirror images of one another. Nonetheless, they can't be combined into one.

Expecting heirs to share. You may think it's a perfectly great idea to split all your assets fifty-fifty between your two children. Each gets half of the house; half of the car; half of the cash.

While cash is easy to split in two, expecting two people to share valuable, tangible assets is asking a lot—even if they get along. That's simply because your two kids are going to grow up and have two separate families. They may go separate ways. One may want to live in the family house, while the other wants to sell. Or worse, they both may want to live in the family house and, in a Dodge City–style showdown, realize that the house isn't big enough for the two of them.

If your goal is to give each child bequests with the same value, consider other ways to do it. And don't hesitate to chat with your prospective heirs to find out how they feel about what you are planning to do.

Surprises. It's nice, but not necessary, to tell heirs what you plan to leave them. But it's a huge mistake to leave executors and guardians in the dark.

Being a guardian to a minor child—or being the executor of an estate—is a big job. You need to discuss it with the person or people involved to make sure they don't mind taking on the responsibility. The last thing you want is to name a guardian, for example, and have them abdicate the job.

On the other hand, if you have a tight-knit or contentious family, your relatives may fight to get your kids. Guardians named in your will have legal "standing" to request custody of your children, but, if there is a dispute, they may have to go to court to enforce that right. If they're prepared and knowledgeable—have a good grasp on why you've chosen them over others—it's a lot easier to argue the case.

Revising Your Will

Certain big events—the birth of a child; marriage; divorce; or moving across state lines—should trigger a rewrite of your will. With births, divorces, and marriages, the reason you need to revise is clear. You've got new—or fewer—heirs. The reason you need to revise—or at least review—your will when you move across state lines is simply because wills are governed by state law. And probate is handled in the state where you die—not where you are buried or where you once lived.

There is a national effort afoot to change will rules in a way that would allow a will written in any state to be valid in any other state. However, for now, the will that you wrote in California may not be valid in New York. Think of it like you consider any other new item on your list of things to do: "Check out local schools; look into state probate laws to see if my will is still valid . . . "

Understanding Probate

When you die, your assets generally go into a sort of legal limbo called probate.

The process boils down to this: Your executor hires an attorney who files your will with the local probate court. The court sends notices to your creditors saying that you've died and that your estate is in the process of being settled. Through a series of legal hearings, the court "proves" the validity of your will, pays your debts, and distributes what's left over to your heirs.

The benefit of probate is that it settles things with finality. Once it's done, creditors cannot go after your relatives for some debt that you failed to pay. It also settles disputes between heirs.

But there are two problems with probate: It's time consuming and it's expensive.

Simple, uncontested wills typically take between nine months and a year to clear probate, attorneys say. If there are disputes—either between creditors or heirs—it can take far longer.

In the meantime, your estate is paying the probate attorney and, possibly, the executor too. How much?

That depends on whether you are paying by the hour or paying according to a formula set up in state law. If your executor does not think to hire the probate attorney on an hourly basis, it's likely the fees will be paid according to the formula, which is designed to set "maximum" probate fees. But, as with many such things, the "maximums" have become the norm and are frequently applied to even the simplest case. Meanwhile, when the estate is unusually difficult to probate—because of disputes between heirs or creditors—judges may award "extraordinary" fees too—making the maximum fees seem paltry.

What are the maximums? They vary by state law. However, in California, probate attorneys can collect fees amounting to 4 percent of the first $15,000 in probated assets; 3 percent of the next $85,000; 2 percent of the next $900,000; and 1 percent of amounts over $1 million.

Technically, the executor is entitled to the same fees. However, executors who are also heirs often don't take the fees. Why? It's better to inherit money tax-free than collect executors' fees, which are taxed just like any other earned income.

One other thing that some people don't like about probate: It's a public process, which means anyone who wants to look up the court records can see just how much money you had and who got it.

Avoiding Probate

If you want to avoid probate, there are a few ways to do it. You can make sure your assets are in nonprobated forms—life insurance, joint-tenancy and "trust"-style bank and brokerage accounts that name beneficiaries. You can give almost all your assets away before you die—assuming you know when you'll die. (Most states don't require probate when the estate's assets are less than certain threshold amounts—such as $50,000 or $60,000.) Or you can set up a living trust.

Living trusts are, by far, the most popular option, partly because they allow you to handle all assets in a single way and partly because they do a bit more than just distribute your stuff when you die. They also help you handle possible incapacity.

Living Trust Basics

A living trust is a three-part document.

The first part of the trust document deals with the distribution of your assets while you are alive and healthy. That may be as simple as naming yourself trustee and giving yourself the right to distribute your assets as you like.

The second part of the document sets up a successor trustee who can handle your financial affairs if you fall into a coma or are otherwise rendered incapable of handling these affairs yourself. The trust can give this successor total discretion or it may impose limitations on what the successor trustee can do.

The third part of the document serves as a will and provides for the distribution of your assets and the appointment of guardians for your minor children after you are gone.

By itself, a living trust does nothing to alleviate estate taxes, which are assessed on estates of more than $600,000. However, at death, you can have assets that are in a living trust automatically transferred into a so-called "bypass trust," which helps married couples pass up to $1.2 million to their heirs estate–tax free. (Correctly drafted, a will can do the same thing.)

Generally speaking, living trusts are revocable, which means you can change or cancel them while you are alive and competent. But they become irrevocable at your death.

To be effective, the trust must own all of your probatable assets. If it doesn't, your heirs could end up dealing with trust administrators *and* probate authorities—a thoroughly unpleasant prospect. Since some people don't remember to transfer all their assets to the trust, many attorneys suggest that you execute a so-called "pour-over" will when you establish the living trust. The pour-over will will transfer any forgotten assets into the trust at your death.

The disadvantage of creating a living trust is mainly financial. They're more expensive to create than a simple will. It usually costs between $500 and $3,000 to set up a fairly simple living trust.

Additionally, some consumers say it's a bit more difficult to buy and sell property that's in a living trust than property that's owned in your own name. That's less true today than it was several years ago, bankers acknowledge, but some are still reluctant to make a home loan when the real estate is owned by a trust rather than you.

If you think the cost or inconvenience of probate would cause a real hardship for your heirs, consider setting up a living trust. If not, don't bother.

If You Are Rich, Cope with Estate Taxes

If you and your spouse have less than $600,000 in assets, you don't need to worry about federal estate taxes. Your heirs won't pay a penny in federal estate taxes when you die.

Additionally, if you are married and plan to leave your assets to your spouse, who is a U.S. citizen, you also can avoid federal estate taxes at your death. There's an unlimited marital deduction for estate tax purposes that enables your spouse to get all your combined assets, tax-free, at your death.

However, if your spouse is not a U.S. citizen, or you have more than $600,000 in assets, your heirs may well be subject to onerous estate taxes that can consume more than 50 percent of the money you left them.

Now, before you gasp and run to a tax accountant or attorney, realize that heirs are not usually going to be undone by estate taxes. They're getting a bequest—found money—from you. Estate taxes only determine the size of this bequest.

Nonetheless, if you are given the choice of leaving more money to your relatives or leaving money to the federal government, you are likely to prefer to give the money to your family.

If that's true, and you've got a lot to give, consider a bit of estate tax planning.

What can you do?

Annual gifts. You can give an unlimited number of people up to $10,000 a year while you are alive, without triggering estate or gift taxes. In addition, you can pay for a child or a grandchild's health care or education without running afoul of the tax code.

In other words, if you have five children and ten grandchildren, you can give each one $10,000 a year—a total of $150,000 annually—until you run out of money. Or you can send all ten of those grandchildren to Ivy League schools and pay their tuition, without facing gift or estate taxes. If you are married, both you and your spouse can give these annual gifts, doubling the amounts you are able to give away without triggering gift or estate taxes.

Bypass trust. If you don't want to give your money away before you die, but you and your spouse have combined assets worth more than $600,000, you might consider a bypass trust.

A bypass trust, which is also sometimes called an A-B Trust, starts out as a revocable trust that splits into two parts—an "A" part and a "B" part—when the first spouse dies.

The dead spouse's portion of the trust takes $600,000 of the couple's combined assets and becomes irrevocable. Eventually, these assets will be given to the dead spouse's chosen heirs. However, while the other spouse is still alive, the money stays in the trust. He or she collects the interest or investment income on the $600,000 in the dead spouse's portion of the trust. When the surviving spouse dies, the assets in both parts of the trust go to the couple's heirs.

In effect, this trust simply creates two separate estates, so that each of you can give $600,000 to your heirs, without triggering federal estate taxes. But it allows you to delay the first bequest until the surviving spouse is sure not to need the money.

Family limited partnerships. If you have substantial assets that require some management and that throw off income—such as rental real estate—you may want to set up a family limited partnership. These essentially work like any other limited partnership—there's a general partner, who manages the assets and distributes the investment income—and there are limited partners, who collect income off the investment.

For estate tax purposes, they're attractive because you can set yourself up as the general "managing" partner, and then systematically give shares in the partnership to your heirs. You don't lose control over how the assets are managed, because you are in charge of managing them.

In addition, when shares in this partnership are valued for tax purposes you're likely to get a break. That's because illiquid—that means hard-to-sell—"minority" investments, such as shares in limited partnerships, are arguably worth less than the pro-rata value of the underlying assets. It's an arcane concept—and one that has little application for most of the world's inhabitants—but if you have a lot of investment real estate or other assets that you're considering putting into a family limited partnership, ask your tax accountant to explain.

The bad news is that family limited partnerships are complicated, only work for certain assets, and cost a small fortune—often more than $10,000—to set up. They're only worth considering if you have a lot of income-producing assets and don't mind paying some legal and accounting fees to protect them from taxes.

Life insurance. If you have a small business that would be devastated by the cost of paying estate taxes—or by delays in paying bills caused by probate—you might be wise to consider what insurance agents call the "1 percent solution."

In a nutshell, you buy a life-insurance policy that you put into an irrevocable life-insurance trust. When you die, the proceeds of the policy pay your estate taxes instead of your heirs.

It's important to stress that this does not *save* taxes. It provides the money to *pay* taxes.

In other words, you are paying *your* money today to save *somebody else* tax payments in the future. That's a reasonable idea only in fairly unusual circumstances. Nonetheless, if these circumstances pertain to you, it can be helpful to your heirs.

The cost varies based on your age, assets, and insurer. The older you are, the more you pay in annual premiums—essentially because the insurance company will have fewer years to invest your premium and allow it to grow.

For example, a fifty-year-old who is buying insurance to pay tax on a $2 million estate might pay $20,000 a year, while a seventy-year-old would pay nearly four times that amount. (That premium payment, however, is low because the insurer that offered it assumed a fairly high investment return. Often the cost is higher.)

Maintaining Quality in Life: Advance Directives

The tragic stories of two young women have brought much needed attention to the fact that medical advances have made it possible to extend your breathing long after the quality of your life is gone.

Karen Ann Quinlan, whose 1976 case launched national debate over the right to die, was kept alive in a coma for ten years through the use of mechanical life-support systems.

Nancy Cruzan, who died in 1990, was left in a permanent vegetative state following a 1983 auto accident. She was kept alive through intravenous feeding for more than seven years. For five of those seven years, her grief-stricken family was forced to battle in court for the right to withdraw the feeding tube and let Nancy die.

If you don't want to be kept alive at a time when your brain has ceased to function—or when the simple act of breathing causes excruciating pain—you should consider an advance directive.

Advance directives are legal documents that spell out for your doctor the point at which he or she should stop trying to cure what ails you. They come in two forms—the well-known living will and the less-understood, but often more valuable, health-care power of attorney.

Living wills usually stipulate that doctors should not treat you to simply prolong your life when the diagnosis is terminal. It can also stop treatment under specific circumstances that you name.

The health-care power of attorney gives a spouse, child, relative, or friend the legal right to make life-and-death medical decisions on your behalf. If you like, you can stipulate in the document how much leeway they're allowed, ranging from total to partial discretion based on specific ailments and expected outcomes. They're often preferable to a living will because it's nearly impossible to anticipate in advance every conceivable circumstance of what could happen and how a doctor should respond. This gives someone you love and trust the ability to make the decision that he or she believes would be best for you.

Notably, if you are able to think and communicate clearly, you have the right to refuse medical treatment. However, if you are incapacitated—in a coma or unable to speak because of a stroke or cognitive ailment—another person must make the decision for you. Without a clear expression of your wishes, a doctor may feel compelled to treat. And, without an advance directive to back them up, a friend or a relative may be powerless to stop treatment—even if he or she knows you wouldn't want it.

Deciding to sign an advance directive is a personal decision, not a financial one. It should be considered only if you can conceptualize situations where you would not want to be kept alive. However, you should know that it does have financial implications.

Aggressive life-prolonging treatments are among the most expensive procedures in medicine. Partly as a result, roughly one-quarter of your lifetime medical costs are rung up in the final twelve months of life—and most of that is in the last month of life.

That's incidental if both you and the quality of your life can be maintained. Unfortunately, sometimes, your life can be saved but the quality of your life cannot.

It's worth mentioning that not all states officially recognize living wills, but they all do recognize your right to refuse treatment. Consequently, doctors will generally follow the wishes expressed in a living will—whether officially sanctioned by the state or not—as long as those wishes are clear.

Making your personal wishes clear is important because the living wills that most people sign—they are forms that you can pick up at most nursing homes and at many hospitals—are vague. They don't specify what "terminal" illness means. They don't specifically say in what circumstances you would want a doctor to withdraw oxygen, food, and hydration devices. In many states, withdrawal of intravenous feeding tubes requires specific consent.

In other words, if you choose the living will, write on the form. Modify it. Make your personal wishes clear. And make sure your doctor knows about the living will and agrees to carry out the wishes you've expressed in it. A recent survey indicated that the vast majority of living wills written are ignored because the attending physician is unaware of its existence.

Where can you get a living will?

Most hospitals and nursing homes give them away. Some states also have nonprofit groups or government offices dedicated to issues of the aging that can provide the forms for free.

You can also buy them at many stationery stores—the ones that stock other forms, such as real estate trust deeds. You can buy them from the American Association of Retired Persons, too.

One other source:

Choice in Dying offers single copies of state-tailored living wills and health-care power of attorney forms for $3.50. Write to: Choice in Dying, Box 397, Newark, NJ 07101-9792. Or call: 800-989-WILL.

Eventually, Somebody Must Deal with Funeral Expenses

Nobody wants to price-check while grieving. But you should know that funeral expenses are stunning—the average funeral costs roughly $5,000 these days. More important, though, the cost varies dramatically from one mortuary to the next.

Indeed, the American Association of Retired Persons surveyed several dozen funeral directors in six major metropolitan areas to determine the cost of a standard funeral. The results: The cost of identical services varied by as much as $2,000 at different funeral homes in the same city. Shopping around can save you a bundle.

Those who want—or need—to cut costs further can do so by watching the services that they buy. Only a few of the costs of a traditional burial are mandatory. Many others are bells and whistles that can certainly make the process more elegant, but are not, in any way, required. You can also save money by using a less traditional process. Cremations, for example, generally cost about one-fifth the cost of a burial.

If you can handle the idea of shopping around at a really miserable time, there's good news. It's easy. Federal law requires funeral homes to readily provide price information in person or over the phone. The only trick is asking the right questions.

To start, determine whether you want a traditional burial or a cremation. Also consider whether religious or personal considerations would dictate a particular choice of a funeral home or cemetery. If so, you don't need to waste time shopping around. To keep costs down, simply buy fewer services or less expensive options.

Unless the funeral home you choose is connected to a cemetery, realize that you'll probably have to buy funeral and burial services separately.

Both funeral costs and burial costs are derived by adding together numerous items, many of which are optional. You can cut out optional items—ranging from cosmetology to flowers and music—if they don't appeal to you or you can't afford them.

On the funeral side, the biggest expenditure is usually the casket—prices range from roughly $250 to $25,000. The funeral home will charge separately for use of the mortuary, services of the funeral director, flowers, music, transportation, preparation of the body, embalming, and obtaining permits and death certificates.

Burial costs include fees for the grave, crypt, or "niche." There may also be a charge for an "outer burial container," for opening and closing the grave, for the marker, and possibly, for recording where the body is.

Some cemeteries and mortuaries offer prepaid funeral arrangements, too. But before you agree to one, be sure to check out the establishment thoroughly. Some consumers have complained that services provided were much less than what was promised to the parents, who paid to have themselves buried. In other instances funeral homes have gone bankrupt. Often, as unpleasant as it may be, the best option is to leave the planning until it is needed.

Funeral Expenses

Mortuary

	____________ (name of mortuary)	____________ (name of mortuary)
Casket	$____________	$____________
Transportation (deceased)	$____________	$____________
Use of facilities	$____________	$____________
Funeral director	$____________	$____________
Music	$____________	$____________
Flowers	$____________	$____________
Death certificate	$____________	$____________
Permits	$____________	$____________
Limousine (to transport relatives to grave site)	$____________	$____________
Other	$____________	$____________
	$____________	$____________
Total funeral	$____________	$____________

Burial Expenses

Cemetery

	__________ (name of cemetery)	__________ (name of cemetery)
Grave/crypt/niche	$__________	$__________
Outer burial container	$__________	$__________
Open/close grave marker	$__________	$__________
Urn (for cremations)	$__________	$__________
Recording fees	$__________	$__________
Other	$__________	$__________
	$__________	$__________
Total burial	$__________	$__________

Will Quiz

Do you need help writing your will, or can you do it yourself? Take the quiz and see.

1. My total assets, including cash, life insurance, securities, equity in real estate, and personal effects, amount to (a) less than $100,000; (b) between $100,000 and $600,000; (c) more than $600,000.

2. My family, to whom I plan to leave the bulk of my estate, consists of (a) my spouse and our kids; (b) my current spouse and kids from both marriages; (c) my spouse, former spouse(s), stepchildren, adopted children, foster children, nieces, nephews, cousins, and grandkids.

3. I would like my will to (a) pass my assets to my family and appoint appropriate guardians for my minor children; (b) pass my assets to family, friends, and charity, and appoint guardians for my children; (c) only pass my assets to beneficiaries who continue to do what I want them to do after I'm gone.

4. I have a family business. (a) No. (b) Not yet, but I plan to start one. (c) Yes.

5. My assets are primarily in (a) cash and liquid securities, such as publicly traded stocks; (b) mixed among stocks, bonds, and residential real estate; (c) real estate, minority interests in partnerships, stocks, bonds, and investments in closely held companies.

6. I hate the idea of my heirs paying tax or probate fees on the money I leave them. (a) No. (b) It doesn't bother me as long as the fees and taxes aren't excessive. (c) Yes. I'll spend what it takes now to make sure my heirs don't have to pay later.

7. My heirs are (a) all responsible people who get along with one another and who are likely to agree to my wishes; (b) some of my heirs are responsible, others are minor children whose ability to handle bequests hasn't been tested; (c) flakes, incapacitated, or reasonable people who simply cannot get along.

8. I would like to set up a trust that will distribute (a) money to my children when they are older; (b) money to charity; (c) income on some assets to my spouse, and equity in those assets to charity or to children.

9. I have used estate-planning or asset-protection strategies with some of my assets. (a) No. (b) Not yet, but I may. (c) Yes.

10. I am uncertain about whether I can create a valid will using a will kit or form and would feel more comfortable if I hired a professional to do it for me. (a) No. (b) It wouldn't make me more comfortable, but my spouse prefers it. (c) Yes.

Scoring: Give yourself one point for each "a" answer; three points for each "b" answer; and ten points for each "c" response.

Key

10–18: You are the perfect candidate for a do-it-yourself will. Your family situation is fairly simple. Your aims are straightforward and your assets may be substantial, but not enough to force you to worry about estate taxes or complicated asset "valuation" issues. But be sure to review your will in a few years, particularly if your assets, personal aims, or family situation changes.

19–49: You are on the cusp—you have a few tricky issues to deal with, but if you're clever and confident, you can probably handle them with a will-writing computer program. If you are scoring near the top of this range, however, you ought to consider having an attorney at least review the will you've written. If, on the other hand, you're in this range mainly because your estate is worth more than $600,000, consider talking to a tax adviser or estate planner.

50–100: Hire an attorney. You either have complex desires, an extended family, or so much in the way of assets that you'd be making a big mistake to go it alone. When considering who to hire, get referrals from friends or the state bar association; then interview potential candidates. The attorney should be able to provide a good estimate of costs and how long it will take to write your will. Some will also provide "engagement letters" that spell out, in writing, what you've agreed to.

Chapter 24

Taxes

You have to pay income taxes. But, if you're smart, you don't pay a dime more than necessary. How do you make sure you don't? Organize.

What the chapter tells you

- Proper organization will ensure you get every deduction.
- It will help you win if you're ever audited.
- It can save you money if you have your taxes prepared.
- It can boost the deductions you get from giving personal items to charity.

What the chapter shows you

- How to do it

Where do I start?

Does spring give you the willies just because that's when taxes are due? Do you wonder whether you're getting the most from your deductions? Are you frightened by the thought of an IRS audit? Do you pay a tax accountant a fortune to prepare your return? If, so there's one way to solve all your tax-related problems: Get organized.

Getting organized is the only way to ensure you'll get every deduction you're due. It's also the best way to prevail in an IRS audit. And it's a great way to save money when getting your taxes professionally prepared.

If you do your own taxes, good organization will also make the process incredibly less irritating. For the first time, you'll actually have all the information you need in one place, at one time. It can transform an all-night return-filing fiasco into a fairly mundane, one-hour job.

The following pages are a modified version of the tax organizers that accountants send to their clients. The organizer has been modified for three simple reasons:

First, it's been simplified to cater to a middle-income reader who doesn't have income from a farm, a foreign corporation, partnerships, estates, trusts, or S-Corporations. It's also *sans* questions about specialized deductions—like writing off part of your home as an office or depreciating business properties.

Could you have these issues and still be reading this book? Sure. But if you do, there are sophisticated strategies that can save you money—not to mention serious tax hazards you'll need to sidestep. You need help from a tax professional, not a book.

Secondly, this organizer includes explanations of the various items you're asked to record.

Whether you prepare your own return or pay someone to prepare it for you, you need to know a bit about the process. These explanations should provide a glimpse of what you need to know.

Finally, though most tax organizers need to be filled out just once annually, this one ought to be used throughout the year to record certain continuing expenses, such as charitable contributions.

The reason is simple. You may otherwise forget.

If you're like most people, some of the money you give to charity is given in cash. You may give a cash donation to the Huntington Library when you visit, for example. You may sponsor a student at the charity jog-a-thon or give cash to a kid collecting for a nonprofit at the door. If you don't remember it, you don't deduct it.

Another significant segment of your charitable contributions may be made in personal items—used books, clothes, and furniture. Although the charity will give you something of a form-letter receipt, it's up to you to establish what the property was and what it was worth. For many people, properly recording and valuing these items can mean hundreds of dollars in deductions. The records will also help you substantiate your deductions if you're ever audited.

Whenever possible, get receipts—even for the smallest deductible expenses. File them away and keep them for four years. That ensures you'll have what you need if you're audited by your state tax authorities or the federal government.

If you write off the business use of your car for work, keep a running tally of your mileage and expenses—but not here. You'll want a separate notebook or calendar in your car, so that it's convenient to jot down the miles on the odometer before and after a business trip. At the end of the year, list the totals in the proper section here.

Avid gamblers should track gambling expenses throughout the year too. Why? If you strike it rich, these records will save you some money. That's simply because you have to pay tax on gambling winnings, but you can deduct gambling losses that are incurred in the same year from the taxable amount. Unfortunately, many gamblers remember neither their winnings nor their losses at tax time. But when they win big, the casino, track, or other gaming establishment reports the gain to the Internal Revenue Service. If you can't substantiate offsetting losses, you're taxed on the entire jackpot. Keep gambling receipts, if you have any. Or simply keep records of the date, where you gambled, and how much you made (or lost) when you get home.

Finally, if you earn less than about $25,000 and have children under the age of eighteen, you would also be wise to keep their school records—report cards and enrollment forms—here too. The reason: The IRS is cracking down on fraud in the earned income tax credit program, which provides lucrative tax breaks for low-income working families.

As a result, the agency is asking parents to provide proof that they not only have children, but that these children live with them and are supported by them. In some cases, that's caused tax refunds to be delayed for months while parents scramble to find birth certificates and school records.

The millions of parents who legitimately claim this credit can save themselves time and trouble with the equivalent of a preemptive strike. If you claim the credit, send a copy (never send originals) of your child's birth certificate and report card with the return. The IRS doesn't require it, but it may head off questions that could delay your refund.

One more thing: This worksheet won't ask for information on how much income you earned from wages, interest, or dividends. Nor are you expected to record how much you have already paid in federal, state, and local taxes through employee withholding. It doesn't have a section to list mortgage interest expenses, either.

You will receive statements—W-2s, 1099s, 1098s, and so on—from your employer, bank, and brokerage firm that will give you this information. As long as you keep these statements where you can find them later, there's no reason to waste time writing these things down.

The worksheet does, however, ask you for information about pension distributions even though you'll get a statement from the IRA or pension plan administrator if you withdraw funds. That's simply because these amounts are taxable only if you fail to roll them into another IRA within sixty days. You must note the distribution on your tax return *and* note what portion was rolled into another IRA within the allotted time. The graph gives you a spot to show where the funds went and when. That's information you'll want to include with your tax return.

To the worksheets.

Tax Organizer

Personal Information

Taxpayers are now expected to include the name and Social Security numbers of every person listed on their returns. If these Social Security numbers are not included or are not correct, the IRS is likely to disallow any deductions claimed for your dependents.

In the following spaces, list the members of your household—you, your spouse, and all your dependents—and their Social Security numbers.

Your dependents can include children, stepchildren, adopted children, and foster children who are under the age of nineteen (or full-time students under the age of twenty-four), provided that they live with you and you pay more than half of their support.

You can sometimes claim dependents who don't live with you, if, for example, a divorce decree stipulates that you get the dependency deductions for your children even though they live with your ex-spouse.

Furthermore, if you provide the bulk of financial support for a parent, grandparent, sibling, step-relative, in-law; or aunt, uncle, niece, or nephew (who is related to you by blood), you may also be able to claim them as dependents. However, a nonrelative, no matter how dependent on you for support, cannot be claimed as a dependent for tax purposes.

The 1040 form requires that you show how the dependent is related to you and what his age is, but there's no reason to list the relationship here unless you are handing this form to a stranger to prepare your return. This listing is simply aimed at giving you the one bit of information that most taxpayers have trouble remembering at filing time—everybody's Social Security numbers.

Name______________________________SSN#_____-____-_______

Name______________________________SSN#_____-____-_______

Name________________________________SSN#______-____-________

Name________________________________SSN#______-____-________

Name________________________________SSN#______-____-________

Name________________________________SSN#______-____-________

Name________________________________SSN#______-____-________

Name________________________________SSN#______-____-________

Name________________________________SSN#______-____-________

Name________________________________SSN#______-____-________

Child Care

If you must pay for child care so that both parents can work (or because one parent is working and the other is in college or is disabled) you may be entitled to child-care tax breaks. To claim them, you must have wage income, one or more children under the age of thirteen (or who are disabled and incapable of self-care), and child-care expenses. Your care provider—whether baby-sitter, nanny, day-care center, or preschool—must also provide you with his or her Social Security or employer identification number. That information must be provided to either the IRS or your employer, depending which child-care tax break you claim.

These tax breaks can come in two forms. One, the child-care tax credit, is claimed on your tax return. For anyone earning more than $28,000 annually, the maximum credit will amount to $960 for two or more children; $480 for one.

The other, a dependent-care account, is offered through employers and simply reduces the amount of taxable income you report. It is, by far, the more lucrative tax break for middle-income parents.

You can contribute up to $5,000 of your pretax wages to the account. That money is then used to pay your day-care provider. Because the money is deducted from your wages before taxes are taken out, you save income taxes on the $5,000 as well as Social Security and Medicare taxes. That's a substantial savings. For someone in the 28 percent federal income tax bracket, that translates into a total tax savings in excess of $1,700 annually. (These accounts can also be used to pay care expenses for a disabled spouse.)

There are some disadvantages to these accounts too. Specifically, once you set your contribution level for the year, you usually can't change it or withdraw money for anything other than dependent care. If you contribute $2,000 to the account and only use $1,500, you lose the other $500. So estimate your expenses carefully, but don't hesitate to sign up. (For more information, see Chapter 14, "Employee Benefits," page 136.)

About 51 percent of the nation's big companies offer these accounts, according to the benefit consulting firm of Foster Higgins. But, inexplicably, only a small fraction of eligible workers use them. If you're not certain whether your company offers one, ask. It can save you a fortune.

If you don't have access to a dependent-care account and you meet the other requirements, you'll claim the child-care credit. To do so, you need to list the name of your child-care provider, his or her Social Security or employer identification number, and how much you paid. (This credit can't be used to offset private school tuition. Once the kids are in first grade, you only get child-care tax breaks if you pay for after- or before-school care in order to work.)

Care provider: ______________________________

Address: ______________________________

____

SSN or EIN#: ______________________________

Number of children cared for: ______________________________

Annual cost of day care: ______________________________

Business Expenses, a.k.a. Miscellaneous Itemized Deductions

Employees can deduct unreimbursed business expenses that exceed 2 percent of adjusted gross income. In other words, if your AGI was $10,000 and you had unreimbursed business expenses of $500, you could deduct $300 of the cost—the portion that exceeds 2 percent (in this case $200) of your earnings.

If you are self-employed or have some self-employment income, your business expenses are subtracted directly from your self-employment income. They are not subject to the so-called 2 percent floor.

However, some major expenses may have to be depreciated—deducted over time, rather than in one lump sum.

Be wary, however. If you have self-employment income, you probably also owe employment taxes—Social Security and Medicare payroll taxes on your net earnings from self-employment. These taxes amount to about 15 percent of your income from self-employment.

In addition, self-employment income is widely considered to be an audit trigger. You'll need to keep good records. And you should realize that if you lose money from your business three years in a row, the IRS may argue that your business is a hobby, rather than a for-profit enterprise. If it's a hobby, you can only write off the losses to the extent that you have income from that "hobby."

If you have any questions about whether your after-work enterprise should be considered a business, consult a tax professional or ask the IRS. The IRS has volumes of free publications that they'll provide to anyone who asks, including one that explains the difference between business and hobby income. To get it, call: 800-TAX-FORM (800-829-3676).

Business Publications (books, subscriptions, magazines necessary for work)

Name:______________________________ Cost:__________

Name:______________________________ Cost:__________

Name:______________________________ Cost:__________

Name:______________________________ Cost:__________

Name:______________________________ Cost:__________

*Meals, Entertainment**

Entertained:______________________________________

When: ____/_____/_____ Why:___________________________

____

____

**Only 50% of the cost of meals and entertainment expenses are deductible. You must retain receipts and records indicating who was entertained, when, where and the business purpose of the meeting.*

Entertained: ____

When: ____/_____/_____ Why: ___________________________

____

____

Entertained: ____

When: ____/_____/_____ Why: ___________________________

____

____

Entertained: ____

When: ____/_____/_____ Why: ___________________________

____

____

Entertained: ____

When: ____/_____/_____ Why: ___________________________

____

____

Office Supplies and Equipment

Item: ______________________________ Cost: __________

Item: ______________________________ Cost: __________

Item:__________________________________ Cost:____________

Item:__________________________________ Cost:____________

Item:__________________________________ Cost:____________

Item:__________________________________ Cost:____________

Auto Expense: ____

Tax advice and preparation fees: ____________________________

Fees for investment counsel: _______________________________

Professional Dues

Organization:___________________________ Cost:____________

Organization:___________________________ Cost:____________

Organization:___________________________ Cost:____________

Organization:___________________________ Cost:____________

Employment-seeking expenses: _____________________________

Safe deposit box (for securities storage):______________________

Other (specify): ____

____

____

____

____

Medical

You can deduct medical expenses to the extent they exceed 7.5 percent of your adjusted gross income—a threshold that's too high for most families to meet. However, if you earned little and were sick a lot, it may be worth gathering together your medical records to see if you can clear the bar—particularly if you don't have health insurance.

What constitutes a deductible medical expense?

Doctor's bills (unreimbursed portion): ____________________

Hospital payments (unreimbursed): ____________________

Prescription drugs (unreimbursed): ____________________

Premiums for medical insurance: ____________________

Dental expenses: ____________________

Medical supplies (crutches/wheelchairs): ____________________

Other unreimbursed medical: ____________________

____

Charitable Contributions

You don't *need* receipts for small, cash contributions (but receipts never hurt.) However, if you give $250 or more at any one time, make sure you get and retain a letter of acknowledgment from the charity.

If you don't have proof of the contribution—which includes mention of whether you received anything of value in return—the IRS now has the power to disallow the deduction.

Cash Gifts

Recipient: ____________________ Amount: __________ Date: ________

Recipient: ____________________ Amount: __________ Date: ________

Recipient: ____________________ Amount: __________ Date: ________

Recipient:____________________ Amount:__________ Date:________

Recipient:____________________ Amount:__________ Date:________

Recipient:____________________ Amount:__________ Date:________

Recipient:____________________ Amount:__________ Date:________

Recipient:____________________ Amount:__________ Date:________

Noncash

To accurately estimate the value of personal items—clothes, books, shoes, furniture, and so forth—contributed to charity, detail approximately what you paid for the item new and what condition it was in when given away. You can reasonably expect to take a deduction equivalent to 10 to 50 percent of the item's original cost, based on when the item was purchased, its condition when donated, and the market value of similar items today. (Actually, you may be able to deduct a higher percentage if the item is in particularly pristine condition. There are no hard and fast rules in this area. Your estimate must be merely "reasonable.")

If you're uncertain about the value of these contributions—but give a substantial amount of personal items away—it may be worth a trip to a thrift store to see how charities price the items you give them. If you contribute any one item of great value, or a group of related items such as clothing or furniture—worth $5,000 or more—you'll need to get a professional appraisal.

Notably, this listing is for your records. It is designed to save you money by reminding you of the actual value of what you're giving away—particularly if you give away sacks full of clothing, furniture, and other personal items each year. However, unless you are audited, you do not need to provide it to the IRS. The IRS requires a separate form (for noncash contributions exceeding $500) that can be completed with significantly less detail.

If your noncash contributions are inconsequential—a few shirts and a pair of shoes here and there—don't bother with the chart. Filling it out would simply be more trouble than it's worth.

Recipient:____

Valuation method: New or nearly new, deduct 50 percent of cost; Excellent condition, 40 percent; very good condition, 30 percent; good, 20 percent; fair, 10 percent. (If an item is in poor condition, toss it. Even charities don't want junk.)

Item:__________Cost:$________Condition:_______Deduction:$________

Item:__________Cost:$________Condition:_______Deduction:$________

Item:__________Cost:$________Condition:_______Deduction:$________

Item:__________Cost:$________Condition:_______Deduction:$________

Item:__________Cost:$________Condition:_______Deduction:$________

Item:__________Cost:$________Condition:_______Deduction:$________

Item:__________Cost:$________Condition:_______Deduction:$________

Item:__________Cost:$________Condition:_______Deduction:$________

Item:__________Cost:$________Condition:_______Deduction:$________

Item:__________Cost:$________Condition:_______Deduction:$________

Item:__________Cost:$________Condition:_______Deduction:$________

Item:__________Cost:$________Condition:_______Deduction:$________

Item:__________Cost:$________Condition:_______Deduction:$________

Item:__________Cost:$________Condition:_______Deduction:$________

Item:__________Cost:$________Condition:_______Deduction:$________

Recipient:____

Valuation method: New or nearly new, deduct 50 percent of cost; Excellent condition, 40 percent; very good condition, 30 percent; good, 20 percent; fair, 10 percent. (If an item is in poor condition, toss it. Even charities don't want junk.)

Item:__________Cost:$________Condition:_______Deduction:$________

Item:__________Cost:$________Condition:_______Deduction:$________

Item:__________Cost:$________Condition:_______Deduction:$________

Item:__________Cost:$________Condition:_______Deduction:$________

Item:__________Cost:$________Condition:_______Deduction:$________

Item:__________Cost:$________Condition:_______Deduction:$________

Item:__________Cost:$________Condition:_______Deduction:$________

Item:__________Cost:$________Condition:_______Deduction:$________

Item:__________Cost:$________Condition:_______Deduction:$________

Item:__________Cost:$________Condition:_______Deduction:$________

Item:__________Cost:$________Condition:_______Deduction:$________

Item:__________Cost:$________Condition:_______Deduction:$________

Item:__________Cost:$________Condition:_______Deduction:$________

Item:__________Cost:$________Condition:_______Deduction:$________

Item:__________Cost:$________Condition:_______Deduction:$________

Recipient:____

Valuation method: New or nearly new, deduct 50 percent of cost; Excellent condition, 40 percent; very good condition, 30 percent; good, 20 percent; fair, 10 percent. (If an item is in poor condition, toss it. Even charities don't want junk.)

Item:__________Cost:$________Condition:_______Deduction:$________

Item:__________Cost:$________Condition:_______Deduction:$________

Item:__________Cost:$________Condition:_______Deduction:$________

Item:__________Cost:$________Condition:_______Deduction:$________

Item:__________Cost:$________Condition:_______Deduction:$________

Item:__________Cost:$________Condition:_______Deduction:$________

Item:__________Cost:$________Condition:_______Deduction:$________

Item:__________Cost:$________Condition:_______Deduction:$________

Item:__________Cost:$________Condition:_______Deduction:$________

Item:__________Cost:$________Condition:_______Deduction:$________

Item:__________Cost:$________Condition:_______Deduction:$________

Item:__________Cost:$________Condition:_______Deduction:$________

Item:__________Cost:$________Condition:_______Deduction:$________

Item:__________Cost:$________Condition:_______Deduction:$________

Item:__________Cost:$________Condition:_______Deduction:$________

If you used your car while conducting business on behalf of a charity and were not reimbursed for your costs, you can take a deduction for the mileage.

Number of miles traveled for charity:________ × $0.12 cents per mile =
Total charitable mileage deduction:______________________________

Other Noncash Contributions (including unreimbursed expenses for a charitable organization or activity)

Description:______________________________Amount:______________

Description:______________________________Amount:______________

Description:______________________________Amount:______________

Description:______________________________Amount:______________

Description:______________________________Amount:______________

Description:______________________________Amount:______________

Description:______________________________Amount:______________

Description:______________________________Amount:______________

Casualty Losses

If your property that's worth more than 10 percent of your adjusted gross income is destroyed or severely damaged by a sudden, unexpected event you may have a deductible casualty loss. Think you do? Then consult a professional. There are several ways to determine and claim your deductible losses. Some people who think they have deductible losses, won't. Others, will have far greater deductions than they imagined. In any case, a top-notch preparer will get more bang from this loss than you could alone.

Pension Income

These distributions are generally taxable at your ordinary income tax rate. Additionally, if you take retirement contributions before you are fifty-nine and a half years old, you may also have to pay a 10 percent federal tax penalty.

However, the tax is not assessed on distributions that are reinvested in so-called "rollover IRAs" within sixty days.

If you are getting a pension distribution and not rolling the money into another IRA account, don't bother to record the distribution here. The retirement plan administrator will provide you with an annual statement showing how much you got and whether taxes were withheld.

If you rolled the distribution into another IRA, list it here so you'll remember to note the transaction on your 1040.

Distributions received from: ______________________

Amount:______________________Tax withheld (if any): ______________

Portion rolled into another IRA: ______________________

Where deposited:______________________When: ______________

Account number: ______________________

Bad Debts/Worthless Securities

Did you lend money to someone you now realize will never pay? Buy stock in a company that liquidated? Here's your chance to let Uncle Sam pay part of the tab.

Make sure you have a good reason for believing the debt is uncollectable–such as, you tried to collect it, but the debtor filed bankruptcy, left the country or is living on the street. This is the type of deduction the IRS is likely to check out carefully. That shouldn't stop you from claiming it. You should simply be extra careful to keep good records.

Amount of bad debt:______________________

Recipient of the loan:______________________

Reason you believe it is uncollectable: ______________________

____

____

____

Original cost of worthless security: ______________________________

Company or security name: ______________________________

Reason you believe it's worthless: ______________________________

____

____

____

Capital Gains/Losses

Here's where you record your net gain or loss on the sale of stocks, bonds, and mutual funds.

Sale price of property $______________________

Original cost –$______________________

Reinvested dividends –$______________________

Trading costs –$______________________

Net gain/loss $______________________

Sale price of property $______________________

Original cost –$______________________

Reinvested dividends –$______________________

Trading costs –$______________________

Net gain/loss $______________________

Sale price of property	$__________
Original cost	–$__________
Reinvested dividends	–$__________
Trading costs	–$__________
Net gain/loss	$__________

Sale price of property	$__________
Original cost	–$__________
Reinvested dividends	–$__________
Trading costs	–$__________
Net gain/loss	$__________

Sale price of property	$__________
Original cost	–$__________
Reinvested dividends	–$__________
Trading costs	–$__________
Net gain/loss	$__________

Sale price of property $____________________

Original cost –$____________________

Reinvested dividends –$____________________

Trading costs –$____________________

Net gain/loss $____________________

Gambling

If you gamble only the occasional Sunday or two at the track, or maybe a weekend a year in Las Vegas—and you don't bet huge amounts—forget this chart.

It's unlikely that your gambling losses amount to much. Only fill it out if you gamble regularly and figure you may hit it big someday. If you hit it big, this documentation will help you deduct past losses from your current gambling winnings. That reduces the taxable amount and saves you money.

Establishment: ____________________________

Date:____________ Gain/Loss: __________________

Establishment: ____________________________

Date:____________ Gain/Loss: __________________

Establishment: ____________________________

Date:____________ Gain/Loss: __________________

Establishment: ____

Date:______________Gain/Loss: ____________________________

Establishment: ____

Date:______________Gain/Loss: ____________________________

Establishment: ____

Date:______________Gain/Loss: ____________________________

Establishment: ____

Date:______________Gain/Loss: ____________________________

Establishment: ____

Date:______________Gain/Loss: ____________________________

Establishment: ____

Date:______________Gain/Loss: ____________________________

Establishment: ____

Date:______________Gain/Loss: ____________________________

Establishment: ____

Date:______________Gain/Loss: ____________________________

Index

D

E

F

G

H

M

N

O

P

Q

R

S

T

U

V